# Dignity, Discourse, and Destiny

President Courtney C. Smith, in a light moment at home, ca. 1960. Courtesy of
Friends Historical Library.

# Dignity, Discourse, and Destiny

## The Life of Courtney C. Smith

Darwin H. Stapleton
and Donna Heckman Stapleton

Newark: University of Delaware Press
London: Associated University Presses

Associated University Presses
2010 Eastpark Boulevard
Cranbury, NJ 08512

Associated University Presses
Unit 304
The Chandlery
50 Westminster Bridge Road
London SE1 7QY, England

Associated University Presses
P.O. Box 338, Port Credit
Mississauga, Ontario
Canada L5G 4L8

The paper used in this publication meets the requirements of the American National Standard for Permanence of Paper for Printed Library Materials Z39.48-1984.

Library of Congress Cataloging-in-Publication Data

Stapleton, Darwin H.
    Dignity, discourse, and destiny : the life of Courtney C. Smith / Darwin H. Stapleton and Donna Heckman Stapleton.
        p. cm.
    Includes bibliographical references (p.     ) and index.
    ISBN 0-87413-833-7 (alk. paper)
    1. Smith, Courtney C. (Courtney Craig), 1916– 2. Swarthmore College—Presidents—Biography. 3. College presidents—United States—Biography. I. Stapleton, Donna Heckman, 1947–    II. Title.
    LD5192.7.S65 S72    2004
    370'.92—dc21

                                                    2003004425

*Honoring our mothers*
*and all those who have taught*
*and mentored us*

# Contents

Preface                                                                    9
Acknowledgments                                                           11

 1. Childhood                                                             15
 2. Harvard, Oxford, and Marriage                                        21
 3. In the Navy                                                          33
 4. Return to Education: Princeton                                       41
 5. The Woodrow Wilson Program Years                                     53
 6. Swarthmore College at Mid-Century                                    59
 7. Swarthmore Looks for Courtney                                        65
 8. Inauguration                                                         70
 9. The Case for the Liberal Arts College                               76
10. Faculty                                                              85
11. "There is strength . . . in having a variety of
      sources of support": Funding the Liberal Arts Tradition            92
12. Networks of Support and Service: Behind the Presidency             102
13. "Nature shaped to advantage": Preserving Campus Viability          118
14. Student Activism: "To care about social justice"                   127
15. Two Decades of Student Life at Swarthmore                           145
16. "Personal things"                                                   154
17. Administration of a College                                         161
18. The Final Year                                                      171
Conclusion                                                              188

Interviews Conducted by the Authors                                     195
Notes                                                                   198
Bibliography                                                            239
Index                                                                   243

# Preface

THIS BIOGRAPHY OF COURTNEY C. SMITH, A MANDARIN OF AMERICAN
higher education for nearly two decades (1952–69), is primarily a study of
a man who was a leading shaper of the educational establishment of his
time—even though much of his activity was just below the threshold of
public recognition. His role in creating the Woodrow Wilson Fellowship
program, in leading the Rhodes Scholar program, in promoting departmental reconfigurations at Harvard University, and most important, in
defending the liberal arts as president of Swarthmore College, place him
near the center of important developments in college and university education in the United States. One would do well to consider today, as well as
historically, Smith's approach to higher education, and his views regarding
why and for whom a truly challenging education is essential.

Equally important, the telling of Smith's life engages a number of important movements and processes not only in higher education, but also in
American society, so that this biography provides certain insights into the
crucible decades of the 1950s and 1960s. Matters of privilege and of race,
for example, were at the heart of much of his life's experience and were the
focus of much of his activity and of his public remarks on education. He
dealt with student activism not only in the storied years of the 1960s, but
also from the beginning of his presidency in 1953. He resisted the lures of
the military-industrial complex that was forever altering colleges and universities elsewhere. And in his own fashion he led an environmental battle
that began fifteen years before the first Earth Day. An examination of
Smith's critique of and engagement with the cold war era will extend our
understanding of how the United States has arrived at where it is today in
important areas such as racial and ethnic diversity and the place of higher
education institutions in American society. It is striking to observe, by
regular reading of the *New York Times* and the *Chronicle of Higher Education,* for example, how many of the issues that Smith dealt with are still on
the public agenda.

9

10

Finally, any study of Courtney Smith's life is at the same time a study of Swarthmore College. As a leading (often regarded as "the" leading) liberal arts institution in the United States for three-quarters of the last century, it has had remarkably little scrutiny and tends to be known only by people who have been innoculated with the liberal arts virus. Why this species of institution, and this institution in particular, has flourished and for decades has produced an outsized number of leaders in almost every category of learning and professional endeavor should be of deep interest to everyone concerned about education in America—and the world. Certainly Courtney Smith's commitment to Swarthmore College as a bastion of liberal education, a place for education through dialogue, is the legacy that he lived—and ultimately—died for.

# Acknowledgments

THIS VOLUME HAS DRAWN ON THE SUPPORT AND ENCOURAGEMENT OF many people, only a few of whom we can acknowledge here. Most important, we sincerely thank the group of Swarthmoreans who first proposed the preparation of a biography of Courtney C. Smith, and who were fully and enthusiastically behind our efforts: Professor James A. Field (deceased), Dr. Gerald Frost, Dr. Elizabeth (Lee) Smith Ingram, Professor Roland Pennock (deceased), and the chair of the committee, Dr. Jeremy Stone. While the committee's emotional and intellectual support were most important, we also appreciate the committee's solicitation of financial support that allowed us to travel to archives and to conduct interviews.

Dr. Ingram, Courtney Craig Smith Jr., and Carol Dabney Smith, the children of Courtney C. Smith, graciously gave us access to and permission to use his personal papers and commented on a late version of the text. Greg Ingram read the manuscript and gave us the benefit of his comments and suggestions. Courtney C. Smith's sister, Florence S. Van Syoc, shared with us her personal collection of documents and her reminiscences. Without the Smith family's generosity this book would not have been possible.

We are also grateful for the cooperation of many people at Swarthmore College. Former president David W. Fraser gave us unfettered access to the Courtney C. Smith Presidential Papers. Various college staff members assisted us on our visits to campus and with other matters, including Judy Pagliaro and Lori Ann Kelley. Jeffrey Lott, editor of the *Swarthmore College Bulletin,* gave us two opportunities to publish our research in progress, one of which (in the spring 1994 issue of the *Bulletin*) was our first opportunity to present a portion of the Courtney C. Smith story.

A number of archivists and librarians significantly aided our research. Most important was Mary Ellen Chijoike of the Friends Historical Library at Swarthmore College (now at Guilford College), who drew our attention to many important resources, and whose knowledge of college history and the library's resources deepened our understanding. Other staff at the Friends Historical Library and the McCabe Library at Swarthmore assisted

us and extended courtesies. At the Rockefeller Archive Center Thomas
Rosenbaum and Emily Oakhill helped us with many of the early research
questions; at the Ford Foundation Archives Alan Divack steered us to the
right documents; and at the Princeton University Archives Benjamin
Primer gave us access to a valuable trove of material. Thanks also to the
staff of various institutions who gave us information or provided copies of
publications and documents: Brimmer and Day School, Des Moines Public Library, Hagley Museum and Library, John F. Kennedy Presidential
Library, Ossining (New York) Public Library, Provincetown (Massachusetts) Public Library, Smith College Archives, Vassar College Archives,
Winterset (Iowa) Public Library, Winterset (Iowa) Historical Society, and
Woodrow Wilson National Fellowship Foundation.

We interviewed over forty people in the course of our research, all of
whom are listed in an appendix. Those who shared with us the story of
their associations with Courtney C. Smith gave us continuing inspiration,
strengthened our understanding, and often sent us in new historical directions. Being welcomed into the homes of so many friendly and helpful
people was the most rewarding aspect of developing this book.

Our friends, colleagues, and family members listened long and patiently
to explanations of our work, suffered our enthusiasms, and asked some of
the hard questions. Of these we want to mention particularly James and
Diana Batten, Julius Gordon, Laura Chernev Gordon, Kenneth W. Rose,
Alice M. Stapleton, Elizabeth R. Stapleton, and Wayne and Nelva te
Brake. At the Rockefeller Archive Center we received assistance and
many courtesies from the staff, especially Marie Callahan, Camilla Harris,
and Pecolia Rieder.

Finally, much of this book was drafted while we were in retreat from the
usual demands of home and work. Bess and Subrata Chakravarty helped
get us started by providing us with the quiet, freedom, and comforts of
their cottage near Rhinebeck, New York, at a critical early point. Carol and
Richard Pesiri's cottages in North Truro, Massachusetts, were the perfect
locale for writing much of the text and for enjoying our own partnership.

# Dignity, Discourse, and Destiny

# 1
## Childhood

IOWA IN THE 1920S AND 1930S CHARACTERIZED MANY OF THE PROMINENT images and leading realities of American life. Its small towns across the predominantly agricultural landscape echoed in architecture and lifestyle the New England roots of the settlers who had arrived scarcely a century earlier. The Iowan communities placed high values on independent farmers, the practice of religion, sound education, and involvement in local government. These values were visibly reflected in silos and grain elevators, church spires, schools, and courthouses scattered over the state's gently rolling land. Thomas Jefferson's ideal of the yeoman farmer as the keystone of American life seemed to be realized in Iowa.

But for anyone growing up in Iowa in these decades it was apparent that there were other images of the state that were equally real and significant. Iowa was a state of immigrants and the dispossessed as well as of the children and grandchildren of settlers. The state capital, Des Moines, had ethnic districts and ghettos, and the state's farmers were increasingly tenants rather than owners. The high point of prices for agricultural products had come early in the century, and farmers were caught between decreasing income and the need to invest in farm mechanization. The clouds of agricultural depression only grew thicker during the 1920s and 1930s, testing the resilience and fortitude of all Iowans.[1] Courtney Craig Smith[2] was born in the small town of Winterset, Iowa (also the birthplace of actor John Wayne) on December 20, 1916.[3] He was the third son, and fourth child, of Samuel ("Sam") Craig Smith and Myrtle Dabney Smith. His father was of Scotch-Irish background and had been born in the Boston suburb of Brookline, Massachusetts, on February 4, 1868. Sam's family moved to Jackson County, on the eastern edge of Iowa, when he was a few months old, then later to Madison County, in southwestern Iowa, when he was eighteen years old. Sam had gone to the country schools, the Dexter Academy, the state normal school in Cedar Falls, and then the University of Iowa in Iowa City, where he earned both his bachelor's and law degrees.[4] After teaching at Fenton Junction in Jones County, Iowa he was admitted to the bar in 1897 and began practicing in Winterset, the Madison county seat. He had a private practice and also served several years as Winterset's solicitor and two terms as the county's attorney. A close acquaintance of his noted that he was quite successful in both his private and public service but also observed that "Mr. Smith . . . never liked the trial table, and preferred the council room; in his business he was thorough, conservative, persistent, and absolutely honest."[5]

Sam Smith served as a director of the Winterset Savings Bank and before his death on December 28, 1929, had become president.[6] He was an active member and trustee of the First Presbyterian Church of Winterset, where he attended Wednesday night prayer meetings, was superintendent of the Sunday school, and was also a teacher of its mens' class. Within the community, he was a member of the Masonic and Pythian orders, and at his death was the grand vice chancellor of the Knights of Pythias of Iowa.[7] He enjoyed golfing as a recreation.

Myrtle Dabney was a woman of French, English and Welsh descent and had come from "a first family of Virginia." She was a capable, resourceful woman who demonstrated her love of learning throughout her life by consistently reading the family newspaper from beginning to end. As a young woman she attended Drake University in Des Moines, afterward returning to Winterset, where she was courted by Sam Smith. Six years his junior, she married him at age twenty-five, on December 20, 1899.[8]

Winterset during the 1920s was a town of about two thousand people that served as a commercial, as well as governmental, center for the predominantly agricultural economy of the surrounding region. Although the town had only been founded in 1846, the Winterset community of the Smith family time already had sufficient sense of its history to begin to preserve the county's numerous covered bridges. In Winterset, a quiet, self-contained, prosperous town governed by the rhythms of farm life, many church dinners, and a great sense of community, the Smiths, for a time, had a tranquil and protected life.[9]

Three other children, Murray, Carleton, and Florence, were born and maturing before Courtney's birth. Their mother, Myrtle, was considered warmhearted, reliable, and energetic when the family was young. She made clothing for the family, made candy for all the children's Christmas gifts, and enjoyed social events with her husband.

Courtney, as the youngest child with significantly older siblings, was a well-disciplined child who went to the Winterset Presbyterian Church and its weekly Sunday school. During his youth he walked to school with his many friends, had an abundance of books and magazines at home, regularly went to the library, listened to a player piano with its many classical and opera rolls, visited his father's law office, and played yard games.

Typical of the period and Presbyterian tradition, Sundays were quieter days for the family (roller skating, for example, was forbidden), household work was kept to a minimum, and the family stayed at home or took walks in the countryside.[10] Myrtle Smith noted that Courtney as a child was "easy to mind," and his uncle told him in his teenage years that he had never brought his mother pain or anxiety.[11] Still, Courtney was remembered by both his sister and his mother as a child who was "persistent" and one who "would never give up as long as there was a possibility" of having what he wanted.[12]

Early in his development Courtney demonstrated oratorical and literary inclinations. When he was in second grade he acted in a high school play called *Daddy Long Legs* with his tenth-grade sister, Florence. Then in fifth grade he was in the operetta *Aunt Drucilla's Garden,* performing the role of Bob, leader of the gang. Courtney was pleased with his fifth-grade performance and wrote gleefully and triumphantly to his siblings, who were all by that time out of the household, that he "had a lot to say in the operetta" and that he had his "name all around town on colored posters" which advertised the performance.[13]

Courtney also enjoyed more tangible achievements, and when he was twelve joined the American Air Cadets, a club that built and flew model airplanes. He was also an active member of the Pioneers and was proud of his success in rapidly acquiring "twelve notches in [his] bronze pin."[14] As a teenager in his freshman year of high school at Winterset he won an essay contest for a piece titled "On Being an Uncle," which he wrote in response to being affectionately named "uncle" by a family friend who appreciated his attention to her new baby.[15]

Courtney was enjoying the Winterset life and his engagement with the community, but all that childhood pleasure ended abruptly. In December 1929, as Courtney was approaching his thirteenth birthday, his father, who had been ill for several months, was hospitalized in the Iowa Methodist Hospital in Des Moines for an operation. Courtney visited his father during his hospitalization and received correspondence from his father during their separation. Sam, in his last letter, shortly before his death, wrote to his teenage son, admonishing Courtney to help his mother during his hospitalization. Sam also reinforced the family's Protestant work ethic by telling Courtney that "it may seem hard at the time when you want to do something else, but afterwards you will feel better than if you had been playing and [you will] get more real pleasure from it."[16]

That winter became difficult. Sam died on December 26, 1929, from cancer. The stock market crash of that fall and its consequences for the Winterset Savings Bank had negatively affected Sam's estate. And, only two weeks after Courtney and his mother buried Sam, Courtney came down with scarlet fever and was quarantined at home for several weeks.

Courtney, just having turned thirteen years old, found himself the sole male of the household and, responding to his father's death-bed admonitions and his sibling's wishes, began to take greater responsibility for monitoring and caring for the home. He wrote serious letters to his brother Murray and sister-in-law Helen, thanking them for paying "Daddy's debt" and telling them that an attorney, W. S. Cooper, was helping their mother sort papers at his father's office; he asked them for grass seed and fertilizer and suggested that the house needed to be painted.[17] He also wrote to his brothers Murray and Carleton regularly in response to their concerns for information about their mother's well-being. These older working brothers had offered to pay him fifty cents per letter received.

Courtney's whole life had changed dramatically.[18] Sam's death and the nation's economic depression significantly altered the course of Courtney's family. Just prior to his death Sam Smith had superintended the merger of the Winterset Bank with another local bank. As a member of the board of directors of the Winterset Bank Sam had invested heavily in the new enterprise and had become its president. With the events of the economic depression occurring, the fortunes of the bank rapidly declined and his estate, which might have provided a comfortable income for his family, was devastated. Myrtle Smith, after thirty years of marriage and homemaking, was left a widow with only $2,000 of oil stock that she had inherited from an uncle and the family home.[19]

After a year and a half of financial struggle in Winterset Myrtle decided to sell the family home for $2500. During the summer of 1931 she rented an apartment in Des Moines for herself, Courtney, and his older sister Florence at 3927 Ingersoll Avenue, in the well-to-do neighborhood on the west side of the city, where Florence was already working and living. Des Moines, only thirty miles from Winterset, was vastly different in size and opportunity. It had a population of nearly 150,000 and was a railroad, meatpacking, and insurance industry center as well as the government center of the state. Des Moines had a "community civil plan of adult education financed by the Carnegie Corporation . . . its special feature [was] the evening neighborhood forum in which noted speakers from all parts of the world [led] programs . . . on political, economic, and social problems."[20]

The Smith apartment was near Roosevelt High School. Courtney began his sophomore year at Roosevelt, and although he was lonely at first he quickly engaged in the school's debating and public speaking programs.[21] Roosevelt proved to be a nourishing environment for Courtney throughout his adolescence.

Sharing a home with Florence was also nourishing and supportive in many ways; Florence eventually joined the Roosevelt High School faculty as an instructor of secretarial subjects and English literature and led group tours throughout Europe during summers. The family income was still limited, however, and typical of many employees during the depression, Florence was paid in scrip. Myrtle was making much of the family clothing, and Courtney, in order to attend dances and parties, collected coat hangers from neighbors and sold them to drycleaners for a penny a piece. His sister recalled years later when reminiscing about the family that in spite of these economies and efforts the family frequently ended the month eating little but cornbread and milk.[22]

Courtney immediately excelled in public speaking and debate at Roosevelt and gained newspaper notoriety. The debates were challenging in the range of subjects which students were required to address on only an hour's notice. In one year the range of topics included "The Dole, Ship Mergers, World Peace, Hoover and Relief, German Conditions, Prohibition, Aviation, Gold Standard, [and] Farm Relief."[23] His debate coach, C. C. Carothers, told Mrs. Smith of "the fine work" Courtney had done and that he was always "well informed and able to deliver his material exceedingly well."[24] Myrtle became engaged in the preparation process for these speeches, attended the local debates, and clipped articles from newspapers on numerous subjects on which he might be called to debate.[25]

In his first year at the high school, he won first place in an extemporaneous speaking contest with eighty competitors and became the Des Moines city extemporaneous speaking champion. Then as a junior, Courtney Smith and Joseph Silver, his partner, won acclaim at an Iowa State Teachers' College Forensic Contest in April 1933 when they "placed first in every argument in which they participated." Although excelling in individual and pair debates, he was also an enthusiastic member of the Roosevelt High School state champion debating team.[26]

Courtney's involvement in debating was just one element of his engagement with Roosevelt High. Having observed the accomplishments of his parents and siblings, Courtney had consciously sought leadership roles throughout high school, believing they "would be quite an asset in applying for [college] scholarships."[27] Courtney, known as "Craig" in high school, was reported in his senior yearbook, *The Annual Roundup,* as having been National Honor Society president, Latin Club president, Student Council treasurer, Sothern and Marlowe (Drama Club) vice president, secretary of Hi-Y, delegate to Missouri Valley Federation, homeroom president, and a member of the tennis, debate, and extemporaneous speaking teams.[28]

By the time that Courtney graduated from high school in the spring of 1934, it was clear that the Protestant ethics of his father and mother and the guidance and examples of his older siblings and family friends provided a strong foundation for Courtney's life. His father had demonstrated a commitment to public service. His mother had exemplified resilience and resourcefulness during the Depression. His older brother Murray had been a law clerk to Senator Albert Cummins of Iowa, later was a secretary to the electrical industry magnate, Samuel Insull, and then had become an official of Commonwealth Edison in Chicago.[29] His older brother Carleton was already a nationally known announcer with the NBC radio network, and Florence had developed skills which she successfully marketed in several ways in a depressed economy.[30]

Courtney had been especially interested in a Harvard education and had set his sights upon that as early as his sophomore year in high school. With his outstanding high school record and the supportive references of family friends such as W. S. Cooper, now a state district judge, he was a strong candidate for admission to colleges. He was eventually offered scholarships at Drake University, University of Iowa, Iowa State Teachers' College, Simpson College, University of Chicago, Carleton College, Swarthmore College, Dartmouth College, and Harvard University.[31]

Financing his education was a major issue for Courtney, however, and he wrote to the dean of men at Swarthmore College and to other institutions to see whether, in addition to their scholarship offers, he could be provided a job to pay for his personal expenses while at the schools.[32] When Harvard assured him a job as well as the promised scholarship he seized the opportunity.[33]

# 2

## Harvard, Oxford, and Marriage

WHEN COURTNEY MOVED ON TO HARVARD HE ENTERED WITH ABOUT A thousand other freshmen who had vied for a place in the university. He was excited to be able to attend the "oldest, proudest, and richest" institution of higher education in the United States, the prestigious, all-male Harvard University.[1]

As a freshman Courtney lived in Thayer dormitory. In lieu of paying for board, Courtney waited tables on Mondays, Wednesdays, and Fridays (and alternate Sundays) in the Harvard Union, wearing a "little white jacket" to serve fellow students. Those who waited tables in the Union not only were distinguishable by their dress and service role but became comrades who shared a need for financial aid and who ate together regularly before serving meals.

Courtney made friends with several of the other waiters, particularly Win Pettingell, John Ashmead, and Bill Murphy. Many of the students who needed financial aid were outstanding students from public high schools throughout the nation and quickly found that they had much in common as they worked among the many other students (nearly 70 percent) who had come from private preparatory schools.[2] Courtney took on the mantle of leadership of this group when he and his friend Bill organized a group that complained to superiors about the "meanness" of the supervisor of the Union dining room staff.[3]

Unhappy with the conditions that he found waitering, in the second half of his freshman year at Harvard Courtney approached the university librarian, Mrs. Florence Milner, and persuaded her to give him another job in the Freshman Union library. Courtney's maturity, elegance, and sophistication impressed Mrs. Milner, who continued to appreciate his qualities and favored him throughout the remainder of his Harvard years by placing him in the Farnsworth Room of the Widener Library and in the library in his own residence, Leverett House. These library jobs allowed him to study between tasks, gave him access to academic materials, and allowed him to engage in conversations with those using the libraries.[4]

21

After their freshman year Courtney and his friends were assigned to new quarters. They had entered Harvard in the early years of the Harvard House Plan, which drew all upperclassmen into seven buildings or groups of buildings named for leading figures in the university's history. Each house held 230–300 men and provided facilities such as libraries, common rooms, squash courts, and dining rooms that were intended to foster social and intellectual life. Every house was supposed to hold a cross-section of the Harvard student body, so that no one major, prep school, or social class dominated, but they certainly did not reflect American society at large or fairly reflect all of those qualified to attend Harvard. A quota on Jewish admissions (roughly 15 percent of any incoming class) had been imposed in the late 1920s, and of the handful of African-American students at Harvard none lived in those houses.[5]

For many students a critical element of the house plan was its academic support. A senior tutor and several assistant tutors were assigned to each house, any one of whom could provide strong guidance and instruction; one tutor of Smith's era was especially remembered for his "impressive display of learning and industry" that challenged students to refine their thinking.[6]

Although students were assigned to their houses by an administrative process, they could request an assignment, and there was competition for the houses deemed most desirable or for those with the best tutors. Courtney and his friend Bill Murphy applied to get into Lowell House, thought at the time to be the most prestigious, but were turned down by the master of Lowell. After that rejection Courtney then went immediately to negotiate a single room for himself in Leverett House.[7]

Although the Smith family had encouraged Courtney to become a lawyer or diplomat because of his skill in public speaking, he quickly decided to study English literature and to become an educator.[8] While commitments to studies dominated Courtney's life at Harvard, he also very consciously took counsel about how to develop professionally, and dressed accordingly.

At Harvard, even though his financial resources were comparatively finite he was known to dress for each occasion in an understated, impeccably fine, although limited, wardrobe of flannels and herringbone, similar to that of the more affluent private school students.[9] He socialized with New Yorkers Morris Lasker and William Murphy, who also studied English literature, and they had both lively academic discussions in the dormitories and many competitive squash games.

As an English major, Courtney began to concentrate on Milton and other authors of seventeenth-century Puritan tracts on education, and he had the opportunity to reflect on liberal arts education and its rationale.[10] At the end of his four years he graduated magnum cum laude in English literature and was elected to Phi Beta Kappa. In his Rhodes Scholar application in the fall of his senior year Courtney summarized his pattern of studies at Harvard:

> Conforming with President Conant's recommendation for greater specialization in the undergraduate's curriculum, ten of my sixteen courses have been in this field [English literature], and all have been passed with honor grades. With my former tutor, Mr. F. W. MacVeagh, and my present tutor, Professor James B. Munn, Chairman of the English department, I have supplemented my course work with additional study. Within this rather broad field of English literature my particular interests are two: first, the Seventeenth Century, an age I find fascinating particularly because of the reflection in letters of England's transition to what in many cases are its modern views on government, religion, philosophy, and the fine arts; and second, modern literary criticism. For my tutors and as optional course work I have made rather detailed studies of Samuel Daniel, John Donne, Restoration prose fiction, and the principles of literary criticism of T. S. Eliot and I. A. Richards. I am a candidate for graduation with Honors, and at present am preparing an Honors thesis on the poetry and literary criticism of A. E. Housman.[11]

His work of thirty hours per week as secretary and library assistant at the Widener Library and Leverett House library occupied most of his free time, but he found time to represent his dormitory, Leverett House, on its intramural squash team, participate in swimming and tennis activities, and serve on class and Leverett House social committees. Feeling that prep school students were dominating campus leadership and activities and not representing him and his friends, he even made an against-the-odds and futile run for a class office.[12]

During his Harvard undergraduate years he also spent time visiting Boston museums and attending concerts, plays, and operas.[13] He took opportunities to learn from peers and to travel with friends. During a winter vacation he spent time with Morris Lasker and Bill Murphy in New York City. They saw New York museums, Fort Totten, Murphy's Flushing home, and Lasker's family's brownstone off Central Park West.[14] During the summer of 1935, Morris Lasker went to Europe with Courtney and Florence's group. Courtney and Morris spent time together during the sail on the *Rotterdam* and during the travel in London and Paris, and then the two of them broke free from the group and bicycled through the chateau country of France for a week.

During his years at Harvard Courtney was actively seeking new relationships. He arrived at Harvard with a well-formed personality; he was physically attractive (tall and slender), had a soft and melodic voice and an "infectious smile." As a gregarious Midwesterner he ran the risk of being considered by prep school classmates as one of the public school "back-slappers," a person who was overly aggressive in making friends. Instead he exhibited a "natural dignity and self-assurance," "seemed to take everything very much in stride," and easily engaged in the casual pipe-smoking and intense bull sessions of the houses.[15]

Courtney developed friendships with a wide range of Harvard men. In addition to Bill Murphy (from Flushing, New York), Morris Lasker (Manhattan), Win Pettingell, and John Ashmead, he was friends with Wiley Mayne (Sanborn, Iowa), Tom Anderson Southwell (Des Moines, Iowa), Al Damon, Robert Parker "Sparks" Sorlien, George Bogardus, Ed Lambert (Spokane, Washington), Alfonso Ossorio, and Robert E. Lee Strider. To this group he seemed "inherently a very moderate and civilized person." These qualities made him such a good companion that in later years some of his friends from Harvard remembered him as someone they not only liked but "loved."[16]

In this Harvard atmosphere Courtney's aspirations and values displayed many facets: he could use his personal charm and good looks in ways that contributed to his individual success but put off others who felt that it was self-centered and self-serving. For example, when his initial plan to room with Bill Murphy in Lowell House fell through, he negotiated for other housing with the dean personally, reserving an attractive single room for himself in Leverett House. He did not share confidences easily and was somewhat distant, making his own way. Although he spent time with these friends none felt that they knew much about his childhood or personal life. Courtney's privacy and independence made some think of him as "too slick," "too careful" about whom he chose to be seen with, and too self-conscious and careful about having a "premeditated plan of appearance." It was a style which some thought was "contrived."[17]

In all, however, the acquaintances respected his personal honesty, his ambition, his clear thinking, his willingness to take on challenges, his charm, and his accomplishments. This circle of associates which he acquired in his Harvard years continued well into the future through correspondence and occasional visits: indeed these friendships dwindled only because of the increasing pressures of his career. In 1962, while telling Swarthmore students of his vision for a vibrant social life on campus, he reflected on how much he enjoyed the intellectual discourse that had occurred in the dining halls of Harvard, as students from various disciplines had socialized and exchanged ideas.[18]

While at Harvard Courtney continued to be close to his sister Florence. When he went to Harvard, Florence took the opportunity to move to Boston and teach secretarial skills at the Katherine Gibb School. She continued her sisterly mentoring and got together regularly with Courtney on Sundays for dinner, visited and played table games with his friends, and discussed books.[19]

During the summers of 1935, 1936, and 1937, between academic years at Harvard, Courtney joined Florence as she continued to lead the group tours of Europe that she had begun while living in Iowa. Courtney was quite good at speaking French so he became the group's courier and earned his tour expenses in that way.[20] Florence's groups now consisted of her Katherine Gibb students, her sorority sisters, and other acquaintances who were taking grand tours through Europe as a traditional element of the social and cultural training for students aspiring to join the business elite. Her groups traveled through England, Scotland, Holland, Belgium, France, Germany, Italy, and Switzerland.[21]

On the 1937 voyage to Europe Courtney met Elizabeth (Betty) Proctor on board ship. Betty was a Smith College graduate from Boston who was traveling independently to meet friends in Europe. She and Courtney enjoyed each others' company and often stayed on deck talking into the wee hours of the morning. Betty was not on the tour so they did not see each other after they arrived in Europe, but after the summer, when they both returned to the Boston area, they began seeing each other regularly and often included Florence in their outings.[22] Courtney and Betty dated while Courtney continued his studies at Harvard and planned for further studies in England. Then in the spring of 1938 Courtney took a position with a wealthy Boston family in which driving a car could be an asset, and Betty, who now had been seeing him for several months, offered to give him driving lessons.

But about that time, the Proctors expressed concern that the relationship between Courtney and Betty was unsettled. Courtney was finishing his Harvard bachelor's degree and was anticipating three years of study at Oxford University in England. Betty was already twenty-three years old and her parents were undoubtedly concerned about her commitment to await his return. In deference to her parents' feelings she called Courtney to tell him "they'd better call it off," but shortly afterward she changed her mind and made a second call to Courtney, saying "This is Miss Change-of-Policy Proctor and I think we should go ahead and have your driving lessons." Soon Betty was wearing, on a chain around her neck, the Phi Beta Kappa key Courtney received in mid-June 1938.[23] The Proctors recognized then that Betty had a love match and that she was effectively betrothed to Courtney.[24]

Increasingly Courtney had been shifting his frame of reference from Iowa to that of the more cosmopolitan Cambridge and Boston culture. He had enjoyed his Harvard friends, the European tours, and his relationship with Betty. But during Courtney's senior year at Harvard he had a further new experience—a extraordinary opportunity to learn about a lifestyle distant from his Iowan roots. H. Wendell Endicott, who had attended Harvard and lived in Dedham, Massachusetts, informed Harvard that he needed a companion for his eleven-year-old son, Bradford, and was put in touch with Courtney. Endicott not only employed him but became a mentor of sorts.

Endicott was vice president of the Endicott Johnson Shoe Company, a director of other companies (such as Sears and Roebuck), a clubman, an avid sportsman, and was interested in arts and philanthropy.[25] Courtney's first major experience with the family occurred in April of 1938 when he joined the Endicotts for a family trip to Bermuda, where they stayed at the Mid-Ocean Club in Hamilton. Both Mr. and Mrs. Endicott were enthusiastic and accomplished golfers: Priscilla Maxwell Endicott ranked among the best of the American women. Courtney, using both his academic and athletic skills, tutored Bradford and played tennis and golf with him. In turn, the Endicotts were very generous to him. As Courtney recalled, the Endicotts "started me on golf, paid for my golf lessons from Ernest Jones [Mrs. Endicott's instructor], bought me an English leather golf bag, three woods and a set of nine matched Macgregor English irons."[26]

The Bermuda trip went well and Courtney thoroughly enjoyed learning the game of golf. He began traveling with the family regularly: their son liked him very much and found him "handsome" and "good humored," as well as "serious." In May of that year he again joined the Endicotts as they traveled by train and then by automobile on dirt roads for a ten-day salmon fly-fishing trip on the Restigouche River in the wilderness of northern New Brunswick.[27]

Then during the 1938 summer Courtney was employed full-time by the Endicotts.[28] He was paid $175 per month and had a room at the family's residence, a fifty-room house on a large estate at 80 Haven Street in Dedham. During most of the summer he golfed early each morning with Bradford at the Dedham Polo and Country Club, but from mid-August to mid-September he again traveled with the Endicotts, going on a big-game hunting trip for grizzly bear, mountain sheep, and deer in British Columbia. Courtney very much enjoyed this introduction to the elite lifestyle, but his selection as a Rhodes Scholar took him to England in the next month.[29]

While Courtney was no longer able to spend time with the family, the Endicott relationship continued to be significant. Courtney kept in touch with the family and four years later in 1942, when Courtney enlisted in the navy, Wendell Endicott, who was then a military consultant, wrote a letter of reference to the War Production Board describing Courtney as a tireless worker, a clear thinker, and a "very attractive young man."[30]

In the fall of his senior year at Harvard, with advice and consultation from Professor F. O. Matthiessen (a former Rhodes Scholar who was chairman of the undergraduate board of tutors in history and literature), Courtney decided to apply for a Rhodes Scholarship to study at Oxford University in England.[31] The Rhodes Trust which funded the scholarships was established by British industrialist Cecil J. Rhodes, who at his death in 1902 endowed the Rhodes Scholarships at Oxford, thirty-two of which were designated to be awarded to Americans for postgraduate study. Scholars were appointed on the basis of intellectual ability, outstanding character and personality, and physical vigor. By the 1930s the American scholars were selected on a regional basis, a process overseen by the American Secretary of the Rhodes Scholar Program, Frank Aydelotte, who was at that time president of Swarthmore College.[32]

While considering this opportunity for study, Courtney learned that the selection process permitted him to apply either as a Massachusetts student or as a resident of the state of Iowa. Displaying his characteristic savvy and calculated long-range thinking, he decided to apply as a resident of Iowa, where he would compete with applicants from a range of institutions in the upper Midwest, rather than applying from Massachusetts, which put him in a region where he would most certainly be competing against numerous applicants from several Ivies and other highly ranked institutions in the northeast.[33]

The Iowa Rhodes Selection Committee did see extraordinary strengths in his application and interview and forwarded his application to the regional committee. As one of two Iowa nominees Courtney then vied with eleven regional candidates for the four scholarships allotted to the entire upper Midwest region of South Dakota, Minnesota, Kansas, Nebraska, Iowa, and Wisconsin.

Courtney worked diligently and presented a comprehensive and well-honed application essay, arguing that a Rhodes Scholarship would give him "the best, and for [him] the only, practical opportunity of reaching an understanding of the temper of the English life and character, an understanding particularly essential to the American student of English language and literature." He stated that he sought "the opportunity at Oxford to gain a deeper understanding of the bond underlying Anglo-American relations and an appreciation of the common heritage of the two nations." He further expounded, "In the field I have chosen for advanced study Oxford is without peer, because of its faculty, its literary tradition, its abundance of manuscripts and original sources, and in no small degree, because of its library facilities, particularly Bodleian, the Library of the English School, and the Faculty Library" and listed a range of student clubs and organizations in which he might participate.[34]

The six-man Regional Rhodes Selection Committee interviewed each candidate about personal interests and ambitions before making the four appointments. Courtney met his competitors for the Rhodes Scholarships during the two-day interview process, some of whom he had known from Iowa debating competitions when he was in high school. He was concerned that there were precedents for distributing scholarships to as many states in the region as possible and recognized that his fellow Iowan, Edward Weismiller, who had studied at Cornell College (Iowa), was a worthy and strong candidate. He was greatly relieved in December of 1937 to find that both Iowans, he and Weismiller, were selected as two of the four upper Midwest regional recipients.[35]

Courtney had reached a rarified place in American academic life. Eight years had passed since his father's death, and now as a result of his constant striving and commitment to his goals, he was in a very select group of thirty-two men who had been given generous scholarships to study in England, and who would be forever recognized as part of an academic elite.

At his time of personal triumph, though, the world was not at ease. Because in September 1938 Europe was embroiled in the Munich crisis the Rhodes Scholars' scheduled late-September departure for England was delayed, and Courtney and his fellow scholars spent nearly a week at Swarthmore College, where the American Office for the Rhodes Scholar Program was housed, awaiting clearance from Oxford to sail.[36] Courtney and the others finally got permission and left New York headed for Britain on October 1, 1938. While traversing the Atlantic the Rhodes Scholars socialized and became familiar with each other. Courtney wrote to his family that while he was at Oxford he would attempt to keep in touch with many of the cohorts he had met on board ship.

Upon his arrival at Oxford, on October 10th, he found that he had been assigned to a very nice St. Alban's Quadrangle room with a study, bedroom, electric heater, and large window seat. In a letter which he wrote to his family soon after his arrival, he described in detail and with a critical eye the ambience and customs of the university in which he found himself:

The room is furnished by the college with a table sort of desk and chair, a comfortable lounge and two large easy chairs, a dining table with three chairs, and a bookcase which has drawers below for my china, silver, and food supplies. . . . Really, the feature of the room is a large window seat (four leaded-windows, and the seat has a thick blue cushion). These windows, facing south and thus catching the sun all day, look down onto a court, which runs into a garden, which runs into a meadow. Thus I have a quarter to half mile vista of green lawn, flowers, trees and meadow. It's the best view I've seen in Oxford so far.[37]

He reported having, as was the custom, "a male servant, called a Scout," who woke him in the morning, made the bed, and helped by serving tea and lunch to his guests. Courtney also noted that he had to adjust to what he called "lots of funny, childish rules," such as attending roll call at eight in the morning, or if he missed it, going to chapel. He expressed surprise and seeming disappointment that the English fellows dressed "very sloppily." But he enjoyed his social life, reporting that he had learned to eat fast, had frequently entertained or was entertained at lunch, and that he had rowed with "the Merton crew" every afternoon.[38]

After classes Courtney met socially with his Rhodes colleagues. One of them, Byron White, described the evening routines at Oxford:

After a quarter of an hour in the store where the fellows go for dessert, they drop off to read or to take coffee in someone's room; with the coffee a glass of port is usually taken. In the evening, when the season permits, the fellows sit out of doors after dinner, smoking and playing bowls. There is no place in which the spring comes more sweetly than in an Oxford garden where the high walls are at once a trap for the firm warm rays of the sun and a barrier to the winds of March.[39]

Courtney and his cohorts obviously were comparing the physical setting with that of Harvard and other American schools and observing the differences in the styles and decorum of the students. Courtney certainly was systematically and automatically exercising his evaluative skills from the beginning of his second campus experience.

Soon after his arrival he was formally admitted to Merton College to work toward a bachelor of letters degree in English literature under the supervision of Professor C. H. Wilkinson and began course work taught by Professors Nichol Smith, E. K. Chambers, one of the leading authorities on Shakespeare and Elizabethan drama, and C. S. Lewis, who was already known for his work in seventeenth-century English literature and Christian themes in fiction. A few months later, in February of 1939, Courtney was authorized to begin his thesis, entitled "Captain William Hickes as Editor of the Seventeenth Century Drollery."[40]

But Oxford was not all classes and campus social life. Courtney purchased a bicycle and took weekend trips through the countryside, including one to Blenheim Palace. He went to London for a week of receptions given for Rhodes Scholars, and during the two six-week holidays between terms (the vacs) he also took opportunities to travel to Ireland and on the Continent.[41] Late in 1938 Betty and her parents took an automobile tour of Europe, and Courtney joined them for a long Christmas holiday of travel through the French and Italian rivieras.[42]

Having completed the 1938–39 year at Oxford Courtney returned to the United States in June 1939, moving in with the Proctor family at their summer home, Sunrock, on Ocean Avenue in Marblehead Neck, Massachusetts. He was anticipating a second Rhodes year when the war broke out in Europe on September 1, 1939, and the Department of State immediately refused to honor passports for study in Europe.[43] What he could and did continue after his return to the United States were his associations with the many fellows he had gotten to know at Oxford, such as Ed Weismiller, Kermit Gordon, Chadbourne Gilpatric, J. Harlan Cleveland, James Nelson, Elvis Stahr, Stephen Bailey, John Luttrell, Fenwick Jones, and Gilmore Stott. Indeed, he had become firmly connected with an elite band of intellectuals who routinely engaged with each other throughout the next half-century to impact government and educational policies throughout the United States.

More important for his life, however, was that he and Elizabeth (Betty) Bowden Proctor announced their engagement on July 16, 1939, the day before Betty's birthday. An announcement party was held, and the wedding was planned.[44] Betty, born July 17, 1914, was the daughter of George Newton Proctor and Emma Bartoll Bowden, whose primary residence was on Beacon Street in Boston. She had graduated from the Brimmer School and then from Smith College in 1936. She had made her debut in the 1933–34 season at a luncheon given by her mother at Sunrock.[45]

With the return to Oxford impossible, wedding plans could proceed quickly. Betty Proctor and Courtney Smith's outdoor wedding took place on October 1, 1939, at the Proctor's beautiful summer home. It was a formal affair that the Boston community read about on the social page of the *Boston Herald:* Edward R. Weismiller, Courtney's Merton College classmate and fellow Rhodes Scholar was the best man; Mrs. George N. Proctor (Rose Stearns), who was Betty's sister-in-law, and Miss Florence Dabney Smith, Courtney's sister, were the honor attendants. According to newspaper accounts, "The bride wore a gown of lustrous ivory satin with a collar of rare old lace that matched the lace in her heirloom veil. She carried a bouquet of lilies-of-the-valley and bouvardia." The honor attendants were gowned in light blue, wore blue feather hats, and carried pink lilies and blue delphinium.[46] Courtney wore a tailed formal jacket and pin-striped trousers.[47]

After the wedding Ed Weismiller, Courtney's Rhodes colleague from Iowa, wrote a poem to commemorate the event:

> Marriage Song
> (For This Autumn Night)
> The fault of birds that have no song
> Leaves yet a singing on this air:
> How dark must think today too long,
> and day think darkness fair;
> How leaves subdue their dusty speech
> And tremble for the night to come;
> How worlds have now but love to teach,
> With the old wars gone dumb.
>
> It is not I alone who sing,
> Nor I who still the winds above—
> The soft song rises like a wing
> Strong and sweet with love;
> And all this singing shall not cease;
> And two shall be no more apart.
> Brother: sister: have you peace;—
> My loves: my other heart.[48]

The joy of the wedding reflected in this poem may have been slightly dampened by uncertainties regarding Courtney's immediate future. With Courtney unable to return to Oxford, Frank Aydelotte, American Secretary of the Rhodes Program, gave Courtney the opportunity to begin a teaching career by recommending him for an opening at the University of Missouri.[49] But instead Courtney decided to begin graduate work at Harvard.

As newlyweds Courtney and Betty took up residence in a small apartment at 353 Harvard Street in Cambridge, and he started a new program of studies in the fall of 1939, and also accepted a position as a tutor for Harvard University. Immediately Courtney began work toward a doctorate in English literature with course work taught by Professors Kittredge, Lowes, Greenough, Robinson, Cawley, Rollins, Munn, Bush, Murdock, Magoun, Whiting, and Jones. After he was awarded a master's degree in

1941 he became a teaching fellow, and he and Betty moved to a larger apartment at 8 Willard Street in Cambridge.

Betty began her role as an academic wife in these years. She assisted him with his manuscript preparation and after he began doctoral work typed his dissertation, as he regularly worked into the early morning hours. Their life was busy, and Courtney's work consumed much of their attention: his teaching fellowship in the English department instructing both Harvard and Radcliffe students required 60 percent of his time, while his own advanced studies consumed (in theory) 40 percent of his time.[50] His doctoral dissertation, "The Seventeenth-Century Drolleries," was supervised by Hyder E. Rollins and his fellowship by James B. Munn.[51]

Two years into their marriage Betty and Courtney enlarged their family and their family life when Courtney Craig Smith Jr. (Craig) was born February 27, 1942. The Smiths by this time had many friends in Cambridge—some former undergraduate friends such as Bill Murphy, John Ashmead, and Al Damon continued to be close, as did the Rhodes Scholars who had come to Harvard for graduate work (James Nelson, Stephen Bailey, Ed Weismiller), and they also began developing a third network of friends, fellow graduate students Walter Ellis, Bob Riesman, Fred Gwynn, and others.[52] Living with the financial constraints of the war and their studies, these men played touch football, walked along the Charles River on Sundays, and frequently visited each others' homes.[53]

Courtney received his earned doctorate in English literature in 1944, and had it been another era he would have sought a teaching position. But he had made a different choice. It was wartime: there were few opportunities in the academic world, and young men like Courtney yearned for military service. In the fall of 1943, although he had been recommended for an appointment at Princeton University, he applied for and received an appointment in the Naval Reserve.[54]

# 3

## In the Navy

COURTNEY FILED HIS NAVY PAPERS ON OCTOBER 25, 1943, INCLUDING A letter from his Harvard advisor describing him as having "a clear and well controlled mind . . . does not lose his head in a crisis and has always shown clear intelligence in planning any course of action."[1] On November 26th he received notice of his commission (dated November 15, 1943) as an ensign in the U.S. Naval Reserve. That wartime Christmas he gave Betty and himself ceremonial gifts—a "Navy pin from-me-to-you [and] Player cig[arette]s for me—for the sake of tradition."[2] The trim, six-foot, 166-pound Courtney passed his entrance physical January 1, 1944, and reported to Quonset Point (Rhode Island) Naval Air Station on January 4th. At Quonset Point he had six weeks of indoctrination training with other entering Naval Reserve officers.[3] Courtney, having finished his Ph.D., had applied to the navy because he felt it offered "opportunities for more immediate and more important service" than teaching at the few civilian appointments available during the height of wartime mobilization.[4] He finished this orientation and was to be sent to St. Simons Island, Georgia, for Naval Radar Training School, but perhaps his references and honors were noted and his orders were modified: instead, he was assigned to the Naval Air Station (established in 1914) at Pensacola, Florida, March 4, 1944, as a liaison officer for Negro personnel. In this shore duty assignment Betty and son Craig could join him.

To equip him for this unusual responsibility, in late April Courtney was sent to the Naval Training School at Hampton Institute (Virginia) for ten days of special training in "the handling and supervision of Negro personnel."[5] Although the navy had had African-American sailors from the time of the Revolutionary War, since the Civil War era, when 25 percent of the enlisted men were black (although none were officers), the U.S. Navy had become increasingly segregated. From 1922 to 1933 the navy did not even enlist African Americans. But by 1943 the demands of the two-front operation during World War II had strained the navy's personnel resources and particularly the staffing of home-front stations. From 1943 to 1945 the navy recruited hundreds of thousands of African Americans with the intent of training them to do menial and custodial tasks associated with shore installations, both to cope with the vastly increased need for labor, and to be the major source of new personnel to replace the white servicemen sent overseas. But the gathering of large numbers of African Americans at bases and their adjoining towns conflicted with the explicit and implicit Jim Crow regulations and social patterns in both military and civilian communities, particularly in the South.[6]

The navy, which could be held accountable to enforce federal laws and regulations against discrimination, such as provisions of the Selective Service Act and above all the Fourteenth Amendment of the Constitution, responded to the dilemma with a temporizing, expedient policy. Avoiding any role as an agent of change, the navy continued existing segregation patterns and kept the assignments of African Americans to traditional roles of mess workers, custodians, porters, and other manual laborers. But recognizing the explosive potential of the situation, the navy trained and assigned some white officers as liaisons between the naval hierarchy and the burgeoning African-American enlisted and draftee population. The liaison officers' school at Hampton Institute, which Smith attended, was held in conjunction with one of two units in the nation established by the navy to train black officers after basic training. The other school was Camp Robert Smalls at the Great Lakes Training Center.[7]

Captain Edwin H. Downes was commander of the race-relations training program at Hampton Institute and taught Courtney's courses. He was described as "enlightened" and "extremely supportive" by an African American who worked under him for two years as a personnel officer and who noted that he "instilled pride and dignity" and worked hard to motivate people and create good morale.[8]

Ensign Courtney Smith found Downes to be a sophisticated observer of Negro society, culture, and social patterns and acutely aware of the difficulties associated with bringing great numbers of African Americans into the service, where there would be intense interracial contacts. In the *Portfolio for Officers in the Negro Personnel Program,* which was the text for Smith's training, Downes noted that "Negroes need a somewhat different approach from that used with white personnel" but not because of indolence, low expectations of officers, or other prejudicial notions. He argued that Negroes needed a different approach by officers, in music and recreation, criticism of their work, education and training, and social opportunities, because "Negroes are sensitive to niceties of appearance and manners; they expect the best of their officers." In a sequence of further observations and pithy comments, he appealed to various widely held values of white Americans as well as stereotypes in order to instill positive attitudes in the race-relations officers: "Negroes prefer to be participators [in sports] rather than spectators," "eighty percent of Negroes are incompetent until they are given the opportunity to be trained—if a Negro is bawled out for incompetency and he is not particularly intelligent, he is apt to misunderstand and to believe that he is being bawled out for being a Negro"; "most of them have had little or no educational opportunity—they cannot visualize conceptions without the help of visual aids and models"; "as a rule Negroes will work harder than whites, because they know they have two strikes against them"; "segregation has worked well both ways [for blacks and whites] and in varying degrees and respects"; "the worse the community is the more a station needs recreational facilities"; "trouble between whites and Negroes hardly ever occurs between educated members of either race, but usually is caused by white 'trash'—we have to be careful to see that whenever a white man steps out of line he is punished promptly and severely."[9]

There was also discussion in Downes's text of some of the more serious racial problems confronting the navy: fights started by "the dancing of Negroes with white girls," "the stupidity of procurement officers in rating good [Negro] electricians as steward's mates," and the unintentional offending of Negroes by Northern whites who were ignorant of Negro culture and life.[10]

Smith found that Downes's approach to racial issues was similar to that of the commander at Pensacola, Captain H. B. Grow, who openly stated his observations that "human beings, regardless of race or color, in a pretty general way react similarly to similar stimuli." In May of 1943 Grow had assumed command of Pensacola and found a large number of African-American sailors were receiving disciplinary action because of their responses to inequities in liberty privileges and to discrimination on public buses, which would "pass up colored people waiting for busses." Grow made some program changes to address these problems: he initiated more on-grounds social events for Negroes with the assistance of the "colored USO," made "representations to the bus company" when occasions of bus discrimination occurred too numerously, and began requisitioning funds to develop more social facilities for the Negro servicemen.[11]

Courtney arrived at the Pensacola Naval Air Station as one of the first specifically designated liaison officers for Negro personnel, trained by the navy. His initial assignment "consisted of morale work with Negro personnel, involving welfare, educational, personnel, and recreational problems, with collateral duties in venereal disease control and liaison activities with civilian health and welfare organizations."[12] Within five months he reported to his commanding officer that his responsibilities were:

1. To supervise the remedial education project for colored enlisted men conducted at the Booker T. Washington High School, Pensacola.
2. To assist in the indoctrination of colored enlisted men newly assigned to the Naval Air Station.
3. To help foster any program which will contribute to lowering the incidence of venereal disease among colored personnel.
4. To advise colored men on advancements or changes in ratings and on their eligibility for various naval training programs.
5. To counsel colored enlisted men who feel that their current assignment to duty does not fully utilize their Navy training or civilian experience.
6. To work with and advise the Commanding Officer's Honor Committee of Colored Personnel.
7. To serve as a member of the Naval Air Station Welfare Board (representing the interests of colored personnel).
8. To participate actively in local health and welfare groups such as the Negro War-Time Health Committee and the Gulf Health and Welfare Council.
9. To meet with and advise the Governing Board of the Colored USO in an attempt to provide better and more wholesome recreational activities for colored enlisted men going ashore.
10. To advise the Petty Officer-in-charge of the Colored Recreation Building on such matters as are not under the cognizance of the Welfare Division or of Ship's Service.
11. To aid the Entertainment Officer in planning recreational programs (for colored personnel) such as dances, USO shows, and special movies.
12. To perform such minor tasks as are deemed conducive to improving the morale of the colored enlisted men by evidencing the interest of officers in their activities—e.g., attending their church services on the station, visiting long-term invalids in the hospital, following their sporting events, and publicizing their activities in the *Gosport* [newsletter].[13]

In general Courtney's role was to optimize the performance of the 2,500 Negro sailors he dealt with and to help them to feel part of the navy team and not outsiders. This teamwork was not easily fostered, since 87 percent of the Negroes came from the South and most of the whites, too, were from the South, where segregation and discrimination were still strongly embedded in the culture. Courtney decided that one way to manage the difficulties was to encourage Negroes to bring their concerns to him instead of trying to resolve personal problems directly. He found most of their concerns related to station policy and procedure and community issues. Concerns were often expressed about the mistreatment of Negro sailors by civilian police in Pensacola and by navy shore patrols, which were staffed by white naval personnel.

As concerns came to Courtney, he recorded them, gathered information, and made proposals. For example, drivers for Pensacola Transit, the civilian bus company, often demanded that Negro sailors sit in the rear of the bus even though they boarded the busses on the air station grounds, where no such discrimination was to take place.[14] Such incidents deeply frustrated and wounded the morale of the African-American sailors. When one Negro sailor was accused of desertion, Courtney Smith reviewed his record, interviewed other naval personnel, and then wrote a report that summarized the sailor's pattern of reactions to discrimination and recommended discharge, in order to both "free [the serviceman] to make his peace with society and . . . unburden the Navy of a troublesome and maladjusted sailor."[15]

Courtney also reviewed the concerns of fourteen Negro men who were assigned to work in the bowling alley, and who argued that they were being given no opportunity to develop naval skills which would prepare them for advancement. Courtney recommended that sailors be rotated off this duty regularly so that they could demonstrate aptitude in other areas.[16] He attempted this kind of creative programmatic and systematic response on other occasions. When a white officer observing two Negro sailors drinking from a fountain insisted that they use paper cups since they were "niggers," Courtney's recommendation read: "Solution: Spigots on all A & R drink ftns., so that everyone has to use a paper cup."[17]

In his work he had the assistance of a confidential Naval Air Station Colored Honor Committee of eight Negro sailors, which had been appointed by the commanding officer February 11, 1944, a month before Smith's arrival. Grow was particularly gratified with the results of the committee's work and urged department heads and squadron and unit Commanders "to permit unit members of the committee sufficient time each day to circulate among their own people [to] disseminate information and investigate circumstances."[18] According to Courtney, however, "Many officers thought the Honor Committee 'too soviet.' 'The idea,' they said, 'of having those niggers sitting up there in the Captain's office trying to tell him how to run the station'"![19]

If Smith's work on the base was not easy, trying to remedy morale damaged by off-base problems was positively forbidding. Courtney himself reminded the Negro men that although they were in a navy community, with some sensitivity to their needs, "outside the gate [it was a] Southern community," with a strong segregationist and discriminatory tradition.[20]

Sometimes the community attitudes reached inside the base with disturbing effects. Inflammatory articles in the *Pensacola News* and *Pensacola Journal* objected to the handling of racial matters at the station. The papers reported that the conservative Democratic Congressman Bob Sikes, who had been elected to Congress in 1940, had wired Admiral George D. Murray, chief of naval aviation training headquartered in Pensacola, about the reported integration and "race mixing" occurring at the station and the postcards he was receiving from his constituents in the community.[21] When assured by the admiral that "naval regulations for the separation of the groups were being adequately handled," Sikes still pressed to have no further interracial quartering, messing, and drilling, saying, "I am vitally interested in the welfare of the station and I want to see us protect the station but we must also protect the traditions of the South."[22] Ensign Smith found such community-based perceptions were overwhelmingly powerful where Negroes had limited voting rights, and "thereafter whenever the 'federal' approach was proposed, it was always met with the objection that some congressman might protest."[23]

Smith even found that many white naval personnel misunderstood the significance and effectiveness of his work. He wrote down the comments of the officer who introduced him to a group at Pensacola. The officer introduced him as "in charge of colored men, now about 700." Smith laconically quoted the officer's praise of his work: "Shines [have been] sent down here in large numbers, not as messmen but in practically all rates. Smith has done a wonderful job 'keeping them in line.' [The] Honor Committee—which may have done some good, though many thought Grow doing too much. Anyhow, [we] have never had any trouble. When men from Washington, etc., inspected [they] always said we had the best setup *re* Negroes in the whole country. Smith is [the] one who has done most all of this."[24] This officer's simplistic racist commentary was certainly not unique to Smith's experience; even the station newspaper published a racist joke.[25]

A special course of lectures and discussions on the G.I. Bill of Rights was instituted by Smith in August of 1945, and he took pleasure in teaching the men about the opportunities that the bill offered them. He prepared posters and movie slides for the Naval Air Station and each of the auxiliary fields and trained several Negro enlisted men to organize discussion groups and to answer questions pertaining to the bill. Smith reported that the future veterans looked "almost flabbergasted when they learn that some form of aid is provided them no matter which way they jump— education, business, apprentice training, and so on." He commented further in writing to his Harvard professor, "It is my impression that almost

30-40% of the enlisted men are headed back [to school], and 90% of the aviation cadets and young officers." "Of the rest (with the exception of older enlisted men who will resume trades and older officers who will go back to business or professions) many will loaf for a while and look about rather idly for those lucrative 'war-plant jobs' they've heard so much about. And then *some* of them will go back to school."[26]

In the context of the many stresses and tensions of his work, Courtney and Betty seemed to enjoy their time and home in Pensacola and developed friendships with disparate groups of navy men and women who had come to Pensacola from around the country. Elizabeth Bowden Smith (known as Lee) was born June 8, 1944, during their time in Pensacola. Courtney wrote to Professor Munn, his doctoral advisor, that "we're leading a normal, healthy life—making speeches to the American Association of University Women, attending conferences of judges and lawmakers in St. Petersburg, nursing our winter grass along, chatting over the back fence with our All-American (Alabama, Tenn, Calif, Conn, Minn) neighbors, and reveling in the wonderful woods at our back door."[27]

The speeches and conferences Courtney referred to were part of his work with the civilian Gulf Health and Welfare Council, established in April 1944 to initiate and develop social resources lacking in the community (which also had 25,000 Negro citizens). The Council sought improvements in the care and treatment of juvenile delinquents, persons convicted of sex offenses, and dependent and neglected children, and to support efforts to insure better health, and particularly to promote a program for the reduction of venereal disease. By the summer of 1946 Courtney had become its second vice president and the Council had expanded public health services, gotten funding for a detention home for juvenile delinquents, gotten day nurseries established for the children of both Negro and white working mothers, expanded educational programs regarding health and welfare, acquired money to hire a medical social worker, and improved the control of venereal disease.[28]

The time, tasks, and experiences of this liaison work honed Courtney's negotiating skills and his understanding of bureaucracies and interpersonal conflict. He had to negotiate the interfaces of multiple cultures: navy-civilian, black-white, bureaucratic-community, federal-local, Northern-Southern. He had intimate dealings with people from cultures with which he had little or no previous contact. He returned to the civilian world with a deepened understanding of the complexity of American culture and behavior and with growing awareness of his own leadership capabilities and the value of analytic decision making. He had had his first taste of administrative responsibilities: serving various constituencies, seeking congruence of policies and procedures, designing appropriate programs, and making effective recommendations.

Courtney began inactive duty April 30, 1946, remained in the Naval Reserve for several years, and was granted an Honorable Discharge in December 1953.[29]

# 4

# Return to Education: Princeton

AFTER HIS APRIL 1946 RELEASE FROM THE NAVY, COURTNEY TOOK A vacation with his family in New England, where they enjoyed the refreshingly cooler climate. He then began searching for housing in Princeton, New Jersey, where he had been offered an appointment to teach in the department of English at the university. First resident at 114 Elm Street in faculty housing, the Smith family eventually settled at 175 Prospect Avenue, near other English department faculty.[1]

While he was at Pensacola, discussing G.I. benefits with naval personnel, Courtney had recognized that more educators would likely be needed at America's colleges and universities if veterans took up their benefits and arrived on campuses in what would be unprecedented numbers.[2] By the fall of 1945 he was actively searching for a teaching appointment, corresponding with his former professor and mentor at Harvard, Hyder E. Rollins, about possibilities. Rollins, who had first recommended Courtney to Princeton's English Department in the fall of 1943, now wrote to Gerald E. Bentley, a member of the Princeton faculty and scholar of seventeenth-century English literature, Courtney's area of doctoral work. Bentley responded with interest, stating "Smith sounds promising," and asked for his records on December 7, 1945.[3] Princeton, a men's university, was recruiting faculty for President Harold Willis Dodd's "Princeton Program for Servicemen," which was intended to make it "easy for men to resume their education almost as soon as they were discharged."[4]

Smith was hired in the following March at the rank of instructor, with the expectation that he would be "most helpful in carrying out the heavy program of teaching that faces the [English] department next year." In July 1946, Smith began his faculty appointment.[5]

Chartered by Presbyterians in 1746, Princeton University is located in west-central New Jersey in a region first settled by Quakers in 1696. By Smith's time the university and the town had become an education and research complex, site of the Institute for Advanced Study, the American office of the Rhodes Scholars Program, the Princeton Theological Seminary, and laboratories of the Rockefeller Institute for Medical Research, in addition to the facilities of the university. As such Princeton was recognized as a leading center of higher education in the United States, although in the 1940s its small-town environment lent a bucolic air to its intense intellectual pursuits. The Smiths immediately adapted to Princeton's vibrant social and intellectual life, which, although similar to their earlier Harvard environment, was far from what they had experienced more recently in Pensacola. They became known for providing gracious entertainment in their home, and the whole family melded with the community by attending the First Presbyterian Church.[6]

Courtney quickly took advantage of the career opportunities that the Princeton environment provided. In August of 1946 Courtney sought out and had lunch with Frank Aydelotte, who had been American secretary of the Rhodes Scholar Program when Courtney had been selected and sent to Oxford. Aydelotte was a Midwesterner, Rhodes scholar, and golfer; had spent time in Cambridge, Massachusetts; and was "vigorous, loyal, contagiously buoyant, courageous, creative in thought and action, [and] a person of convictions with great understanding, tender tolerance, and love of individuals."[7]

Although until 1939 the Rhodes Scholar Program office for the United States had been at Swarthmore College while Aydelotte had been its president, Aydelotte had moved the office to Princeton when he was appointed director of the Institute for Advanced Study.[8] Aydelotte had followed Courtney Smith's career (as he had followed the careers of many former Rhodes Scholars), so when Courtney resumed his contact with the Rhodes Program after his naval service, Aydelotte unhesitatingly drew him into the ex-Rhodes group that helped him administer the program in the United States, which included Courtney's Oxford classmate Gilmore Stott. Intentionally seeking out this connection with the Rhodes office is early evidence that teaching responsibilities alone were insufficient to sustain Courtney's energies.

In the English Department Courtney followed a normal progression. He was reappointed instructor in 1947–48, then appointed assistant professor in the Department of English in July 1948.[9] During that time he attended many university and department meetings, went to meetings of Phi Beta Kappa, saw sports events, and served as an advisor to the English Club, which had undergraduate seniors, officers of literary clubs, graduate studies, and some humanities faculty as members. His scholarly interests ranged widely, as he published pieces based on his Rhodes experience and on his doctoral work on seventeenth-century English drolleries but also drafted an article on "stereotyped characterizations (according to nationality, religion, or race) in American fiction" and an essay about his naval liaison experiences and reflections, began a book of criticism of American social fiction, and studied the novels and poetry of twentieth-century writers.[10]

This broadening range of expression reflected Courtney's recent past. While out of academia his skills and experiences had grown markedly. He had administered a complex program of race relations, had dealt with the wide range of people brought into the military as servicemen, and had read literature on African-American society and culture, such as Richard Wright's *Black Boy,* W. E. B. Du Bois's *Color and Democracy,* and Gunnar Myrdal's *An American Dilemma.*

Smith's new interests made him a natural ally of those in the English department who believed that American and twentieth-century texts needed to have a larger role in its curriculum. In February 1949 the convened department formally adopted a new four-course sequence for majors, including American Literature, Modern Dramatic Art, English Thought during the Last Hundred Years, and Modern Literature.[11] Immediately Modern Literature, regarded as a "key course" in the sequence, was entrusted to Smith, who taught it for two years.[12] The university catalog described the course as providing "critical interpretations" of "Yeats, Eliot, Frost, Joyce, Hemingway and Steinbeck, or Farrell."[13]

Smith was carving out a significant identity for himself in the department by taking a visible role in the new curriculum, an initiative that few could have anticipated when he was hired. Moreover, he moved even further from his graduate school focus by participating in his department's American Civilization Program. Founded in January 1942, the program at its inception trained British and American military officers as well as regular undergraduates. Princeton faculty from departments as diverse as art and archeology, economics, English, history, philosophy, and politics oversaw classes on, among other topics, racial, group, and ethnic issues and their impact on American civilization.[14]

Courtney was asked in May 1949 to be the English department's representative on the American Civilization Program's board for 1949–50, and then became acting chairman and conference director of the American Civilization Program in spring 1950, throwing himself into the role with enthusiasm. The program's conference director ran the senior-year seminar for program majors, with the seminar's topic announced annually: for 1949–50, when Smith supervised the second semester, the topic was "The Issues of American Life, 1918–1948, and their Expression in Literature and the Arts."[15] According to the former chairman of the program, Willard Thorp, Courtney performed services for the program "in and out of season way beyond the call of duty" and quickly got to "know more about the Program and what it may do for its students than anyone."[16] A Princeton colleague later recalled that in that role Smith had demonstrated that he was a "natural administrator."[17]

In the spring of 1951 Courtney was appointed a bicentennial preceptor. Preceptorships had been established by Princeton University President Woodrow Wilson in 1905 and were designed to provide tutors (mentors) to undergraduate juniors and seniors who would guide them in their reading for both course work and independent studies in their major field.[18] The preceptorial system was expected to "promote intelligent discussion based on or springing from a specific body of reading"; assure "the expression of opinion, and of difference of opinions"; assure expression of individual ideas; and to develop the skill to defend one's own ideas against conflicting ideas. Preceptors working with seven to ten men were to suggest "new questions" and act as "informal umpire[s]," in order to "give practice to the art of conversation, in exchanging opinions and reaching conclusions in intelligent, civilized, and courteous fashion."[19]

Courtney's preceptorship, part of a new class of preceptorships at Princeton created with alumni gifts, was a position at the assistant professor level but provided a higher salary; it also was a three-year appointment with one year devoted to a leave for scholarship. The purpose of a preceptorship for junior faculty was "to provide outstanding young men the opportunity to advance in both teaching effectiveness and scholarship thereby strengthening the Faculty and the quality of undergraduate instruction."[20]

Courtney, having experienced and appreciated guidance from professors at Oxford and having done similar work at Harvard before joining the navy, clearly enjoyed his preceptor role. His students commented on his ability to instill the highest ideals of the academic profession and on his "quiet and perceptive brilliance" as a mentor, his thoroughness in reviewing their work, and his receptive demeanor.[21]

Some of his colleagues were struck by his evident teaching ability and commitment to the educational process. A fellow junior faculty member described him as "one of the very best preceptors in the university, and that principally because he [was] one of the most patient, gentle (in the best sense), understanding, helpful teachers I have ever run across"; similarly, another peer described him as "the greatest listener I've ever met."[22] A senior colleague stated that he was "one of the best of our younger teachers in the English department. I have taught with him in several courses, and in every way he has pleased me. I have always asked for him as a preceptor in my courses . . . he [has been] outgoing in his relations with students, always willing to spend extra time with those who need extra help"; a third colleague noted, "he [had] an unusually strong interest in students . . . much more than most teachers have."[23]

Although Courtney himself characterized his years at Princeton as an outstanding experience, it was not idyllic, particularly in regard to income. He struggled with what he believed to be the inadequacy of his salary to meet the needs of a family. When Courtney was hired as instructor in 1946 his salary was $3,000, and it was increased annually until as an assistant professor in 1950 he received $4500. His subsequent preceptorship yielded about $5,000 with an additional $500 for research expenses.[24] After his first year at Princeton, he recorded in a dismayed note to his department chair that "our living expenses between 15 September 1946 and 15 May 1947 have taken *all* my salary plus *all* the money we have received from our 'investments' plus *all* the money we were given at Christmas to 'go out and buy books and records with' plus $1,620 in war bonds which we saved during the war. What price glory!"[25] He thought that academic salaries in general needed to be increased, and when Courtney left the Woodrow Wilson Fellowship Program in 1953 he emphatically recommended a higher salary be provided for his successor, Robert Goheen. He argued that $6,000 per year was too low and $8,000 a year was adequate, but $10,000 was "proper."[26]

Whatever the salary struggles at Princeton, while he was there he did enjoy the extra challenge of working with the Rhodes program. Aydelotte was a formidable leader who developed talent not only by the selection of Rhodes Scholars but also by identifying promising future academic leaders and taking them on as his assistants. Smith seemed to recognize that working with the Rhodes program offered the opportunity to become a protégé of a stimulating and well-connected leader in the American academic community.

Beginning in 1947 Courtney served as the secretary of the New Jersey Committee of Selection for the Rhodes Scholarships, and that same year attended the grand reunion of two hundred twenty-two former scholars at Princeton. He later became quite involved in the national program and by 1952 became Aydelotte's assistant. Courtney was the last of a series of Rhodes Scholars who assisted Aydelotte and then went on to distinguished careers in academic administration: Alan Valentine became president of the University of Rochester, John W. Nason followed Aydelotte as president of Swarthmore College and later became president of Carleton College, James Hester became president of New York University, Henry A. Moe became president of the Guggenheim Foundation, and Gilmore Stott served in the Swarthmore College administration for forty years.[27] When

Aydelotte retired in 1952 after thirty-five years as Rhodes secretary, Courtney Smith was appointed the new American secretary of the Rhodes Scholar Program and began his international duties effective January 1, 1953.[28]

Smith in the meantime had not remained in his preceptor position very long, evincing an inclination toward administration that was stronger than his commitment to teaching. In February 1952 he took a partial leave and began helping Whitney Oates, the director of the Woodrow Wilson Fellowship Program, to develop its new national program.[29] These new administrative roles tapped Smith's attributes that made him not only an excellent teacher, but also a fine future administrator: personal warmth and charm, an interest in others, an ease in meeting people, and a ready ability to articulate program ideas and procedures.[30]

Smith's professional growth was accompanied by family growth. While at Princeton, Courtney and Betty saw the enlargement of their family with the birth of Carol Dabney Smith (known as "Dabney") on October 15, 1947. The family began taking summer vacations at Squam Lake, New Hampshire, in 1950, and Betty continued to focus her attentions on being an excellent mother to the three children, a skilled homemaker, and an academic wife. The Princeton community knew Betty as gracious, lovely, and attractive. Betty was both a socially and financially supportive partner for Courtney, since she had an inherited independent income that afforded their family some relief from the burdens of typical academic life.[31]

For 1952–1953 Courtney took a full leave from his preceptorship in order to assume the challenge of developing a national program for the Woodrow Wilson Fellowships. It was apparent to much of the Princeton community that Courtney's gravitation toward administrative positions was complete, and many of his colleagues thought that it was in such roles rather than scholarship where his greatest skills lay.[32] The Woodrow Wilson Fellowship Program was about to test those observations.

Courtney C. Smith's home in Winterset, Iowa, prior to his father's death. Courtesy of Elizabeth Smith Ingram.

Smith at play in Winterset, Iowa, ca. 1926. Courtesy of Elizabeth Smith Ingram.

**Smith about the time of his move to Des Moines, Iowa, ca. 1931. Courtesy of Elizabeth Smith Ingram.**

**Smith bicycling during a Rhodes Scholar weekend in his Oxford year, ca. 1939.
Courtesy of Elizabeth Smith Ingram.**

**An exuberant Elizabeth (Betty) Bowden Proctor, ca. 1938. Courtesy of Elizabeth Smith Ingram.**

**Courtney Smith, in his navy uniform, with Betty and Craig (Courtney Craig Smith, Jr.), ca. 1945. Courtesy of Elizabeth Smith Ingram.**

A professor and his family: (left to right) Lee, Betty, Craig, Dabney, and Smith at Princeton, New Jersey, ca. fall 1948. Courtesy of Elizabeth Smith Ingram.

The Smith family, late 1951 or early 1952, in Princeton, N.J. Front (left to right): Carol Dabney, Courtney Craig Jr., Elizabeth (Lee). Back (left to right): Courtney, Betty. Courtesy of Elizabeth Smith Ingram.

# 5

# The Woodrow Wilson Program Years

THE WOODROW WILSON FELLOWSHIP PROGRAM, WHICH COURTNEY WAS to develop, was inaugurated in the autumn of 1945 by Whitney J. Oates, a professor of classics and humanities at Princeton University, and was named by Oates's wife in honor of the former president of Princeton. Oates was chairman of the university's the special program in humanities, "an interdisciplinary plan of study that exerted lasting influence on the form and spirit of education at Princeton." He had a special concern for the development of support for the humanities in the post–World War II era, and in addition to creating the Woodrow Wilson Fellowship Program Oates was a leader in creating both the National Endowment for the Arts and the National Endowment for the Humanities.[1]

The Woodrow Wilson Fellowship Program was in origin a Princeton program to identify and give financial support to first-year Princeton graduate students in the social sciences and humanities who "possessed the highest qualities of intellect and character." It was designed to support "those in particular, who had never thought of an academic career, or at least were undecided upon it" and could be encouraged to pursue graduate education, if they had assurance of an adequate living for a year. Initial funding was provided by gifts from Isabella Kemp and Mr. and Mrs. Randolph Compton (New York City), William D. Sherrerd Jr. (Philadelphia), and the trustees of Princeton University.[2]

The program, however, soon took nominations from other institutions in the mid-Atlantic region, and in consequence of its broader reach received $100,000 in March of 1949 from the Carnegie Corporation of New York to support the expanded program. Later, on May 5, 1951, representatives of Princeton University, the Carnegie Corporation, the Rockefeller Foundation, the General Education Board, the American Council of Learned Societies, the Association of Graduate Schools in the Association of American Universities, and the Woodrow Wilson Fellowship administrative committee met and decided that the program should extend nationwide. They agreed that the Association of American Universities (AAU) was "the logical body to carry on the operation of the program in the future," should "seek support for the program from foundations and other sources," and should "determine the extent to which the member institutions of the AAU would be prepared to underwrite the program." On November 20, 1951, in response to a proposal from Oates and the AAU the Carnegie Corporation made a further one-year grant of $50,000 to fund the 1952–53 fellowships and "explore the ways and means for establishing an enlarged program in the future and its financing by institutions and foundations." In December 1951 with the Woodrow Wilson Fellowship Program having grown substantially, its board decided that the program should find a national director, develop policies for future operations, and meet the new funding and program objectives.[3]

Professor J. L. Shanley of Northwestern University was initially asked to become its national director but upon his declination, Oates and Smith, both at Princeton, were appointed co-directors to run the program for the remainder of the 1951–52 academic year. Smith was assigned to take on the crucial task of visiting thirty-seven members of the Association of Graduate Schools, which were scattered throughout the country, to ascertain views on selection of a national director, the organization of regional committees for the selection of fellows, suggested modes of institutional support, the problem of distribution of fellows, and the cooperation of other foundations in the program. Courtney was specifically to assess the financial support each graduate school would offer the fellows.[4]

Princeton had already developed the tradition of waiving tuition payments for Woodrow Wilson fellows. Courtney obtained commitments from the graduate schools of $46,920 in support, and that, along with a new Carnegie grant of $100,000 and a General Education Board grant of $60,000, allowed the program to dramatically expand from twenty-nine fellows in 1952–53 to one hundred one fellows for the 1953–54 year![5]

When Oates went off to the American Academy at Rome for 1952–53, Smith was appointed the national director (July 1, 1952) and managed the program's expansion.[6] He developed functional regional selection committees and processes and pursued long-range funding that would put the program on a permanent footing.

Smith had been concerned for some time about the postwar economic and demographic conditions that would challenge the teaching profession. In the fall of 1952, Courtney wrote specifically about these concerns and the potential of the Woodrow Wilson program to address them. He expressed his concern that "the rewards of teaching are far from obvious, we have difficulty in maintaining our [teaching] ranks, and revitalizing our forces, and competing with the more lucrative professions and the journalistically more glamorous professions for the talent we want and need."[7] He knew that higher education enrollments were building up, and he was concerned about whether high-quality people could be drawn to the challenge of teaching in the humanities and social sciences. He and others saw that science, with its industrial fellowships, sponsored research, and hundreds of fellowships given by the National Science Foundation, was able to attract many students with intelligence, character, and personality to graduate school and thence to teaching. Courtney hoped that the Woodrow Wilson fellowships for social sciences and humanities students would do the same.

Courtney worked with Whitney Oates to design a regional nomination process, similar to that of the Rhodes Scholars program, for the United States and Canada. It had allotments of fellowships for each region, assuring maximum outreach and geographic distribution of not only the fellowships, but also the impact of the program. He had experienced the benefits of that system when selected as a Rhodes Scholar and later when serving as a Rhodes Selection Committee member. He knew that such a selection system generated enthusiasm and competitive standards.

In the fall of 1952 Smith appointed the members of the twelve Woodrow Wilson fellowship regional selection committees and had them visit the colleges and universities in their areas in order to talk about the fellowship program and encourage the nomination of outstanding male and female students. This outreach was crucial since students could not apply for fellowships; they had to be nominated for them by their professors.

He was very concerned about the quality of those that the program was drawing into the teaching profession. Courtney admonished the members of the regional selection committees "not to fill their quota if the quality of the candidates does not merit it." He stated flatly, "If a candidate is not clearly first-rate he should not be given a second thought. The number of teachers in the profession is not our concern; the quality is."[8]

The deadline for the 1953–54 nominations was January 5, 1953, and Smith was delighted to find that his efforts had brought the names of one thousand two hundred sixty-three men and women to the twelve regional committees. Three hundred nineteen nominees were invited to be interviewed by their committees; the committees found that the interviews allowed them to see individual characteristics and brilliance not identifiable on paper nominations, and they were enthusiastic about the process. By February the regional selection committees had completed their interviews and filled their quotas by choosing seventy fellows and identifying sixty-two alternates. Because in January additional funding from the General Education Board was available, Courtney was able to enlarge the program even further by creating a national selection committee that granted awards to an additional thirty-one of the designated alternates.[9]

Courtney's review showed that the fellows included twenty-four women and seventy-seven men who had come from seventy-four institutions and who would go to forty-one different universities in the United States, Canada, and Europe.[10] Smith commented to Hugh S. Taylor, chair of the Fellowship Committee of the Association of Graduate Schools, that in his opinion "the selection process functioned smoothly. . . . and the system of quotas assigned on the basis of the undergraduate population in appropriate institutions assured each region of its fair share of the awards." The fellowship program was also considered successful because the admitting graduate schools were reportedly "enthusiastic about their 'haul'" of highly qualified students.[11]

In addition to setting up this smooth selection system Courtney contributed to the stabilization of the program by successfully gaining long-term support from two major American educational foundations. He was able to build upon the relationship and credibility that Whitney Oates had established with both the Carnegie Corporation and the General Education Board. The Carnegie Corporation had been established in 1911 to support educational programs and institutions in the United States and typically supported initiatives that it believed would eventually become self-sustaining. The General Education Board was created in 1902 by John D. Rockefeller to support secondary and higher education throughout the United States but particularly in the South.[12] Courtney persuaded both of them to make five-year commitments to the Woodrow Wilson Fellowship Program.

Courtney found it easy to work with the Carnegie Corporation for it had shown continuous interest from the time of its first grant to the program in 1949, prior to Smith's involvement in the program. Carnegie had a tradition of supporting Princeton initiatives, and Charles Dollard, the president of Carnegie in the late 1940s and 1950s, was a personal friend of Hugh S. Taylor, the dean of the Princeton Graduate School, who initially helped Oates create the Wilson program.[13] Carnegie gave initial support of $100,000 in 1949 and $50,000 in 1951; then while Smith was director of the Fellowship program, Carnegie agreed to make the substantial commitment of $100,000 annually for five years beginning in the fall of 1952.[14]

The General Education Board (GEB) needed more persuasion to join in the funding of the fellowships, because it had had its own fellowship program for three decades. Its fellowships initially gave support especially to promising black students from the South, who would go on to do graduate studies, but in 1950 the GEB initiated a new program to encourage approximately forty white and black students from the South to enter the teaching profession and modeled it on the Wilson program. In the early 1950s, under the direction of President Dean Rusk, the GEB was intentionally spending out its endowment and was considering how it could leave its legacy to other active programs.[15] Oates had already had discussions with the GEB, starting in 1950, about the potential for merger of the two fellowship programs.[16] It is likely that Oates felt he could raise such a possibility because the president of Princeton University, Harold W. Dodds, was a trustee of the General Education Board.[17]

By the time Courtney Smith became national director there were long discussions about exactly when and how the programs could be merged and yet guarantee the same number of fellowships for the Southern students. Courtney and others involved with the Woodrow Wilson program had many communications with the General Education Board's program officer, L. F. Kimball. And on November 10th, there was a particularly critical encounter: it seemed that the GEB would give no immediate funding to the Woodrow Wilson Fellowship Program because the GEB was reluctant to provide money when it felt that other already-committed institutions could give support to the Wilson program. All signs indicated that the GEB was inclined to maintain its own program for at least another year.[18]

But Smith's defense of his proposal had in fact turned the situation around. As Kimball noted in his office diary, "I raised all of the tough questions I could think of and they were all answered promptly and satisfactorily."[19] Within a brief time the GEB decided not only that it would not withhold its financial support from the Woodrow Wilson program, but that it would make a considerable commitment to support the program. In December the GEB made a $300,000 grant for three years, 1953–1955, and GEB president Dean Rusk gave private assurance that there would be a further $200,000 grant for 1956–57.[20] With that support in place, Courtney was able to work out an allocation plan to assure the GEB that the Wilson program could offer the desired level of Southern fellowships.[21]

Courtney had come to the Woodrow Wilson position wanting "to see people selected who were intellectually first-rate, intellectually powerful, people who had an insatiable curiosity in their field and a passion for the field which would be communicated to others and would also stimulate colleagues in other disciplines to see new possibilities, and ask new questions, in their own fields. And [he] wanted to see people selected who were not only first-rate in intellect but first-rate in character and in personality."[22] Courtney also had clearly demonstrated his ability to develop programs and work with national funding agencies. When he left the national director position, a year earlier than he expected, to take on his new responsibilities as president of Swarthmore College, he said, "It's been great fun administering the Program this year, and what I lose on the swings in leaving the program I hope in a few years from now to make up on the roundabouts by attempting to hire all of this year's Fellows for the faculty of a certain college in Swarthmore, Pennsylvania."[23]

Courtney had made strong connections throughout the United States, had become an able fund-raiser for programs, and had been recognized as having a personality that developed the confidence of those he was leading. As one of his contemporaries commented as he departed from the directorship: "you held the Fellowship Program together by your own personality last year . . . [with] the quiet way in which you ran it. . . . We felt that you were in touch with us all the time, that you were giving us complete support, and yet there was no sensation of being pushed."[24] Courtney had developed a style of leadership that others admired.

# 6

# Swarthmore College at Mid-Century

SWARTHMORE COLLEGE WAS FOUNDED IN 1864 BY A GROUP OF THE Hicksite branch of Society of Friends (Quakers) intent on providing a higher education institution for both men and women, but never was under the aegis of any governing body of the Society of Friends. Named for the home of George Fox, the founder of the Quakers in England, the college in its early years was supported by a group of Philadelphia Quakers who provided both financial underpinning and family members as students. For its first three decades the college had a solid reputation, but it was not particularly distinguishable from other small sectarian colleges throughout the United States. It struggled with integration of women into an institution of higher education (when there were few co-educational institutions in the United States), with the degree to which Quaker traditions and faith should shape the policies of the college, and with the means of assuring financial security for the institution.[1] The college made an important decision in 1902 when for its new head, it hired away from the presidency of Indiana University Joseph Swain, a mathematician who had studied in Europe.

Swain set higher academic standards for the college, hired outstanding new faculty, and insisted that the college's Board of Managers find ways to significantly increase the endowment. During the early years of the century, the college became known for its outstanding football teams, but Swain's leadership also set it on a course of increasing academic standards. When Swain left in 1921 the college had five hundred students, a strengthened faculty of forty-five, and an endowment of $3,000,000. By 1915 the General Education Board ranked Swarthmore as one of the first-class American colleges.[2]

Swain was succeeded by Frank Aydelotte, the first president without a Quaker background. He came to the attention of the Board of Managers by Swain's recommendation. Aydelotte was a Harvard graduate, a Rhodes Scholar, and a former professor at both Indiana University, where Swain had known him, and the Massachusetts Institute of Technology.

Frank Aydelotte had grown up in Indiana and received his bachelor's degree from Indiana University in 1900; he had studied classics at Harvard and received a master's there in 1903. He had taught high school in Louisville, Kentucky, and after hearing about the institution of the Rhodes Scholar program sought and obtained one of the first appointments. His two years at Oxford University, 1905–7, permanently changed his views of higher education. He developed a lifetime commitment to the Rhodes Scholars program, organizing returning scholars, serving as editor of *The American Oxonian,* and in 1918 becoming the administrator of the program in the United States.

Aydelotte's intellectual orientation was not a perfect fit for Swarthmore, which Abraham Flexner, his longtime friend, called "a 'football' college." But Flexner later realized that "Aydelotte shrewdly perceived" that Swarthmore could be transformed into a quality institution that would perform an "important service to American education and American life"—a function that he believed was "the justification of all professions and all occupations."[3]

According to one commentator, "Aydelotte was looking for a place where he could put into practice his conviction that the Oxford System of intense study for honors could be adapted to American colleges. He said time and again, before and after his arrival at Swarthmore, that American colleges were very good at mass education but not very good at educating superior students to their potential."[4]

In considering the presidency Aydelotte asked the Swarthmore faculty members whether they would work with him to develop an intense honors program, and it was their affirmative replies that convinced him to accept the position. The college, under the following two decades of Aydelotte's leadership, transformed itself into a leading intellectual undergraduate institution with a reputation that extended throughout the United States.

The honors program he initiated at Swarthmore addressed his concern about the need for American colleges to better educate superior students to their potential. Faculty selected outstanding students at the end of their sophomore year and put them in an honors-track curriculum; in their third and fourth years they then took only two intense reading seminars each semester. The honors program thus accelerated and focused their studies, climaxing with examinations administered at the end of the fourth year by visiting committees of professors from other institutions. The students who passed the examinations were then graduated from Swarthmore "with honors." This program with its national visiting committee component dramatically increased applications to the college and made it possible for the college to enlarge its constituency. Students applied from throughout the country and competed with the traditional Quaker students for both admission and recognition.

The honors program significantly changed the college.[5] Many alumni expressed concern that their children and grandchildren, under this new system, were not being admitted to the school as expected. They were also concerned about the increased emphasis upon academic achievement and its consequential threat to traditional college activities. They voiced annoyance that sports, particularly football, were increasingly regarded as adjunct activities on campus and that the school no longer competed with Ivy League and Big Ten institutions on the gridiron. Many were also dismayed that students attacked the system of sororities on campus and during 1933–34 voted to eliminate them.[6]

Aydelotte pushed forward despite these criticisms. For him, the primary concern was the need for extra funding during the transition while the college did not have full alumni support. He wanted to attract outstanding faculty and students and sought funding from the General Education Board, the largest private philanthropic foundation already committed to improving standards at the leading higher education institutions throughout the United States. Believing that if one "make[s] the peaks higher" other institutions will rise to the new standards, the General Education Board found at Swarthmore an exemplar for its program. Aydelotte, who had known the longtime GEB trustee, Abraham Flexner, since they had taught together in Louisville, was able to convince the GEB to grant Swarthmore $240,000 of general support over five years, starting in 1925.[7] The GEB's support of Swarthmore continued during Aydelotte's successful $4,000,000 capital funds campaign (begun in 1929), when it gave an additional $675,000 to the college's endowment.[8]

Aydelotte, who demonstrated that he was "an engine of inexhaustible energy" who could involve his colleagues "in prodigious undertakings with an air of inviting them to share in a lark" had, with the support of the faculty and managers, transformed the college into an academic form almost unique in America.[9] He led this new Swarthmore until 1940, when he resigned to head the Institute for Advanced Study (Princeton, New Jersey), replacing the Institute's founding director, Abraham Flexner.

A new joint committee of the Board of Managers, faculty, and alumni met to consider Aydelotte's successor. They selected John W. Nason, who had been a Rhodes Scholar in 1928–31, had taught philosophy at Swarthmore for eight years, and had assisted Aydelotte with the administration of both the Rhodes Scholar program and the college in 1937–38 and the spring of 1940.[10] Nason had served Aydelotte as a "troubleshooter" and liaison with college administrations involved in the Rhodes Program. The committee knew that Nason was a supporter of the Aydelotte vision for the college and would provide continuity.[11] Nason had graduated Phi Beta Kappa from Carleton College (1926), studied at Yale Divinity School (1926–27), gotten a master's degree in philosophy at Harvard (1928), and had a degree from Oxford University in philosophy, politics, and economics (1931). Along with his wife, Bertha Dean White, a 1926 Swarthmore graduate, Nason sought to improve the level of trust and sense of community at Swarthmore.[12]

Nason was a "Quaker by convincement" and married to a Quaker. He focused upon the expansion and cultivation of alumni support and worked to integrate some alumni wishes with the newer academic thrusts. He appointed an alumni director and strengthened the Alumni Association. In 1941 the college resumed its Haverford-Swarthmore football rivalry, and in the second year of Nason's presidency the college had its first Alumni Fund Drive, collecting $17,454 from 27 percent of the alumni.[13] Although he found it difficult to build up the endowment as rapidly as needed for the changing times, Nason was successful in rekindling the interest of many alumni.[14]

Nason later recounted one vignette that illustrated the change: "I can remember an alumnus coming up to me on a cold Saturday afternoon and saying, 'you know I'm glad to be back on the campus to see a football game. I vowed I would never come back to this campus as long as Aydelotte was President. . . . I have to admit, I think, publicly, Aydelotte was right and I was wrong.'"[15]

John Nason had an agenda when he took office in 1940 but found that "One year after I became president much of what I had intended to do was simply put aside because of the war."[16] The draft and war work took 25 percent of the faculty away, male enrollment dropped precipitously, and the college struggled with finances, its response to the war, and its role as a service institution. After considerable discussion and consideration by the faculty, the college decided to take on a navy training unit of three hundred officers, instituted summer sessions so that students could graduate within three years, and accepted a unit of forty-nine Chinese naval officers who were to be taught English on the campus.

This bought another wave of dramatic changes to Swarthmore. Most men on campus were now men in uniform. The navy integrated the campus by bringing three blacks to campus in its unit. The college and government became integrally bound for the first time, and it was clear that at least temporarily it was a financially necessary arrangement. The Quaker college, known for its pacifist expressions in World War I, broadened its position by both affirming on the one hand its commitment to peacemaking, but on the other hand accepting its role in the education of servicemen. And although the college had not felt ready to accommodate Negro students in 1940 when there was discussion of minority enrollments, it was soon thrust into the experience of having Negroes on campus.[17]

From 1940 to 1952 Nason worked hard not only to maintain student enrollment and the college's solvency but also academic standards. He asked the Alumni Council to study the academic program in 1943 and worked with a faculty curriculum committee as it recommended mandatory courses in the humanities, social sciences, and natural sciences for freshmen and sophomores.

The end of the war brought certain questions about the changes the college had experienced. The Student Association established a race relations committee in 1946. The *Phoenix* ran an editorial in 1947 regarding discrimination against Jewish and black applicants to the college. Applications for enrollment again increased and there was renewed pressure to accept more students. There were large percentages of veterans (51 percent of the men in 1947) in incoming classes, and Nason noted in 1949 that veterans "returned [to college] with an intensity of purpose hardly known before on campus . . . their greater maturity has been a stimulus to their instructors, a wholesome goal for freshman straight from school, and a valuable influence within the student body in general . . . at no time has the public discussion of current issues been more vigorous or more intelligent."[18]

The college was simply beginning to confront some of the same emerging issues as the rest of the nation, all of which raised questions about the function and responsibilities of educational institutions in society. Throughout the United States, not just at Swarthmore, faculties were encountering veterans who "revealed unprecedented enthusiasm for learning" and who "brought into what had been relatively sheltered academic communities experiences and knowledge of distant parts of the world."[19] In 1942 "Edwin Embree, president of the Julius Rosenwald Foundation, criticized Swarthmore for not admitting blacks, causing the *Phoenix* to write an editorial urging their admission."[20] In 1949, the faculty and students voted unanimously to support those on the faculty of the University of California who had refused to sign the state-required loyalty oath. In 1950, with the developing perception that communists had significant influence in American colleges and universities, Nason responded publicly that communism was incompatible with free inquiry on campuses.[21] And in 1951 the fraternities were criticized by students for being discriminatory, and there was a movement, supported by both nonfraternity members and fraternity brothers, to question the membership policies of national fraternal organizations.[22] These matters were not easily resolved and continued to affect the college throughout the next decade.

By 1952 the college was in excellent financial condition, had a fine faculty, was known for its strong academic program, and again had sound alumni support. The honors program was vigorous, and the college's reputation was generating a strong applicant pool. In November Nason announced his intention to leave Swarthmore and become president of the Foreign Policy Association.[23] Swarthmore College set about a search for a new leader. The history and the traditions of the college set many of the parameters for the presidential search, but the search was open.

# 7

## Swarthmore Looks for Courtney

When the Board of Managers received Nason's resignation on November 29, 1952, they drew together a presidential selection committee composed of managers, faculty, and alumni, just as they had upon the resignation of Frank Aydelotte twelve years before. The managers were represented by Boyd T. Barnard, Richard C. Bond, Eleanor S. Clarke, Hilda Lang Denworth, Thomas B. McCabe, and Claude C. Smith (chairman of the Board), *ex-officio;* the faculty by George Becker, Howard Jenkins, Clair Wilcox; the alumni by William F. Lee, Richard W. Slocum, and William H. Ward. (All except Becker and Wilcox were Swarthmore alumni and most were Quakers.)[1] Thomas B. McCabe, a graduate of Swarthmore in 1915, a manager since 1935, former chairman of the Board of Governors of the Federal Reserve System, and president of Scott Paper Company, was made chairman of the selection committee.[2]

The committee deliberated in the Quaker tradition, seeking input from the entire community. After discussing the qualifications it sought in candidates, the committee wrote to all alumni to solicit nominations. It brought into consideration as many viewpoints as possible, attempting to reach a general consensus and to act with a sense of unity.[3]

The committee found it difficult to define what sort of person it was searching for as president other than for "an outstanding human being, not for an embodiment of a particular philosophy of education or specialized skill in administration."[4] The members generally agreed, however, "that he be no more than 53 or 54 years old, that he be an educator . . . , that he come from outside the college, and that it would be desireable, though not mandatory, that he be a Quaker."[5] (It seems that the committee never considered the possibility that it would have a female candidate who would meet the criteria.)

The alumni of the college responded to the search enthusiastically, submitting dozens of nominations, and indeed the committee soon accumulated 236 potential candidates for the presidency.[6] But the nomination that bore the most weight came from former Swarthmore president

Frank Aydelotte, who had been serving on the Board of Managers since 1945.[7]

Aydelotte told the committee that "the one person whom I should most enthusiastically propose as president of Swarthmore is Professor Courtney Smith of Princeton, who has acted as my assistant for some time in the Rhodes Trust office and who has succeeded me as American Secretary. Professor Smith was a Rhodes Scholar himself. . . . He seems to me to have just the qualities which would be wanted at Swarthmore and his wife and family [are] admirably suited to help him in the job. . . . I feel quite certain that Courtney Smith will become a college president somewhere and I should like to see Swarthmore [be] the place."[8]

This recommendation was immediately taken seriously by the committee in part because Aydelotte was known personally by several of the board members and was held in highest respect due to their own experience with his remarkable educational leadership. Further, Aydelotte was known to have a keen ability to identify talented young educators. His former protégé, John Nason, had been highly successful as president of Swarthmore, and through the years Aydelotte, by bringing them into his office, had trained other men who had taken on leading educational roles throughout the country: at this point his former assistant, Detlev Bronk, was president of Johns Hopkins; Alan Valentine was master of Pierson College at Yale University and then president of the University of Rochester; James Hester was president of New York University; and Henry A. Moe was president of the Guggenheim Foundation.[9]

Comments about Courtney Smith quickly began coming into the committee. On January 22, 1953, Courtney was interviewed at Swarthmore by Thomas McCabe, who according to Boyd Barnard was assigned to "look into Courtney Smith's politics."[10] McCabe did not get answers about Smith's politics but was impressed by him, and at the next committee meeting "urged that close scrutiny of Smith's capacities for the Presidency be carried on rapidly."[11] Indeed, McCabe was so impressed by Smith that at the same time he gave only cursory notice to the committee regarding the other four candidates who were under consideration at the time.

Further comments about Courtney were solicited both directly and indirectly, but primarily the committee relied on the views of Princeton faculty colleagues and Rhodes Scholar classmates.[12] George Becker, secretary of the committee, provided a written summary of the feedback for the committee: Courtney was described as "an extremely hard worker, a very able teacher and a very level-headed person," "soft-spoken, gentle, gracious, sensitive, considerate, tactful, well-mannered in every way . . . [with] a strong moral sense, a strong interest in social problems," "[having] an excellent understanding of the problems and objectives of a liberal arts college," "[having] convictions about things . . . [and] capable of standing his ground on things that really matter," "a man of principle [who] has a quiet force and can be firm."[13] Even those who commented about his youthfulness and his lack of scholarship and publications balanced those remarks with commentary about his energy, commitment to education, strong ethics, and good judgment. Many commented as well on Betty Smith, who was described as "a good academic wife, a good . . . hostess, . . . an excellent mother and housekeeper," and "very attractive and nice," "gracious, poised, dignified," and "perfectly lovely." Some commentors anticipated that Betty would be "an asset to Courtney and the college," and that she "would be universally adored."[14]

The full selection committee proceeded to interview Smith on February 23d, and by March 16th the committee was enthusiastically planning to invite Courtney (their front-running candidate) and Betty Smith to meet the deans, officers of the college, department chairs, and leaders of the Board of Managers.[15]

On March 23 Courtney spent the afternoon and evening at Swarthmore meeting those constituencies. According to the memorandum sent to Courtney by Clair Wilcox, the faculty representative who organized the visit, the faculty was told that Courtney was visiting in order to meet people and learn about Swarthmore before deciding on whether he would like to be considered for the position, but in fact the committee's purpose was "(1) to give key members of the administration and the faculty . . . the feeling of being included at a stage prior to final decision and announcement, and (2) to break the ice for you [Courtney] and [to enable them to] greet you with familiar rather than strange faces in the fall."[16] It was clear that the managers had already made a de facto decision to invite Courtney to become president.

On April 7th, Courtney and Betty went to the Swarthmore campus for another full day and the final stage of the courtship. The Board of Managers, concluding a four-month search, voted to appoint Courtney Smith president of the college, stating:

We were looking for Mr. 'Super-Man' himself . . . the best prospect almost from the beginning of our deliberations . . . was Courtney C. Smith. . . . a man of outstanding character, ability, personality and vigor.

Courtney C. Smith's home environment and small-town background have developed in him the traits of human understanding and common sense so necessary to a realistic approach to his administrative and education problems. His New England wife, with her gracious manner, conservative background and social charm, will contribute much to making the President's home the social center of the college.

Courtney C. Smith is unusually conversant with the rich and unique traditions of Swarthmore College, and has visited our campus on several occasions. He has expressed a strong desire to preserve the high standards and the great heritage which will be handed him by our able and beloved John Nason. He is favorably known to some of our faculty."[17]

The Managers also noted with pleasure some of his expressed visions for the college: "The keystone of his program is great emphasis on human relations as they encompass student welfare and the vitalizing of a strong mutual understanding and confidence among students, faculty and alumni. . . . Smith intends to 'beat the bushes' (using his own words) with his fellow administrators at Swarthmore to find and select students with character and fine personality and the spiritual, mental and physical vigor necessary to the accomplishment of his program."[18]

John Nason told the faculty about the new presidential appointment, and the Smiths spent the remainder of the day socializing with board members, faculty, and the Nasons. In the evening, as president-elect, he greeted faculty and staff and spoke a few minutes at a special Collection, Swarthmore's all-college gathering.[19]

The college community learned more about Smith through extensive biographical articles in the *Phoenix* and the alumni issue of the *Swarthmore College Bulletin.* His upbringing in Iowa, his working "thirty hours per week to support himself through Harvard," his war-shortened time at Oxford, his race-relations work in the navy, and his academic and administrative work while in Princeton were noted. Alumni and students also learned that Courtney's father had died when Courtney was only thirteen, that one brother was a vice president of the National Broadcasting Company, that another was an official of Commonwealth Edison (of Chicago), that his sister was married to an English professor at the University of Michigan, and that his hobby was sports, particularly squash. The articles also noted that Courtney was only thirty-six years old, had three children, Craig (age eleven), Lee (age eight), and Dabney (age five), that his wife was a graduate of Smith College in the class of 1936, and that he was American Secretary of the Rhodes Trust.[20] The article did not reveal that Courtney's presidential salary was set at $16,000 a year, and that he would receive allowances for the expenses incurred for the operation of the president's house and for entertainment responsibilities.[21] Courtney was interviewed about the appointment and gave comments to the *Philadelphia Evening Bulletin,* whose editor (Richard W. Slocum) was on the selection

committee, to *Time* magazine, and to the *Newark Sunday News,* a paper
read within the Princeton community.[22] Courtney shared his enthusiasm
for the Swarthmore College opportunity, noting that although he was very
sorry to leave teaching, "Swarthmore's something special."[23]

This was a particularly exciting time for Courtney and his family, for in
the same month, he was also involved, as the newly appointed American
Secretary of the Rhodes Trust, in the final planning for a gala at Oxford,
England. The Rhodes Scholars were having an international reunion in
recognition of Cecil Rhodes' one hundredth birthday and the fiftieth anniversary of the establishment of the Rhodes Trust.

On April 24th, Courtney and Betty sailed for Britain on the *Mauretania*
and arrived at Oxford by May 5th. The Smith family took a temporary
residence in a 250-year-old house with a thatched roof in the village of
Standlake, twelve miles from Oxford.[24] During their time at Standlake,
Courtney not only completed the details for the Rhodes reunion, but Craig
learned to play cricket, Lee and Dabney learned to "ask for thrupences for
popsicles," all three played with all the village children, and Betty served
as a judge for the village children's costume contest on Queen Elizabeth
II's Coronation Day. Courtney characterized it as "a busy time, and a
wonderful one."[25]

In June, 400 returning scholars and 274 spouses from Australia, South
Africa, Canada, and the United States held what was regarded as the
largest banquet in Oxford history, met in numerous garden parties, and
observed the awarding of honorary degrees to five scholars of international
fame, including Senator J. William Fulbright of the United States.[26]

Betty and Courtney then left Oxford on July 14th for a two-week holiday on the Continent, sailed on the *Queen Elizabeth* from Cherbourg on
July 29th, and by August 3d they were back in New York. Courtney spent
his first day on campus as president of Swarthmore on August 9, 1953.[27]

# 8

# Inauguration

OFFICIALLY TAKING OFFICE SEPTEMBER 1ST, 1953, COURTNEY BEGAN getting to know his constinuents and learning about the institution that he was to lead. John Nason gave him some pointers in a summary he prepared the day before. "I hope I have left the college in reasonably good shape," Nason wrote. "There are problems ahead, some in the near future. But the faculty, for all the weak points here and there, is excellent. Claude is a wonderful Board chairman and should be a tower of strength. The alumni are closer to the college than they have been for a long time. And the raison d'etre of the college, the students, are a highly educable bunch."[1]

Smith's immediate assessment of the situation agreed with Nason's, and he wrote to many of his friends about finding a "house in good order."[2] He kept the entire administrative staff in the same roles, quickly built a positive relationship with the board chair, Claude C. Smith, and found that his initial enthusiasm about the quality of education available and ongoing at the college was well merited.

For the eight months prior to Courtney's arrival, Nason had been granted a half-time leave in order to assume his Foreign Policy Association role, and Vice Presidents Edward Cratsley and Joseph Shane had taken day-to-day leadership of the college.[3] Smith immediately began to rely on Cratsley's and Shane's expertise and began having regular staff meetings with them and Deans Susan Cobbs, Everett Hunt, and John Moore. From the beginning Smith's high expectations and standards were evident, and the staff recognized his striving for "perfection."[4]

Together, Courtney and Betty spent September getting to know the leadership of the college personally by plunging into a series of teas and dinners with faculty and staff.[5] In that first month Joseph Shane, the vice president for alumni relations, also hosted a gathering of alumni officers in order for them to meet the new president. Courtney greeted and thanked them for the support they provided the college, which kept the college in the black and out of the red, saying, "It's a tough business running a non-profit, idealistic, often misunderstood enterprise like a college these days."[6]

On the 23d of September Courtney addressed the Swarthmore faculty. He spoke about the inevitable anxiety of change and, drawing upon a metaphor from his navy years, assured them that "I have no intention of swashbuckling around simply to make it clear that there's a new skipper aboard . . . my desire is, very simply, to help out . . . my first job is, therefore simply to take inventory, and the major excitement is likely to be in my own blood vessels." He shared his initial observations of his work as president of the college and interjected, with humor, that in coming and going from his office, which was adjacent to a women's dormitory hallway, he was "only now learning what stairways in Parrish are safe to use."[7]

He next spoke to the college at the year's First Collection (October 1), which was also the annual Freshman Talent Program. Again he used humor to introduce himself, opening his remarks by reading "The Scotty Who Knew Too Much" from James Thurber's *Fables for Our Time*. But he also warned students about concerns he had regarding dangerous behavior, such as climbing the college watertower, which he then emphatically forbid.[8]

Courtney soon was fully absorbed in his new position and wrote to his former associates about his delight and awe regarding his new position. Courtney told one alumnus that he was committed to a "sixteen hour a day process of learning by doing."[9] He informed an acquaintance at Oxford that "Swarthmore is actually the closest thing to a cross between the English and American systems of education!"[10] He told W. Wendell Endicott, his former summer employer in Massachusetts, "I'd give anything if I could show you this college—which for its combination of intellectual distinction and fineness in its daily life really stands, I am convinced, in a class by itself."[11]

On the morning of October 17, 1953, in the college's outdoor amphitheatre, Courtney C. Smith was inaugurated as the ninth president of Swarthmore College in a ceremony with attendance of two thousand. Nason introduced the new president as one having an "instinctive flair for asking the right questions and arriving at the right decision."[12] What transpired next immediately provided a glimpse of Smith's character. The *New York Times* reported, "Dr. Smith began to speak but the public address system had broken down and no sounds reached the audience. Dr. Smith waited for workmen to fix the microphone. It took a minute. Dr. Smith began again. 'Whatever I was going to say about modern science would be pertinent now,' he declared. The audience applauded."[13]

Having shown his good humor, Courtney went on to give a strong address to the gathering of distinguished guests, alumni, managers, administration, faculty, and students. He began by commenting that he was both humbled and excited about the conditions of the college and by invoking his need for both God's help and the help of those gathered. He then began the core of his remarks by speaking of the crises that faced colleges in the past and present. Smith referred to an issue that confronted all colleges and universities at the time—the civil liberties of faculty and staff, telling those present that "[In our] time . . . the former president of Wellesley College and wartime head of the Waves cannot take up the United Nations Economic and Social Commission because she was not 'cleared' of possible disloyalty in time. It seems indeed to be a time described by William Butler Yeats's lines of some years ago, a time when 'The best lack all conviction, while the worst are full of passionate intensity.' 'Things fall apart.' as Yeats put it. Or perhaps we should be more dynamic, more modern and say that things look as though they might blow apart."

Smith noted that "our colleges and universities . . . are now held more or less directly responsible for what is wrong in the modern world." While suggesting that "I don't think we need be so generous as to assume all the blame," he quoted T. S. Elliot's remark that "Education is a subject which cannot be discussed in a void: our questions raise other questions, social, economic financial, political." Arguing that it was appropriate "to try to think beyond the cliches to what it is we really mean by a free and democratic society under God," Smith pointed out that higher education's usual response to social problems was to reevaluate curriculum in order to sustain its relevance.

Smith told those gathered that he was more "inclined to think that if we bring together the right students with the right teachers in the right atmosphere we won't have to worry too much about what 'education' is." He then said that, in his view, education could be defined "quite simply as the development of self for the sake of others. . . . I simply believe—as indeed Quakers have always held—that there is something of God in each of us to which we can and must appeal."

He went on to set a context for effective education: "We must develop the character which makes intellect constructive, and the personality which makes it effective," by creating the conditions under which intellectual development can occur. He argued that the college campus should provide "the personal experience of living in an integrated community where there is a healthy respect and a lively concern for values."

Smith elaborated that he believed one maintained values on the campus by making individual values known to others. Smith argued that to not acknowledge values would allow students to graduate without "religious or moral or ethical or political commitment," and might encourage them to choose materialism or sentimentality as guides to life, or to use statistics to set standards of behavior.

Smith stated that he believed that Swarthmore could "make its major contribution to American education through continuing to maintain intellectual distinction within a conscious, and indeed life-giving, context of meaning and value." He argued that the college should continue its mission of creating leaders for the future, which he regarded as "the most urgent need of our society." He told his audience that that goal required the utmost of the institution, a striving for perfection, but that "perfectionism is the very essence of the Quaker tradition, and thus of this campus. To strive for less, when we have been given so much, would be unforgiveable."

Smith reflected on how a college with 0.0004 percent of the whole United States college population could hope to fulfill its high goal. Primarily, he said that it could be done by seeking "students with high potential for distinction in intellect, character, personality, and leadership . . . not forgetting, either, that it is a balanced community which will give us the best chance of developing the balance of qualities we hope for in our graduates."

Turning to the kind of faculty that would educate this student body, he remarked on the widespread public impression that leftist professors were teaching America's young. Indirectly, he was commenting on the McCarthyism that pervaded higher education at the time, and which drove away or intimidated some of the best faculty at his alma mater, Harvard.[14]

Stating that "we must *insist* on the necessity of academic freedom," Smith argued that rather than questioning a teacher's political affiliation, it was better to ask "the questions which must at *all* times finally determine our evaluation of any teacher:

(1) Is he a man of character and integrity?
(2) Is he professionally competent?
(3) Is he intellectually free?
(4) Is he forthright and candid in expression, making no mental reservations?
(5) Has he engaged in illegal activity?"

Smith emphasized that Americans should be careful not to prejudge individual actions or expect too much conformity, and that colleges needed to clarify what they do and why they are important. He argued that colleges needed "to make [their] function understood," and to teach the public "what freedom is."

Smith said that he wanted a college to be understood as a place where students learn, not mainly as a place where teachers teach. Teachers, he argued, need to enable questioning students. "A college is, by its very nature, the most conservative and, at the same time, the most liberal force in a free society: conservative insofar as it fulfills its responsibility of preserving and passing on the inherited wisdom of the ages, liberal insofar as it fulfills its responsibility of constantly reassessing the old, judging what endures, discovering and testing and evaluating the new." Smith set these remarks in the context of his future leadership of the college, noting that Quakers had from their origins as "Friends of Truth" adhered to a spirit of "questioning the accepted and of trying out new ways of doing things."[15]

Courtney Smith's address was indeed an outline of his values, beliefs, commitments, and principles—the fundamental precepts that guided his administration for the next fifteen years. Smith had made the most of his opportunity to address the college community, sharing his opinions and principles in an open and forthright manner and hoping to rally his audience to support the broad goals of his presidency.

He knew his job was not going to be easy. The evening after his inauguration address he spoke to a dinner gathering of alumni in the college's field house. With some humor and wit, he shared his awe regarding the magnitude of the expectations before him and asked for their understanding and insights as he exercised his new responsibilities:

> If it's true that the only real cause of fear is the unknown, I suppose it would follow that there's nothing to fear about being a college president. In fact, it's very simple. All he has to do is—Administer the college so as to meet the high marks of the trustee body which has the ultimate responsibility for the preservation and progress of the college.
>
> All he has to do, in addition is to—Know so intensely in every bone and tissue what a teacher lives for that the faculty feels that it is but an extension of themselves that sits behind that big mahogany desk and pushes rows of flashing buttons.
>
> All he has to do, in addition is to—So thoroughly understand that cluster of short circuits we sometimes call students that each short circuit, who knows he is really a tremendous voltage carrier, knows that the president is quite a live wire himself.
>
> All he has to do, in addition, is to convince the public at large that even though it is too bad they didn't get to the college they can still salvage something by doing and giving their all for the college.
>
> And all he has to do, in addition, is to—Convince each member of the alumni that since he, Alumnus A, or she, Alumna B, cannot at the moment give full time to running the college it probably is no worse off in President S's hands than it would be in many others.
>
> So you see—it's all very simple—superimpose in one picture:

The wisdom of Solomon
The patience of Job
The goodness of the Samaritan
The leadership of Caesar
The courage of Horatius
The fortitude of the Boy at the dike.
And frame it all with the Wizardry of Oz—and you have the picture of a fair to middling college president.

Frankly I don't recognize myself in the portrait—and I shall need some help.[16]

Humor aside, there clearly were troubling issues in higher education during this period. College and university leaders throughout the nation had identified several dangerous trends, including threats to academic freedom, pressures toward conformity and value-free education, and the promotion of "practical" curricula.[17] One contemporary leader of higher education, for example, saw Americans as ignorant of the role of the educator in a free society, as becoming depersonalized due to patterns of industrialization which promoted regimentation, and warned of the steady growth of militarism "with its emphasis on conformity and unquestioned acceptance of ideas" and "the canonization of the informer."[18]

Smith had shown the Swarthmore constituents that he understood the threats to higher education in America and had the courage to confront those threats directly and assertively. Moreover, he enunciated a vision of excellence that he expected the college to sustain through his presidency.[19] Smith had sketched out his mission and the college's and now had to fulfill both!

# 9

## The Case for the Liberal Arts College

COURTNEY SMITH WAS A STRONG ADVOCATE FOR A LIBERAL ARTS EDUCA-
tion, and he believed the small college was the right setting for it. He
wanted to promote an environment which would raise the right questions
in a setting that allowed freedom of thought and had an ambiance which
would facilitate the development of enlightened leadership for society.

When Courtney immersed himself in his first year at Swarthmore he
became part of an academic environment that had espoused the pursuit of
an ideal liberal arts education for three decades. Aydelotte's institution of
the honors regimen in 1923 had transformed Swarthmore from one of the
better American small colleges into a leader, a place that attracted students
wanting a demanding curriculum and professors wanting a challenging
classroom. Under the guidance of Aydelotte, the American secretary of the
Rhodes Scholar program and an admirer of British tutorial education,
Swarthmore's approach to education entailed heavy reading lists, frequent
writing assignments, and seminars emphasizing professor-student and
student-student dialogue.

These innovations brought considerable attention to Swarthmore as an
institution that was approximating the ideal of liberal arts education as it
had developed in the United States. Aydelotte himself wrote a great deal
about the honors program and Swarthmore's educational style, promoting
it as excellent training of the mind's critical faculties as well as the best
possible training for future leaders of the nation. Aydelotte may be regarded as an exponent of the "philosophical tradition" of liberal arts education, which promoted individualistic inquiry, in contrast to the "oratorical
tradition" (epitomized in Aydelotte's time by Robert Hutchins), which
argued for the critical examination of classical texts in a search for unifying ideas. Aydelotte was also candid about his belief that intellectual
ability was unequally distributed throughout the American population, and
that Swarthmore's exacting curriculum was appropriate only for a select
few whose preparation and demonstrated skill had made them equal to the
challenge.[1]

Courtney Smith, steeped in the preceptorial systems of Harvard and Princeton and appreciative of his Oxford experience, largely agreed with Aydelotte's approach to liberal arts education. However, unlike the extreme proponents of liberal education who thought that any hint of utilitarianism tainted learning, he generally argued that the ultimate test of education was whether it prepared an individual for a life of service and critical engagement with matters of the world. Smith's experience in working his way through Harvard and in serving at a grassroots level in the navy, always tempered his idealism.

Certainly his decisive and clear commitment to liberal arts education was rooted in his life experiences. He had grown up in the Presbyterian Church, which highly valued liberal education, his ideas and intellectual skills had been honed and sharpened by his high school teachers' mentoring, he had matured in his awareness of social skills through his association with H. Wendell Endicott, and he had discovered the benefits of an extraordinary education at Harvard and Oxford and while instructing at Princeton.

At Harvard he experienced tutorial work both as a tutee and as an tutor. As a senior he had intensive personal preparation in English under the guidance of F. W. MacVeagh and the chairman of the English department, James B. Munn. They directed his studies of seventeenth-century English literature and guided work on his honors thesis.[2]

At Oxford while on his Rhodes Scholarship he was exposed to a similar tutorial approach to education as he studied research methods, paleography, history of English studies, the biography of Shakespeare, and bibliography at Merton College. Indeed he found that many of the Oxford tutors had done work at Harvard.[3]

Upon returning to Harvard from Oxford he assumed tutoring responsibilities for both Harvard and Radcliffe undergraduates. He described his personal satisfaction and comfort with this close teacher-student instruction when writing to his brother Murray:

> I meet with most of my tutees, individually, weekly or bi-weekly. I assign them work, have them prepare papers, discuss English literature with them, and give them more than the equivalent of several lecture courses. I don't actually grade them on the work, and, am not supposed directly to prepare them for their general exams, but my estimation of them bears a great deal of weight in whether they graduate, whether they get Honors, whether they make Phi Beta Kappa, etc. Usually I take a tutee when he begins his specialization in his Soph[omore] year, and have him or her until he graduates. It's precisely the type of teaching I enjoy—sitting down comfortably with one student and discussing the work as if it were something a little bit human and enjoyable.[4]

Indeed, Courtney had long enjoyed the life of the mind and frequently seized upon opportunities to discuss ideas informally but intensively. Fifty years later he was remembered by those who knew him during his Harvard years as one who energetically and forcefully discussed ideas when he was socializing with fellow dorm residents and other students.[5]

Even when confronted with practical, stressful, and mundane tasks in the navy, he continued to expand his knowledge. During those years, working with African Americans in the South, he read Negro literature (including W. E. B. Du Bois's *Color and Democracy*) to sharpen his perception of Negro culture, beginning scholarly pursuits and interests that continued for several years.[6]

When he moved to Princeton he again had chance to see and participate in models of liberal arts education. In 1905 Woodrow Wilson, as president of Princeton, had instituted the preceptorial method of study in which small groups of students met regularly with faculty members to discuss lectures and readings. Courtney taught standard classes in the English department and in the American Civilization Program, but he told his department chairman that he gathered greater satisfaction from his preceptorial responsibilities—where he gave no quizzes, did no scolding, gave "no dope" or inside information, stayed with three main issues and points, and prohibited note taking—and that this gave him "more breadth and variety of teaching."[7]

Indeed, Courtney was described by one of his students as a preceptor who was a "true mentor" with enlightened moderation, who was always sympathetic to undergraduates and welcomed students to his house, and who encouraged and inspired students by "recounting his own adventures and excitement as an intellectual neophyte, as an undergraduate in Europe, as an evaluator of the American scene."[8]

The preceptorship program was so important at Princeton that in 1950 ten additional bicentennial preceptorship positions were established. Courtney then was appointed to one of them in 1951. The new bicentennial positions were three-year appointments designed to support "the development of a man as a teacher-scholar" at the assistant professor level prior to tenure, but with salaries about $500 higher than the regular assistant professor level. During the third year there was expectation that the full year would be devoted to scholarship.[9] Courtney had fulfilled his preceptor roles so well that in 1952 he was chosen, along with Edgar Stephenson Furniss Jr. and Robert Francis Goheen, to discuss the preceptorial method at a meeting of the National Alumni Association in Chicago.[10]

His participation in the American Civilization Program first challenged him to better conceptualize his understanding of American culture and higher education's impact upon it. That and the forceful impressions of his preceptorships provoked him to think seriously about the interrelationship of culture—the forum in which the educated person acted—and the mind, which shaped that person's values and attitudes.

Smith hoped to spend his scholarly year of the preceptorship engaged in writing a book on the techniques of American social fiction. He planned "to analyze novels grouped according to similarity of intention (novels about racial and religious minorities, strikes, migratory workers, class distinctions, etc.) to see if there [were] any principles that determine the effectiveness of social fiction and draw the line between art and propaganda."[11] In 1950, as acting chairman of the American Civilization Program, he had the opportunity to delve into these issues when he directed the annual conference for seniors majoring in the program. The conference included joint study and presentations by students, faculty from the thirteen departments cooperating in the program, and leading commentators on American society and culture.[12]

As he was formulating his own ideas about liberal arts instruction, Courtney started reading about the broader issues in liberal arts education in America. In 1947, for example, Courtney read the report of the President's Commission on Higher Education, *Higher Education for American Democracy.* He marked, as important, the passage: "If our colleges and universities are to graduate individuals who have learned to be free, they will have to concern themselves with the development of self-discipline and self-reliance, of ethical principles as a guide for conduct, of sensitivity to injustice and inequality, of insight into human motives and aspirations, of discriminating appreciation of a wide range of human values, of the spirit of democratic compromise and cooperation."[13]

It was a combination of his personal experience with teaching and his reading that he brought to his presidency of Swarthmore. One of Smith's earliest public formulations of his view of liberal arts education was presented in New York at the Fifteenth Annual Forum on Education of the Tuition Plan in February 1955. He appeared on a panel with Nathan Pusey (Harvard University), Henry Wriston (Brown University), and Father Theodore Hesburgh (University of Notre Dame). He began his remarks by outlining aspects of the public's misunderstanding of liberal education, saying, "the public remains essentially afraid of expanding horizons, afraid of the questioning spirit, afraid of the thought that perhaps all truth has not yet been discovered. . . . They remain disturbed by the pattern of undergraduate development familiar enough in any college worth its salt, the pattern of the student who enters college with certain inherited beliefs and values, with everything he has ever believed seriously questioned."[14]

He argued however that a liberal education provides the tools for destroying the status quo, but that it is, at the same time, a powerful force for preserving culture and traditional ideas and values. As Smith put it, rephrasing slightly a line from his inauguration speech, "a college is . . . conservative insofar as it fulfills its responsibility of preserving and passing on the inherited wisdom of the ages, [yet] liberal insofar as it fulfills its responsibility of constantly reassessing the old, judging what endures, discovering and testing and evaluating the new."[15]

Courtney went on to suggest that such a well-balanced and responsible college would be primarily a place where students learn, rather than where teachers teach, and where knowledge is felt to be a continuum rather than what is just between the covers of books. He held up a vision of an institution where there is a meaningful pattern of study leading to a final comprehensive examination, where there are facilities for challenging and holding the interests of above-average and superior students, where independent work is permitted under knowledgeable and sympathetic supervision, and where there is "an atmosphere which respects academic accomplishment, which knows the excitement of ideas, believing that man was endowed with reason for a purpose."[16]

He also argued that liberal education required the broadest understanding and permission for intellectual freedom.[17] Echoing the issues of the McCarthy era he remarked that

> it is all too easy for a college—faced with critical financial needs, beset by restrictive pressures, and engaged at all times in trying to give stability to a mercurial community—to avoid exposed places and to take on the protective coloring of its surroundings. But surely this is to abrogate our responsibility, our responsibility to speak out against anything which would bind the minds and spirits of men: to speak out against outside control through investigations, oaths, and intellectual bullying; to speak out against the growing notion that although there may still be two sides to every question only one is entirely respectable; to speak out against the profession of false witnessing and of intimidation.[18]

Courtney's remarks at the Tuition Plan Forum were the first in a series of colloquies about the essence of the liberal arts and the liberal arts college that included presentations at the Los Angeles Town Hall (1956), the Pennsylvania Association of Colleges and Universities (1960), and the Association of American Colleges (1961), a Voice of America address (1960), and a speech to students and faculty at Swarthmore (1962).[19] In these remarks there was a continued elaboration and refinement of his ideas, culminating with his identification of community dialogue as the core concept of liberal arts education.

Smith came to this conclusion by the pursuit of two ideas. First, he discussed the necessity for freedom of speech in education. Initially his comments simply asserted freedom of speech as a right and were framed in terms that suggest a response to the perceived threat of McCarthyism, but later he argued that freedom was a necessary precondition for "freeing the mind from ignorance and prejudice," as well as for a critical approach to received knowledge and culture.

Second, Smith argued that liberal arts education had a special role in developing what he called "character" through the provision of a caring and values-rich environment as the context for education. In order to define character Smith frequently drew on Woodrow Wilson's 1913 address at Swarthmore in which he said,

> What a man ought never to forget with regard to a college is that it is a nursery of principle and of honor . . . I cannot admit that a man establishes his right to call himself a college graduate by showing me his diploma. The only way he can prove it is by showing that his eyes are lifted to some horizon which other men less instructed than he have not been privileged to see. Unless he carries freight of the spirit he has not been bred where spirits are bred. . . . You are here [he said to the Swarthmore students] in order to enable the world to live more amply, with greater vision, with a finer spirit of hope and achievement. You are here to enrich the world, and you impoverish yourself if you forget the errand.[20]

In Smith's view, a liberal arts college like Swarthmore had an obligation to develop a faculty with strong moral and ethical standards and a sense of concern about issues of current importance, such that in classroom discussions the students were bound to be challenged to sharpen (and perhaps change for the better) their own values and attitudes.

These two lines of thought came together in what Smith believed to be the epitome of education and what he thought was the goal of education at Swarthmore—a dialogue. Clearly operating within the Aristotelian tradition that unfettered but systematic search for truth leads to the highest levels of knowledge, Smith argued that a community like Swarthmore's, which he thought had unusually close teacher-student relationships, strong interdisciplinary contacts throughout the faculty, and a commitment to personal caring for each other, provided a fertile environment for continuing and fruitful dialogue.

In his speech to the college in the fall of 1962 (later disseminated to the Swarthmore constituency through publication in the *Bulletin*) he told the students and faculty that to preserve this dialogue they needed to value and preserve intellectual honesty, and openness to new ideas. Recognizing that the dialogue took place in particular temporal and social frameworks, Courtney argued that dialogue required a willingness to recognize a range of political views. He showed particular concern about the last point, arguing that the college had largely been captured by a politically liberal viewpoint and needed to include and consider more conservative views in its community dialogue. Smith also inveighed against students' tendency to look beyond their undergraduate years toward graduate school, because he thought it turned education into a pursuit of vocation rather than a pursuit of understanding.

Yet Smith reserved his closest examination of the style of dialogue at the college for the faculty, not the students. He explored the basis for the faculty's interaction with students and asserted it had responsibility for maintaining dialogue in and out of the classroom, arguing that "the student-faculty dialogue comes best when there is substance—when it starts, for example, with an intellectual question the student wishes to carry further, or when it involves a problem the student has a reason to believe the faculty member could help with."[21] It should not be surprising, given Smith's veneration of Oxford-style education, that he thought one-on-one interchange provided the highest level of dialogue.

At the same time, Smith worried that the faculty at Swarthmore did not meet his expectations for intellectual engagement with each other. Putting himself in the same category, he ventured that "most of us in the faculty would agree that we may well be farther from this ideal here than in any other category I have so far discussed."[22] He wondered whether anyone could claim legitimately to be a generalist, and asserted that it was "not enough . . . to say that in many fields knowledge has become so specialized that the man who has gone far in it can no longer profitably communicate with non-specialists."[23]

Courtney's views on the liberal arts were strongly informed by his reading of the modern writers Jacques Barzun, a professor at Columbia University, and José Ortega y Gasset.[24] Barzun, one of the severest critics of higher education in the United States, argued that higher education should be demanding, honest, personal, and focused on ideas. The reality, he thought, was that the modern American university had been "captivated by Art, overawed by Science, and seduced by Philanthropy."[25] It was possible to prevent the total subversion of higher education only by a constant insistence on the primacy of intellectual discourse and excellence in expression in the classroom. Barzun was unabashedly elitist in his prescription for solving the ills of higher education, stating that "the only answer is the selection and special schooling of those with a talent for abstraction, articulateness, and the pursuit of ideas in books."[26]

Smith clearly took comfort from Barzun's views, but it was Ortega y Gasset who sketched out what was for Smith a fuller philosophy for the intellectual man in the modern age. Ortega y Gasset was a Spanish intellectual steeped in the German philosophical tradition who wrote two influential works on education and society in 1929–30, *Mission of the University* and *Revolt of the Masses.* In general, he criticized modern higher education for failing in its traditional and, in his view, necessary role of educating the political, economic, and social leadership of the Western world.[27]

The cause of the problem, Ortega y Gasset asserted, was that higher education had become too particular in its subject matter and thereby had lost its mission to serve as the means of instructing successive generations in the central tenets of culture, which he defined as "the system of ideas *by* which the age lives."[28] According to Ortega y Gasset, so-called educated persons now were "more learned than ever before, but at the same time more uncultured."[29] He castigated such persons as the "new barbarian[s]" and believed that scientists, "knowing much of one thing" because they were more concerned about inquiry than knowledge, were particularly likely to deserve that label.[30] For many of his contemporaries, the recent use of chemical warfare in World War I probably made this characterization seem apt.

Ortega y Gasset's prescription for the problem of cultural transmission was to make the teaching of ideas the center of a university education and to reduce or eliminate the growing influence of scientific inquiry. Moreover, because he thought that within the normal framework of a college or university education it was impossible for a student to learn everything a subject had to offer, he thought it was imperative that educators focus on teaching only what was essential to pass on the cultural heritage. He included among the essentials physics, biology, history, sociology, and philosophy but discarded laboratory science and other training that focused on methodologies or techniques.[31]

Ortega y Gasset justified this scheme by stating that the true aim of higher education was to train persons for the professions—primarily medicine, law, education, and government service. Persons entering these professions, who effectively constituted the elite of modern society, were in Ortega y Gasset's view not only responsible for maintaining an orderly society based on the best ideas of the times but were also the purveyors of those ideas to the next generation.

Thus educational institutions were critical to the survival of modern life, particularly in light of the enormous stresses and strains on the social fabric that were visible in the first three decades of the twentieth century. For

Ortega y Gasset, higher education had to be a rock *and* a beacon in the turbulent sea of modern life. As he unflinchingly described it, an institution of higher education "must assert itself as a major 'spiritual power,' higher than the press, standing for serenity in the midst of frenzy, for seriousness and the grasp of intellect in the face of frivolity and unabashed stupidity."[32]

Together Barzun and Ortega y Gasset made strong claims for the importance of higher education in training the next generation's elite leadership while making searing critiques of higher education's current direction. They called for creating cohorts of generalists who appreciated the power of ideas rather than training students in technique or attempting to make them specialists.

Without question Smith was drawn to these writers because they presented a program compatible with the preservation of the small liberal arts college committed to making its students undergo a rigorous intellectual challenge. Personally Smith found Barzun and Ortega y Gasset attractive because as a trained humanist and a product of a broadly cultural education himself, he saw the post–World War II American drive toward scientific-technical education as a threat to the nurturing of the life of the mind that he cherished.[33] Approaches to education that seemed intent on dividing knowledge into smaller and smaller units that could be inaccessible to the average intellectual, in a way parallel to what physics was doing to the basic particles of matter, seemed to Smith to violate the joy of engagement with ideas that, though potentially large or small, were more educationally valuable when large and requiring interpretation. Pointedly, Smith once told a member of Swarthmore's physics department that modern science was eroding the poetry of language.[34]

Smith also valued the writings of Barzun and Ortega y Gasset because they supported his vision of the college as a citadel, a beacon, a holy place of learning. Against an apparently rising tide of mediocrity or perhaps even barbarism (as Ortega y Gasset saw it), Smith understood that the college's mission was to stand fast, to be an oasis of calm, and to be a preserve of culture. Whether rebuking McCarthyism, staving off the incursion of an express highway, or chastising students for slovenliness, while at Swarthmore Smith found comfort in the notion nurtured by his reading of Barzun and Ortega y Gasset that he was an advocate for an institution entrusted with the preservation and transmission of the core values of Western civilization. From the beginning to the end of his presidency at Swarthmore, Smith not only acted with a belief that he knew the right direction for the college, but with a philosophical certainty that the college's commitment to the liberal arts was on the right side of history.

# 10
## Faculty

Central to Courtney Smith's work at Swarthmore, and to a significant degree his success there, was his concern with and commitment to supporting the faculty of the college. Courtney, as a former teacher, was very concerned with improving the status of faculty members, challenging them to reach for the highest standards of instruction and encouraging open and honest inquiry.

Almost immediately upon appointment Courtney began to look at the salaries being offered to faculty at Swarthmore and five other liberal arts colleges in the Northeast: Amherst, Bowdoin, Haverford, Wesleyan, and Williams. He found that Swarthmore salaries were below the average of this group for all professorial ranks. He also compared endowments and found that Swarthmore's endowment per student ranked significantly lower than the other colleges.[1] He quickly concluded that the endowment needed to be increased to sustain any significant increase in faculty salaries and began talking with major financial supporters of the college.

He began his campaign to develop support for increased faculty salaries when he told the Alumni Council in June 1954 that "reality" was different from the "delusion" that Swarthmore's finances were on par with other institutions. He offered his projection that the endowment needed to be increased by $8.75 million, in order to pay faculty appropriately and to upgrade academic facilities, a matter that Courtney felt was directly related to improving faculty resources.

In July 1954 he extended his campaign when he spoke to a group of Quakers at Buckhill Falls, a Quaker summer community in the Pocono Mountains. He argued that accounting for inflation faculty salaries had actually declined since 1938 and (echoing his complaint to his department chair at Princeton in 1947) said that he "would like to challenge anyone who regards himself as practical to see if he can manage to live in as much dignity as faculty people somehow do" on the existing salaries.[2]

Smith certainly was not alone in defining faculty salaries as a primary problem of higher education. Indeed, major figures and organizations fastened on it as a critical area for colleges and universities to address in the 1950s. In the first year of Smith's presidency the theme of the Association of American College's annual meeting was "Financing Liberal Education," and one of the three major issues on the table was "Low Salaries of Professors." The association said that professors were "woefully underpaid" and warned that "many top-flight teachers have left—and many more may follow suit—for high-priced jobs in government or industry." The result, accordingly, would be a shortage of qualified educators in a decade when enrollments were expected to increase dramatically.[3]

This pronouncement was repeated over the next few years by various authorities. At the beginning of the 1954–55 academic year the United States commissioner of education stated that faculty salaries had to be raised in order "to attract and hold required faculties" for future burgeoning enrollments.[4] In a front-page article in the *New York Times,* the chancellor of New York University, Henry Heald, argued that increases in the cost of living in the postwar decade had far outstripped his institution's salary increases, with the result that "the student's education has been in part subsidized by the teacher."[5]

Such remarks were solidly supported in the fall of 1955 when the Fund for the Advancement of Education, a research arm of the Ford Foundation, reported that its study of the last half-century of higher education had revealed that professional salaries had deteriorated relative to those of other occupational groups. In ominous language suitable to the era of anticommunism, Beardsley Ruml, the author of the report, warned that low salaries had created a "disaffection" in the professorate that contributed to a "pervading pessimism, extending in extreme cases to subversion, fellow-traveling, and other educational sabotage."[6] In later remarks, Ruml characterized the salary problem as urgent, but speaking before the Association for Higher Education, he used a less politically charged image in predicting that "if meager financial recognition of college teaching is permitted to prevail the liberal college will settle into a dreary mediocrity."[7]

On the eve of the Sputnik crisis in the fall of 1957, just as the entire American educational system came under intense scrutiny, a government report appeared that certified the prevailing wisdom on faculty salaries. President Eisenhower had appointed the Committee on Education Beyond the High School to study the role of the federal government in higher education and to make recommendations for future policy.[8] Crawford Greenewalt, a member of the committee and president of the DuPont Company, recruited Courtney Smith to serve on a subcommittee focusing on college finances.[9] Although the sub-committee's report was not published, it influenced the final report, which stated definitely that increases in faculty salaries of 75–80 percent were required if professors were to be recruited competitively in the professional job market.[10]

Smith was successful in raising faculty salaries. A substantial increase in Alumni Fund giving occurred after his challenge to the alumni, and it was earmarked to support a 20 percent increase in salaries from 1953–54 to 1956–57. Although this kept pace with national increases reported by the federal Office of Education, Courtney was still dissatisfied. These increases had provided "only a slight gain on the loss of purchasing power" experienced by professors over the previous twenty-five years.[11]

Then, learning about a Ford Foundation program to upgrade faculty salaries, Courtney applied for a grant. Swarthmore's proposal was well written and well- received, and it was a recipient of an endowment grant of $430,000 in 1956. Later the college received $277,000 from Ford as an "accomplishment grant," given to institutions that had made an "outstanding effort throughout the period since World War II to raise the economic level of their teachers, and to recognize in other ways the central importance of the faculty in the educational process." Both grants were added to the endowment for faculty salaries by the Board of Managers.[12]

In January 1957 when Courtney spoke in Atlantic City at a Joint Conference of the American Alumni Council and the American College Public Relations Association he was still voicing his concern regarding faculty salaries. He argued vehemently that faculty salaries needed to be doubled so that colleges could successfully compete with business and industry in capturing the bright and able people and curb the drain out of higher education.[13] As another strategy for improving faculty salaries, Swarthmore decided in the spring of 1957 to increase tuition 25% (to $1000 a year) for the following year. In writing to a fellow college president, he expressed satisfaction that Swarthmore was no longer "letting faculty members subsidize" higher education.[14]

In April 1957, he announced his intention to raise Swarthmore salaries for faculty by "at least $500 [for instructors], Assistant Professors $1,000, Associate Professors $1,500 and Professors $2,000," which allowed some Professors to make as much as $14,000, and 25% of the faculty to earn $10,000 or more in 1957–58.[15] Salaries were further increased the next year (1958–59), and Courtney was proud to note that a comparative study of twenty-seven similar liberal arts colleges in the United States showed that Swarthmore's mean annual salary of $8640 was then "#1 by a very big margin."[16]

These challenges to support faculty fueled the amazing growth of the Alumni Fund that sustained Courtney's initiative. In the three years after

1954–55, the fund's annual giving had doubled and alumni participation had gone from 44% to more than 51%.[17] By 1959 Smith proudly announced that Swarthmore was a leader in improving faculty salaries, and in 1962 he told alumni that Swarthmore salaries were at leading levels and should be kept there so that they were something "which the raiders [from business, industry, and large universities] have to reckon with."[18] Swarthmore remained in the top rank of faculty salaries for the remainder of the decade.[19]

Courtney read professional journals, newsletters, and major newspapers regularly and kept notes on trends and dilemmas confronting higher education. A continuing theme in this literature was the problem of faculty salaries.[20] Certainly Courtney fought for improved faculty salaries in part because he understood the situation at Swarthmore in the context of the situation nationally. But Courtney also was willing to go to bat for higher faculty salaries was because he had tremendous respect for faculty members individually and as a body. In 1953, when he spoke about the Swarthmore faculty, he noted that they were "better integrated" than most college faculties, had "little factionalism," and had committee meetings with "no arguing for victory." He proudly stated that the faculty "Suffers less than most from rigid departmentalization. In fact there is (I believe) a situation conducive to a meaningful cross-fertilization." He also saw that the faculty's overall style was already close to his ideal of the "teacher-scholar" model.[21]

When new faculty had to be appointed, Courtney encouraged departmental searches to be broad, and he personally solicited nominations from alumni, faculty, and his network of Harvard, Oxford, Rhodes, Princeton, and Woodrow Wilson colleagues. In searching for new faculty he took seriously his role in selecting faculty who met his standards. Courtney was more active than his predecessors had been in this role and was "in the thick of every new appointment" at the college.[22]

Typically when a vacancy occurred, several candidates were invited to come to campus, where they would meet with department members, deans, and other faculty who were interested in the candidates' fields of work. Courtney was known to rule out invitations to candidates whom he felt did not have proper credentials or dossiers: he strongly favored those with Ivy League and British training and readily dismissed those from state universities. At times he inserted his own candidates into the process, particularly those who were Rhodes Scholars or who had Harvard and Princeton connections.

When the department faculty had sifted through the names and qualities of each candidate for the open position, had shared their comments about the strengths and weaknesses of the candidates in writing, and had identified a few outstanding candidates, Courtney arranged personal interviews with those candidates. After he met with them, he refused to permit any further consideration of candidates about whom he had reservations, because he, in fact, made the recommendation to the Board of Managers that a candidate be hired.[23]

In those personal interviews Courtney routinely and intensely inquired about candidates' professed interests, actualized interests, and potential to become more generalized, "grade A" men. He also considered their age, "conversational" characteristics, and ways in which they would "add anything very positive" to boost the faculty, and whether he found himself "wanting to sell the college" (because he learned through experience that this was a measure of his enthusiasm for the candidate).

He was not interested in candidates whom he felt had "pedestrian" scholarship or unfavorable social characteristics. He distinguished "'scholarliness' as a cast of mind, a cast characterized by a passion for one's field of learning, an insatiable curiosity, a compulsion to keep moving ahead in one's field, as contrasted with mere 'productivity' as an expedient accommodation—sometimes cynical, sometimes fearful—to what is expected."[24]

For Smith, the entire interview process was an inquiry into each candidate's integrity, values, character, competency, intellectual freedom, candidness, and ability to be a catalytic agent within the college.[25] In February 1962, Courtney recorded in his interview notes a typical comment about a candidate whom he had interviewed and who met his tests for qualities he wanted at Swarthmore: "I was very favorably impressed by him. He is composed, strong, attractive, and I think quite able. I liked his values, and the way he talked."[26]

Courtney believed that character and ability to strengthen the faculty body were the critical factors in determining new appointments. He chastised faculty for talking and thinking about salary and rank during a search, before he had an impression of the candidate:

> To mention a particular rank or salary in advance of the time when we wish to make a definite offer often seriously misleads, perhaps most seriously when it shuts off the interest of someone we might on further acquaintance wish to offer a higher rank and salary than the one that had been mentioned to him or contemplated by us.
>
> I can assure you that this policy works, and we have never failed to secure someone we have wanted for the faculty because of rank or salary.
>
> I have not only been able to test our own policy in practice but have noted my own reaction whenever I have learned that some other institution is seeking

someone at a particular rank or salary: I always get the feeling that the institution seems more interested in the niche than the individual.[27]

This faculty interview process was a powerful introduction to Swarthmore and President Smith's style. One interviewee recalled that: "The interview process was long and very exacting, and I can honestly say that the best part of the whole episode was meeting Dr. Smith. We had a very long talk and chatted about mutual friends. . . . He had the mark of quality in his person and in his intellect, a quality orientation that was very marked and distinctive. . . . His leadership was marked strongly by this quality and it went down to all levels of the school."[28]

Some faculty regarded this process as too controlled by the president and as deprecating of faculty opinion.[29] Although he routinely sought faculty input and feedback regarding faculty change, in the end he usually followed his own lights. According to Clair Wilcox, who taught at the college for forty years (retiring only in 1968) and who was one of Smith's strongest supporters, Courtney was a benevolent dictator in the end.[30]

Indeed the astuteness of Courtney's interviews was in at least one instance validated quite concretely. Ten years after Courtney had interviewed one candidate and rejected him, noting his sense that he was "hostile to board and administrations and department chairman . . . suspicious, ungenerous, belligerent," Roland Pennock, professor and chair of political science, told Courtney that the former candidate had published a book in which he admitted that he was "suspicious of people in positions of power and authority . . . [and sought] to penetrate their pretenses and shatter their legitimacy."[31]

Smith wanted faculty who valued the liberal arts tradition and who would respect fields of inquiry outside of their own. He expected faculty to be in contact with other institutions and colleagues and to be visible leaders in their fields of inquiry. He felt that the small faculty and intimacy of Swarthmore should not only provide interdisciplinary discussions on campus and lead to excellent liberal arts instruction, but that it should also lead to critical questions and studies that would stimulate cross-departmental inquiry and study.

Given Courtney's concerns, faculty responsibilities and expectations needed constant review. In the spring of 1956, the third year of his administration, a Teaching Load Committee was established; the faculty-administration committee consisted of Mary Albertson, Edward H. Cox, Edward K. Cratsley, John M. Moore, Edith Philips, Howard M. Jenkins (chairman) and Courtney Smith (*ex officio*). They polled the Swarthmore faculty members about their teaching loads and sought comparable information from other institutions such as Amherst, Brown, Bryn Mawr, Harvard, Haverford, Princeton, and Wesleyan.[32] Smith, in soliciting information from Princeton, wrote: "I said in my earlier letter that our loads seemed to me heavy: I might better have said that they seem to me in some departments excessively heavy, and in certain others really rather on the light side. And perhaps our first step ought to be recognition of different loads by ranks, which we have not done."[33]

In the end the committee noted that there were many variables when it compared the various college and university data, but that the teaching loads at Swarthmore were indeed a little heavier than those at comparable institutions. In the fall of 1957 the committee recommended standardizing the Swarthmore teaching load at nine classroom hours a semester for humanities and social sciences and twelve classroom hours a semester for sciences and engineering classes with laboratories. With Courtney's support the recommendation was adopted by the full faculty.[34] It soon was clear that this new standard led to appreciable reductions in department teaching loads, with the biology department being the leading example.[35]

Having supported changes in salaries and teaching loads, Courtney expected the faculty to maintain and continue the ideal of a liberal arts community—an ideal that ran counter to the increasing disciplinary specialization occurring in higher education throughout the United States. In 1961 Smith again encouraged the college community "to be experimenting constantly with cross-departmental and interdepartmental courses and seminars." He stated that he was convinced that "Our faculty . . . is ready and willing to fight the artificial barriers created by departmental lines." He recognized that interdisciplinary work was time-consuming and expensive, often to the point of seeming extravagant, but he supported his view with interdepartmental appointments and by seeking foundation funding for interdisciplinary seminars at Swarthmore.[36]

Ultimately Courtney was highly successful in his efforts to create and maintain a strong Swarthmore faculty dedicated to both teaching and scholarship. An accreditation review by the Middle States Association in 1958 described the faculty as "notable for its devotion both to sound learning and to the College and its distinctive aims."[37] By the usual measures of higher education, Swarthmore's faculty in the Smith era was to be envied and admired.

# 11

## "There is strength . . . in having a variety of sources of support":
## Funding the Liberal Arts Tradition

COURTNEY SMITH RECOGNIZED IN THE FIRST YEAR OF HIS PRESIDENCY that low alumni giving and a modest endowment would make it nearly impossible for the college to maintain its high ranking in the academic world by competing successfully for the best faculty and the brightest and most challenging students. Salaries needed to be raised significantly. Library and scientific research facilities needed to be renovated and greatly expanded. Dormitory overcrowding needed to be alleviated.

A fundamental problem was that annual Alumni Fund giving had not reached a level comparable to that of other small, competitive-admissions liberal arts colleges. Much of the alumni support of the college had fallen away during the Frank Aydelotte era (1922–40), when he instituted the Honors Program, downplayed the traditional role of sports in college life, approved of the elimination of sororities, and limited the preferential admission of students from the Quaker community and alumni families.[1] What Aydelotte had accomplished was initiated primarily with General Education Board support and other outside funding, rather than major gifts from alumni.[2]

During the Nason years (1940–52), when the war reduced enrollments (and thus tuition), the college had received funds from the federal government to defray the costs of educating navy officers coming to the campus for specialized training, and Nason created both the Alumni Association and Alumni Fund. In a capital campaign, 1946–48, with a goal of $5 million, however, the college was only able to raise $1.5 million. That disappointment was later reported to have made some leading alumni "gun shy" regarding fundraising efforts, and no major campaign was launched for fifteen years.[3]

Smith nonetheless took on the challenge of alumni fundraising directly and vigorously. With the constant support and encouragement of Joseph

Shane, vice president for alumni relations, he began to cultivate alumni support by speaking regularly to regional alumni clubs, Quaker schools and organizations, and Philadelphia-area organizations in which alumni were prominent. Smith made a good impression on his audiences: he was physically elegant and fastidious in his dress, a polished speaker, and an engaging conversationalist. His addresses made a strong case for sustaining Swarthmore's unyielding commitment to excellence in faculty and students while retaining its small size and liberal arts traditions. Moreover, Courtney believed that specification of needs generated giving to the college, and in his remarks routinely outlined both the physical and programmatic goals that he felt needed to be met in order to maintain Swarthmore.[4]

Smith's evident dedication to the college and his candor were effective. In December 1955 he reported that alumni giving in 1954 had been $100,000 but had increased to $127,000 in 1955, and he challenged alumni to give $200,000 by 1957. He declared that alumni gifts would be earmarked for better faculty salaries, stating, "we cannot, as a practical matter, lag behind other colleges and universities; we should not, as a humane matter, shut off our faculty from the benefits of the growth of the American free enterprise economy."[5] The alumni met Smith's challenge; the $200,000 was raised. In fact, 1957 was the fourth year in a row during the Smith administration in which alumni giving increased at approximately twice the rate of the college's budget growth.

Over the next decade the alumni continued to give in excess of $200,000 annually,[6] and in 1966–67 Alumni Fund giving reached $250,000, with an additional $400,000 of designated gifts for buildings, endowments, and special purposes.[7] The next year the Alumni Fund reached a record level, totaling $275,000 in unrestricted monies and winning the American Alumni Council's Award for Sustained Performance in Annual Funds among large co-educational colleges.[8]

In the 1950s and 1960s Swarthmore's success with its alumni was modest in the context of broader changes in higher education funding in the mid-1900s. Many institutions of higher education turned to the postwar flood of sources federal funding to support growth and development, especially the Defense Department, the National Science Foundation, and the National Institutes of Health. Even Harvard, with its ample endowment, depended heavily on the federal govenment in the 1950s, when three-fourths of its research funding came from that source.[9]

This new funding atmosphere led many analysts of higher education to predict the relative decline of the small college, particularly the liberal arts college. Most notably, in 1963 Clark Kerr, chancellor of the University of California (and himself a Swarthmore graduate who "had a keen appreciation and indeed affection for the great traditions of liberal education"), nonetheless confidently proclaimed that the true future of American higher education was to be found in the conglomerate "multiversity" of undergraduate and graduate schools, research laboratories, extension programs, and multiple services to society that were shaped by federal grants.[10]

While at Princeton University in the late 1940s Courtney Smith could not have avoided observing these massive changes occurring in higher education. In 1946, the year Smith arrived at Princeton, President Harold W. Dodds had established a committee to investigate "the proper balance between Princeton's educational responsibilities as a liberal arts university and the extent to which it can enter into research partnerships with government and industry."[11] Several leaders at Princeton believed that greatly expanded federal funding and secret military research threatened the traditional liberal arts curriculum and teaching milieu on their campus. Dodds's solution to the problem was to create a nearby research campus, the Forrestal Center, to house new research activity funded by government and industry. But Dodds's effort backfired when the science faculty's time and energy quickly shifted to the Forrestal Center. Princeton University's dynamics had been fundamentally altered, and the humanities faculty, of which Smith was a member, became "conscious of the shifting balance of campus power and the redistribution of resources, that appeared to threaten honored Princeton traditions and established principles."[12]

Swarthmore, a co-educational, Quaker institution of nine hundred students that had for thirty years been dedicated to what many regarded as one of the purest expressions of liberal arts education in the United States, certainly was an unlikely candidate for participation in the massive, national defense-related research funding that began with the Korean War. Nonetheless, Smith was consciously resistant not only to the scientification of higher education but also the snares of federal funding.

As president of Swarthmore College, Smith faced most directly the difficulties accompanying federal funding when the National Defense Education Act (NDEA) of 1958 took effect. The NDEA provided colleges and universities loans for students of superior academic background who intended to teach after graduation or students of superior capacity who intended to work in science, engineering, or modern languages.

Swarthmore students clearly qualified but Smith was concerned about the provision in the NDEA that required every student receiving a loan to sign an affidavit certifying "that he does not believe in, and is not a member of and does not support any organization that believes in or teaches, the overthrow of the United States government by force or violence or by any illegal or unconstitutional methods."[13] In mid-November

1958 Courtney shared his understanding of the implications of the NDEA loan requirements with Swarthmore faculty and asked for legal advice from Claude Smith, chair of the college's board of managers. Hearing their responses (which were divided regarding the constitutionality and morality of the NDEA provision), Courtney asked the Board of Managers to create a joint committee of the managers, administration, faculty, and students to "consider the college's position with care and formulate a recommendation to the faculty and the Board."[14]

With the joint committee's supportive feedback and drawing on the Quaker belief in resistance to any oath taking, Courtney then began to investigate the possibility of having the affidavit provision repealed. Within a few days he was contacting public figures he knew who might be able to assist in the matter. He turned first to Senator Joseph Clark (Pa.), whom he had served with on the Harvard Board of Overseers, and then asked the executive director of the American Civil Liberties Union (ACLU), Patrick M. Malin, for advice on how to proceed.[15] Malin was an alumnus and former professor at the college and the son-in-law of Clement Biddle, a member of the Board of Managers.

Senator Clark told Smith that the repeal effort would only succeed in Congress if there was strong opposition throughout higher education, including Catholic institutions, and if support for repeal could be gotten from Republicans (such as Hugh Scott [Pa.] and Jacob Javits [N.Y.]), as well as from Democrats. Malin was more pessimistic: he told Smith that "there was not even a 1% chance of getting repeal" and that support from colleges to fight for repeal seemed unlikely.[16] But Smith was not discouraged. When he attended the Association of American Colleges meeting in Kansas City in January 1959 he helped to put the issue on the table and found that "it was the consensus of a substantial portion of the members attending the meetings that the affidavit in particular constitute[d] a serious infringement of and threat to individual liberty and freedom of conscience."[17] By March 1959 the ACLU, too, made a formal protest of the "superficially attractive . . . [but] harmful" provision of the NDEA.[18]

There was in fact sufficient public reaction to the affidavit that Senator Clark and Senator John F. Kennedy (Mass.), who also served on the Harvard Board of Overseers with Courtney Smith, introduced a Senate bill to repeal the affidavit provision of the NDEA. In April 1959 the bill was brought before the subcommittee for education, chaired by Senator James E. Murray of Montana. Kennedy began the hearing by arguing that the NDEA had no provision for checking the veracity of the affidavits, that it singled out students for such affidavits when other federal loan recipients were not required to make such affidavits, and, indeed that "card carrying members of the Communist Party, of course [will] have no hesitancy about perjuring themselves in such an affidavit. This provision will not keep them out of the program. But it may well keep out those who resent such a requirement, those who find it distasteful or humiliating, those who are overapprehensive in their interpretation or who fear unnecessarily the Government's interpretation of their views, or those who are conscientiously opposed to test oaths."[19]

Smith worked closely with senators Clark and Kennedy to prepare comments for the hearings on the bill and recruited testimonies from the presidents of Bryn Mawr, Haverford, University of South Dakota, and other higher education institutions. Those recruited by Smith were then invited by Kennedy to appear at the hearings. Kennedy later wrote to Smith that "all agreed to testify or submit written statements. Your suggestions have been of considerable assistance."[20]

Courtney himself was called to testify before the sub-committee on May 5, 1959. He informed the panel that

> Swarthmore College, on the action of its board of managers and faculty, has voted not to participate in the student loan program of the act unless section 1001 (f) is repealed. . . . Swarthmore College is opposed to the requiring of any commitment from students as to belief or disbelief as a condition to their receiving loans made in aid of their education. The freedom, privacy, and integrity of individual beliefs is a crucial aspect of America's constitutional tradition, and these aspects of belief were precisely what the men who wrote the Constitution and the Bill of Rights intended to protect. . . . As an educational institution Swarthmore College believes that strong citizens in a democratic society are produced in an atmosphere of freedom where ideas do not need to be forbidden or protected. The college has confidence in its students and in the educational process itself, confidence in the efficacy of free inquiry and debate to reveal error.[21]

The bill did not pass in 1959, but a broader groundswell of support for repeal was evident in the similar bills introduced in the House of Representatives by congressmen such as John Brademas, who knew Smith through the Rhodes Scholar Program. President Eisenhower and Vice President Nixon endorsed the elimination of the disclaimer affidavit, and in 1960 repeal of the affidavit provision was a plank in John F. Kennedy's presidential campaign platform. The disclaimer affidavit, which Courtney had felt so strongly about, and which Swarthmore sought to nullify, finally was eliminated in 1962.[22] Swarthmore College, having lobbied for the repeal for three years, then agreed to accept NDEA loans for its students.[23]

Smith's response to the federal monies available to higher education was exemplified by his *National Defense Education Act* endeavors. He knew that great possibilities were being given to higher education, but as early as 1954 he told supporters of the college that he described himself as "lukewarm" regarding federal funding.[24] He believed that little thought had been given to the effect of federal aid on higher education in general, and he did not want funding to shape the future of the liberal arts in America.[25] Certainly he was resistant to creating and relying on a system that could make education less intellectually free and less intimate, and he believed that the mission of the college would be seriously distorted by undertaking the massive staff and facilities commitments required to operate apparatus such as a cyclotron (an example Smith used frequently) and other manifestations of big science.[26] He favored individual faculty research that drew on students as collaborators and which was directly related to teaching, and he enthusiastically supported grant applications for such purposes.[27] Indeed, many faculty members received National Institutes of Health and National Science Foundation monies during his administration, and the physics department had Atomic Energy Commission support. In spite of his concern about supporting a science establishment the college even sought and received federal grants for two larger projects that provided infrastructure for frontier research—an animal research laboratory and a mainframe computer.[28]

But Smith's attention was focused on ways to develop private funding for Swarthmore's needs. He thought that private sources always gave Swarthmore more ability to control and determine the use of the monies than did federal sources, and he fought with determination to clarify the terms of private grants and gifts. For instance, he had a running debate with Amos Peaslee, a scholarship donor, about the conditions of his gift and its impact upon Swarthmore curriculum standards. Smith would not accept the donor's money on the donor's terms, which required recipients to do an internship, until he was satisfied that the internship would not dilute the rigor of the required academic curriculum.[29]

Similarly, in the mid-1960s when the college joined the University City Science Center, a scientific research consortium led by the University of Pennsylvania, Smith quickly became concerned about Swarthmore's lack of control of the kinds of research being conducted there. He argued for review of the founding charter and a return to the consortium's originally specified focus on industrial research rather than continuing the classified military research it had begun to do.[30] In most instances, however, Courtney found that there were fewer problems in receiving privately donated individual and corporation funds than government funds, because those donors gave greater latitude and authority to Smith and the college.

Smith's search for private support for the college went well beyond the Philadelphia region: he also drew upon a nationwide network of higher education leaders, foundation officers, and funding sources, whom he had known before taking the presidency at Swarthmore. When he was assistant to the American secretary of the Rhodes Scholarship program he had become familiar with foundation funding expectations, and then as director of the Woodrow Wilson Fellowship Program Courtney had generated foundation support from the General Education Board (a Rockefeller philanthropy) and the Carnegie Corporation. In 1953 he was elected a trustee of the Markle Foundation, and he continued to serve on that board throughout his presidency. In 1953 he was elected trustee of the Eisenhower Educational Exchange Fellowships, and in 1955 he was elected to the Harvard Board of Overseers. At Swarthmore he became active with Quaker College Presidents, Association of American Colleges, American Council on Education, and Pennsylvania Association of Colleges and Universities and was a frequent speaker at college commencements, inaugurations of college and university presidents, and conferences of educational leaders. This network of contacts and his regular reading of the *New York Times* and other news accounts of philanthropic matters kept him abreast of funding trends in education.[31] He knew that opportunities to tap private giving to higher education were expanding rapidly.[32]

During Smith's leadership of Swarthmore private foundation and corporate support grew at least as rapidly as alumni giving. In the fourth year of his presidency, 1956–57, at least sixteen foundations and twenty-seven corporations gave grants to Swarthmore.[33] This source of support continued to grow throughout Smith's presidency.[34]

Perhaps Smith's greatest success with a private foundation resulted in funding for a new science building. Smith knew of the long-standing need for new science facilties on campus and included it on his earliest list of funding priorities. There was greater impetus for a new science building when in the fall of 1957 the Soviet Union successfully launched the artificial satellite *Sputnik* and the American public focused its attention on improving scientific education.[35]

A search for possible funders led him to the Longwood Foundation, a du Pont family philanthropy. He got advice from Walter O. Simon (Swarthmore alumnus and Du Pont Company official) about the Longwood Foundation's interest in funding science facilities. Smith then had vice presidents Joe Shane and Ed Cratsley develop a grant application in a format which Simon told Smith would be appreciated by the Du Pont Company officers and executives who sat on the foundation's board. Two of the officers were Crawford H. Greenewalt, whom Courtney knew from collaboration on a subcommittee of the President's Committee on Education beyond High School, and William Ward, a Swarthmore graduate, Du Pont Company executive, and member of the college's Board of Managers. The Longwood Foundation approved a grant to Swarthmore of $1,800,000 in December 1957, within three months of the application.[36]

Smith quickly notified the members of the Board of Managers of the approval of the application, concluding his letter with "Isn't it a Merry Christmas?"[37] He quickly appointed a science faculty committee to work with the administration and then selected an architect, Vincent G. Kling. The committee and architect worked together to design the long-needed science building, which was named for Pierre S. du Pont, the leader of the Du Pont Company through most of the first half of the twentieth century. Ground was broken July 1958 and the building was dedicated April 1960, giving new a new appearance to the north campus and a new life to the science curriculum.[38]

This success gave Smith encouragement to take on a major funding drive to address long-term capital needs that the college had had on its agenda for more than a decade. He began seriously thinking about a campaign in May 1959 with manager Thomas B. McCabe, the college's most generous financial supporter, and the next month he outlined his vision to the Board of Managers.[39] After considerable preliminary effort, in the fall of 1961 Smith announced a campaign that would conclude in 1964, the centennial year of the college's founding.[40]

Smith soon told the alumni in his annual report that "Much of the year 1961–62 went . . . to intensive, detailed planning for the *Centennial Fund* campaign. The members of the Board of Managers have accepted a commitment to support the college with the utmost generosity in this effort, an effort essential to our reaching a new level of performance in our program, and we shall soon be approaching every alumnus and parent and good friend of Swarthmore."[41] Smith, who had developed regionalized national recruitment plans for both the American Rhodes Trust and the Woodrow Wilson Fellowship Program, now set up an elaborate nationwide communication and solicitation network to systematically approach alumni about Swarthmore's needs for financial support.

Smith formed a Centennial Fund Council, comprised of leading members of the alumni and Board of Managers, to plan and implement outreach and hired a professional fundraiser to manage the campaign. The council, which met regularly with President Smith, designed a program with separate financial quotas for each region, including overseas areas. Five hundred volunteers were recruited to contact eight thousand one hundred alumni, alumnae, and friends of the college scattered throughout the United States and in foreign countries.

Each region arranged meetings so that all alumni could be engaged and solicited and leadership gifts could be sought. The strategy for solicitation was to outline the college's specific building and program needs and the funding required to accomplish each one. The campaign sought funds or matching funds for endowed professorships; additional faculty appointments in new fields of learning, research, and academic equipment (including a computer); a language laboratory; endowed scholarships; an enlarged library; a Friends Historical Library expansion; an animal laboratory; an addition to the Sproul Astronomical Observatory; additional offices and classrooms; a hydraulics laboratory; a dining hall; a men's dormitory; and an infirmary. President Smith spoke directly to many of the groups but also made a long-playing record of his talk so that groups that he could not visit personally could listen to his remarks on "The Things Swarthmore Believes in."[42]

The Centennial Council members each solicited leadership gifts, but Courtney specifically took on the task of seeking out the largest donors and foundation contributions. He contacted a number of Philadelphia, New York, and Midwest foundations, including Dana, Independence, Donner, Presser, Sloan, Danforth, Kresge, Lilly, and Mellon. The campaign leaders were very conscious of the value of Smith's personal charm and national prestige in this process. According to Thomas McCabe (chairman of the Board of Managers, the Centennial Campaign and the Scott Paper Company), Courtney's "influence and prestige could be used most advantageously" if he focused on "$100,000 prospects, but not on $10,000 ones."[43]

Courtney was extremely successful in sharing his vision and generating enthusiasm for Swarthmore when he contacted potential supporters of the campaign. The Centennial Fund campaign not only reached its $10 million goal, with contributions from 6,870 alumni and other donors, but exceeded it by $2 million because the Ford Foundation made a matching $2 million grant to Swarthmore as part of its $100,000,000 program of general support for higher-education institutions. Campaign Council members also made significant gifts that changed the physical character of the campus: during the campaign Philip Sharples gave $1,200,000 for a new dining hall, and Thomas McCabe gave nearly $2,000,000 for the new library.[44] The success of the campaign was much celebrated on campus, so much so that the editors of the *Phoenix,* the student newspaper, reported in their 1964 April Fool's edition that their college had inadvertently been sold to the Ford Foundation for $3 million due to a clerical error during a flurry of final centennial gifts![45]

Some of Smith's efforts in fund-raising did not pay off until after the close of the Centennial drive. During the 1964—65 academic year the Dana Foundation gave $200,000 for a men's dormitory; Thomas Hallowell, co-chairman of the campaign, made a gift for a second men's dormitory; the Kresge Foundation gave $25,000 for a professorship; and the James Foundation gave $500,000 in two unrestricted gifts.[46] Some contacts took even longer to mature. During 1966—67, the Danforth Foundation gave $60,000 to help underwrite three major studies of the curriculum, library needs, and student life; the Old Dominion Foundation gave $125,000 for faculty study and research in the humanities; and the Sloan Foundation gave $375,000 for equipment, library resources, and staff support that was intended "to provide increased chance for professional and research opportunities for the natural sciences."[47]

As a result of the Centennial Fund Campaign and its immediate aftermath, Swarthmore College in the latter 1960s had a solid financial underpinning in virtually all areas and had renewed, replaced, or enlarged several outmoded elements of the college campus, including dormitories, the dining hall, and the library. Smith's search for funding was not only outstandingly successful in a financial sense but also had been a means of further articulating and defining Swarthmore's educational mission and institutional character. Carefully choosing a variety of sources of support and making clear what was unacceptable, Smith chose a path for Swarthmore that was distinctive in an age of rapid changes in higher education funding. Swarthmore, unlike numerous other elite institutions, including Harvard, Princeton, and Stanford, was not substantially altered by federal funding in the postwar era, nor was it required by financial exigencies to give up its central commitment to the liberal arts.[48]

# 12

## Networks of Support and Service:
## Behind the Presidency

DUE TO HIS FATHER'S EARLY DEATH COURTNEY SMITH WENT THROUGH adolescence without the strong support and guidance of a father figure, but he was advised by teachers, community leaders, his mother, older siblings (notably his sister), and extended family; he also developed a knack for developing and sustaining lifelong relationships. He was guided by his mother and sister throughout his formal secondary and post–high school education, and when he entered college and adulthood he quickly associated himself with strong men with mentoring values. Courtney, throughout his career, developed widening circles of support and advisors. Although the relationships he created were largely invisible to the Swarthmore community in the 1950s and 1960s he was continually engaging the infrastructure of higher education and thriving on its discourse.

His networking efforts began at Harvard when he was away from home. In the unfamiliar Eastern culture, he worked on the Harvard campus and began seeking adult guidance to realize his personal and professional visions. Then when he was a Rhodes Scholar he was inspired by the quality of the repartee he found in the deliberate teacher-scholar discourse that he found at Oxford. Throughout the remainder of his career he attempted to replicate that type of relationship in other settings. He seemed to thrive on the intimate, intensive discourse offered by twosomes and small groups. He reflected upon others' ideas and found they stimulated his own creative thoughts. What he learned from his conversations with others, he often transformed into practical responses to challenges he faced.

When he was in leadership roles Courtney sought to develop programs that would encourage and sustain mentoring relationships. He argued for intentional interviewing of candidates for the Rhodes Scholar Program and the Swarthmore faculty. He argued for the retention of a small student body and low student-faculty ratio at Swarthmore. He argued for the validity and reliability of the liberal arts education as a force creating the best citizen in the face of postwar concerns about deteriorating patriotism and democratic values. His ongoing and conscientious outreach and responsiveness to constituencies of the college and American higher education all seem to relate directly to his personal appreciation of professional mentoring and the networks of people who sustain it.

As an undergraduate at Harvard, Courtney was advised by F. O. Matthiessen, and upon his return to Harvard for doctoral studies professors James B. Munn and Hyder E. Rollins supervised and encouraged his work. These relationships were maintained for many years after leaving Harvard. Courtney corresponded with Munn and Rollins to share his experiences and seek their advice. They responded with encouragement, support, and approval of his endeavors. Rollins, who was clearly touched by their relationship, wrote to Courtney upon his appointment as the president of Swarthmore, "My Boy already knows what I think and how proud I am of him."[1]

While at Harvard, Courtney had also been socially mentored by H. Wendell Endicott, the wealthy Harvard alumnus and avid sportsman who had hired him to become a companion for his young son, introduced him to several outdoor sports, and taken him on Endicott family trips.[2] Endicott continued to be invested in Courtney and became his advocate. Endicott wrote to the War Production Board about the possibility that Smith could be appointed to serve on it and commented enthusiastically about Smith's proficiency in research, his reading knowledge of several languages, and his habit of being a tireless worker and a clear thinker.[3] He also recommended Smith for a naval officer position, commenting upon his conscientiousness, dependability, and ability to "handle with tact delicate situations."[4]

As Courtney was nearing completion of his naval service in 1945 and was hoping to obtain a teaching position, Hyder Rollins, with whom he had corresponded, became his champion. Rollins wrote to the Princeton English department and successfully recommended Courtney for an appointment there.

While at Princeton teaching English, Courtney developed collaborative relationships with two popular teachers who were leaders in the liberal arts: Willard Thorp and Whitney J. Oates. Thorp's interest was American literature and he had initiated the American Civilization Program; Oates was an ardent advocate of humanities, who had conceived of and found the money to develop the Woodrow Wilson Fellowship Program. Oates drew Courtney into the Woodrow Wilson program and valued his contribution to administering its expansion.[5]

As a Rhodes Scholar teaching at Princeton, Courtney sought further contact with Frank Aydelotte, the American secretary of the Rhodes program, who at that time was director of the Institute for Advanced Study in Princeton. By 1952, Courtney had become assistant to Aydelotte and in the next year succeeded him as the American secretary. It was Aydelotte, a former Swarthmore College president, who then strongly recommended Courtney's appointment for the presidency of Swarthmore. Clearly, by the early 1950s, Smith had in place a significant network of educators and administrators derived from his Harvard-Oxford-Princeton years and his experience with the Rhodes and Woodrow Wilson Fellowship Programs. He was connected and admired enough to make him a prime candidate to serve as a trustee for like organizations.

The first program to draw upon his expertise was the Markle Medical Scholars Program of the Markle Foundation, which late in 1952 asked him to serve on its fellowship screening committee. The John F. and Mary Markle Foundation was established in 1927 by John Markle, who had made a fortune in Pennsylvania coal mining. The foundation originally spent its money on social welfare programs, but in 1935 it shifted to focus to grants for medical research. In 1947, it began devoting all of its funds to five-year fellowships for young physicians who agreed to forego the higher remuneration of private practice in order to pursue careers in medical research. Fellows were chosen from a group of candidates who went through an intense screening process carried out over several days by a group of academicians and physicians selected by the foundation.

Smith spent four days early in 1953 at the Arden House in Harriman, New York interviewing and selecting candidates for the Markle fellowships.[6] He apparently impressed the Markle trustees by his performance and knowledge from the Rhodes and Woodrow Wilson fellowship programs because he was elected a member of the foundation's Board of Directors on October 29, 1953.[7] He was highly regarded by the foundation's president, John Russell, who described Courtney in 1955 as having "a very high order of ability, and an effective, relaxed way of talking business."[8]

Smith served as a Markle director for sixteen years, attending most directors' meetings (held three times a year) and many scholar selection meetings. The Markle board was relatively small and composed mostly of financiers from J. P. Morgan and few academicians. While participating in funding discussions Smith made efforts to separate his allegiances. He abstained from decisions about Harvard, and he rejected another director's notion that Swarthmore apply for a grant to support research at the college.[9]

In 1967, after twenty years of awarding Markle medical fellowships, Smith and his fellow trustees recognized that medical research was being increasingly funded by public monies, and concluded that the Markle Foundation could no longer make a significant difference in that field; they wanted to identify, support, and impact new areas of need in American society. In 1967–68 Courtney took the significant leadership step of chairing the ad hoc Committee on Future Plans.[10] In the chairing role he contacted many leaders in higher education, the arts, and government to ascertain their views of the pressing needs in American society.[11]

Although the Markle Foundation was his primary commitment, Courtney also served several other nonprofit organizations. In August 1953, Courtney was approached by Ward Wheelock, an advertising executive in Philadelphia, and asked to serve on a temporary Policy, Plans and Operations Committee for the proposed Eisenhower International Exchange Fellowships. Thomas McCabe and Philip Sharples (both members of the college board of managers' committee that had recruited Smith) and other leading Pennsylvania Republicans had conceived this new organization. They wanted to honor President Eisenhower, whose new farm in Gettysburg had made him a resident of the state. The Eisenhower Exchange program was intended to provide "potential leaders" in developing nations the opportunity to come to the United States for "first-hand observation of our developments in their fields" of interest.[12]

Courtney agreed to serve on the Eisenhower Exchange's temporary committee and during September 1953 met at the Union League club in Philadelphia with a small group of men who had been Republican financial supporters. There, Courtney helped to organize the program and select the first Executive Committee and Board of Trustees.[13] Courtney was elected to both and was very involved in the process of clarifying and establishing criteria, critiquing proposals, making suggestions for improvement, and setting standards for the international exchangees. Indeed, as late as 1968 he was making recommendations about the countries that should be involved in the 1969 exchange.[14]

As president of Swarthmore, Courtney also attended meetings of the Quaker College Presidents and the Pennsylvania Association of Colleges and Universities. In 1956 and 1957 he chaired the nationwide Quaker College Presidents' Group, and in 1957 he hosted the presidents at the Friends Historical Library and at his home, where he and Betty had a buffet dinner. Although he attended further meetings and encouraged the participation of all Quaker college presidents, Smith and Joe Shane were disappointed that the group discussed general issues related to college administration rather than focusing on educational issues specific to Quaker colleges. They also felt that Swarthmore was in an elite class of Quaker colleges (with Haverford and Bryn Mawr), so that collaborative ventures with the other institutions would yield no particular benefit to the college.[15]

With Swarthmore situated in Pennsylvania, Claude Smith, the chair of the college's board of managers, recommended that Courtney also get involved with the Pennsylvania Association of Colleges and Universities (PACU) as an organization that attempted to unite the state's higher education institutions in order to effectively address common problems. Courtney responded to Claude's advice and became involved with the association. He attended the October 1954 meeting, and the president of the association immediately noted that Courtney had dealt with some "very knotty problems" regarding the future of higher education in Pennsylvania.[16] PACU routinely monitored higher education activities of the state government, so Courtney found that the organization allowed him to lobby effectively and efficiently for legislation that would affect Swarthmore directly. During his Swarthmore presidency he wrote to legislators expressing his views in opposition to the establishment of a regents-like program and in support of bills directed toward the elimination of the 15 percent inheritance tax on charitable bequests, the formation of a State Council of Higher Education, and the inclusion of independent colleges in the establishment of a statewide community college system.[17]

In 1957 he was consulted by the executive director of PACU about the governor's proposal of a major new loan program for higher education and how it could be facilitated. Following that consultation he went to a luncheon at the Executive Mansion to hear about Governor George Leader's plan.[18] He also made a major address for the Pennsylvania Association of Colleges and Universities when it held a special assembly for new faculty in 1960. His remarks on the nature and challenges of teaching in liberal arts colleges were well received.[19]

Throughout his presidency of Swarthmore, Courtney was more interested in national organizations than state ones and regularly went to meetings of the Association of American Colleges (AAC) and the American Council on Education. He attended his first Association of American Colleges meeting in the fall of 1953 and shortly thereafter was asked to serve on its Commission on Liberal Education. In 1956 he participated on a panel discussing alumni funds and annual giving.[20] Then in 1957 he was appointed to the AAC Board of Directors for a term ending in 1961. And although he turned down a request that he become vice president of the AAC, as a board member he helped the AAC to get Carnegie Corporation support for the 1961 Annual Meeting in Denver and was one of three AAC leaders who conducted merger discussions between the AAC and the Council for the Advancement of Small Colleges.[21] Participation in AAC conferences allowed Smith to attend the 1956 and 1958 Pugwash conferences scheduled in conjunction with the AAC meetings.[22]

In the fall of 1954 Courtney attended his first meeting of the American Council on Education (ACE), a national group of private, public, and business education associations and institutions promoting cooperation and supportive legislation. The local Quaker colleges were active in this organization, and Smith's colleague, Katharine McBride, president of Bryn Mawr College, was elected its chair in 1955–56.[23] In 1957 Courtney was asked to lead discussions regarding "Cooperative Education Activities among Institutions at the Same Level" at ACE's annual conference.[24] He was on the Council's Commission on International Education from 1962–65, and although he went to further national meetings he was apparently not directly involved with the organization's leadership.[25]

Courtney, a member of his Class of 1938 Alumni Committee, was nominated in 1955 by the Harvard Alumni Association to be a candidate for the Overseers of Harvard College; he ran against Senator John F. Kennedy and eight others, who vied for five seats. He won his election to a six-year term as an overseer, a position that required attending six meetings a year and entailed reviewing the curriculum and faculty appointments at Harvard College.[26] Smith was an active member of the Harvard College Overseers, attending nearly all the meetings and serving separately as chair of the Divinity School and the philosophy department visiting committees.

David Rockefeller, who was also on the Board of Overseers during Smith's term, has recounted that the overseers always met in University Hall around a large table headed by the president of the university, Nathan Pusey. There were lively discussions that included reviewing visiting committee oral reports about the departments in the college. When the college was considering reorganization or redirecting a program during the Pusey era, the overseers and visiting committees, which brought outsiders to campus, often were of significance in acquiring funding and providing rationale for change.[27] Pusey, an Iowan like Smith, also knew Courtney as a fellow member of the Commission on Liberal Education of the AAC, which Pusey chaired. He called on Smith and the chancellor of Vanderbilt University, Harvie Branscomb, to appear with him when he announced a major capital campaign for Harvard in October 1956.[28]

Chairing the two visiting committees for Harvard was Smith's most important service to Harvard College. The committees, which were mechanisms for the faculties to communicate with the overseers, gave both constructive criticism and assistance to the college's units. Committees were composed of five to twenty people not necessarily connected to the university but with interest in the specific field or discipline being reviewed. They held meetings with faculties, considered problems of the department, brought new ideas, provided liaison functions, and helped to raise monies for the departments. Each visiting committee chair, who was usually an overseer, chose the members of the committee and was responsible for both the yearly oral reports and triennial written report to the board.[29]

In 1955 Courtney succeeded the famous scientist Robert Oppenheimer as chair of the Visiting Committee for the Philosophy Department. Morton White, the chair of the department, gave Courtney a summary of the functioning in the department, especially the split between the older and younger philosophers in the department at the time. White reported that faculty attrition meant that the department was not as strong as it had been in the past and that the previous visiting committee's report had "let the department off rather easily."[30] White himself wrote a defense of philosophy and a warning that it needed to be better understood as a discipline being shaped by issues in the modern world.[31] Courtney took the view that the department was increasingly more relevant to students' preparation, a perspective supported by the increased enrollment in philosophy undergraduate classes.

In his first triennial report, Courtney reviewed intensively the multifaceted nature of philosophy at Harvard and noted that "it is the opinion of the Visiting Committee that the Department is strengthening itself, that it is seeking to rethink its aims and functions, and methods."[32] McGeorge Bundy, then dean of the Faculty of Arts and Sciences and later an advisor to Presidents Kennedy and Johnson, wrote Courtney that the report was "without question the best single document of the kind that I have seen in my six years in the office. There have been many good reports, and many helpful ones, but none which combined understanding of a very complex and difficult situation with a skillful choice of the right things to say about it."[33]

Since Courtney had responsibility for selecting members of the visiting committees that he chaired, he asked John Nason (his Swarthmore predecessor), Morris Lasker (his Harvard classmate and a lawyer), and Chadbourne Gilpatric (a Rhodes Scholar classmate and Rockefeller Foundation officer) to join him on later visiting committees to the philosophy department. In his committee's second triennial report (drafted in 1961), Smith noted that "the most dramatic and popular expansion of philosophy has been in the General Education program . . . [where the course taught by Albritton, Cohen and White,] Ideas of Man and the World in Western Thought, . . . [had an enrollment of] close to 700 students," demonstrating that philosophy "can be a strong component in the main stream of college education."[34]

The chairmanship of the Visiting Committee to the Divinity School, which Courtney assumed in October 1956, was even more challenging for him because he came into that role just as the Divinity School was beginning a rebuilding and restructuring process, after completing a successful 1952–55 fund-raising campaign.[35] The Divinity School, which was founded in 1816, had gone through a period of neglect and stagnation prior to the beginning of Pusey's presidency in 1953, and the previous visiting committee had been critical of a number of aspects of the school.[36] Upon taking the chairmanship of the committee, Smith heard criticisms regarding the dean of the school, Douglas Horton, who had been with the Divinity School since 1955. Faculty described Horton as likeable but also as a pacifier who lacked leadership skills and consistency during the planning and implementing of programs. Courtney met with Horton and found that he agreed with the faculty criticisms, noting additionally that Horton was "misleading to work with" because the dean did not follow up on their agreed agendas, meeting plans, and commitments.[37]

Overall, Courtney and the Visiting Committee were concerned about the nature and demands of contemporary theological training, the coherence of the school's curriculum, the relationship between the Divinity School and the churches, and the qualities of the students enrolled in the school.[38] During Courtney's chairmanship of the Divinity School Visiting Committee, Dean Horton retired and there was a search for a new dean who could meet the changing needs of the school.

Samuel H. Miller, a minister who had held four pastorates and most recently had been at the Old Cambridge Baptist Church while also a member of the Divinity School faculty, was appointed to the deanship. Although Courtney did not appoint Swarthmore faculty to the visiting committees, he did consult with Swarthmore staff about issues and proposals being made for the Divinity School. Courtney was also particulary anxious to appoint to the visiting committee George William Webber, a Harvard graduate serving the East Harlem Protestant Parish in New York City, and others who would be active in their deliberation about theological training and the administrative issues of the church.[39] In its 1962 report, the committee was enthusiastic about the directions that the school was taking and called for even greater funding of the school.[40] After three years of Smith's chairmanship of the committee, Elliott Dunlap Smith, one of the most influential members of the Board of Overseers and the Divinity School Visiting Committee thanked Courtney for "what your leadership is doing for the School in this [time of] crisis."[41]

Courtney had given Harvard a substantial amount of attention for several years, and in the view of his peers had served Harvard well. In his last year of chairing both the Philosophy and Divinity Visiting Committees, he was appointed to the Harvard overseers' English department Visiting Committee. However, in spite of his English literature background, he was less active on the committee and attended only four meetings during his six-year term.[42] His commitments to Swarthmore's Centennial Campaign in the early 1960s clearly overrode undertaking further substantial service to his alma mater.

Courtney had less intense relationships with other academic and scholarly organizations in the mid to late 1950s. During Courtney's presidency of Swarthmore he had many occasions for correspondence and involvement with the American Friends Service Committee regarding educational matters, and he supported the involvement of faculty and staff, such as Registrar John Moore's membership on the AFSC's Educational Advisory Committee.[43] Although he cooperated with many of the AFSC requests for information and served on its Educational Advisory Committee beginning in 1955, he frequently expressed concern that he did not have enough time to engage in their activities to a depth that would make him feel comfortable and like a significant contributor. He told George Mohlenhoff, director of college programs at AFSC, "I don't like 'nominal memberships' . . . I am likely to miss a good many meetings," when Mohlenhoff asked him to remain on the Advisory Committee despite Courtney's absence from several meetings.[44] Although the committee met at Pendle Hill, just a few miles from the college, Courtney apparently felt that few of the meetings could justify his time away from more pressing matters and institutional responsibilities.

Courtney assisted other organizations in limited ways. He served briefly in 1955 on the General Electric Educational Foundation's Fellowship Selection Committee. He sat on a Lilly Endowment grant review committee (1956–58) that made recommendations for the distribution of $149,000 to eight liberal arts colleges in Indiana for experiments in curricula and teaching. He accepted an appointment to the National Committee for the Florence Agreement, an organization urging U.S. acceptance of an international agreement on the importation of educational, scientific, and cultural materials. And in 1962 he met with the representatives of colleges who had received Ford Foundation Endowment Grants.[45]

In February 1957, after Smith had been president of Swarthmore for several years, he was asked by Alfred H. Williams, president of the Federal Reserve Bank of Philadelphia and a Swarthmore College manager, to participate in discussions "to consider the explosive growth of Philadelphia and the Delaware Valley region and the problems which attend [that] growth" in the tri-state, eleven-county region.[46] Courtney agreed to join the group of businessmen, planners, labor and industry leaders, government personnel, and higher education leaders (including Hugh Borton [Haverford College president] and Katherine McBride [Bryn Mawr College president]). The group soon prepared a Ford Foundation grant application asking for funds to develop a program that would pursue research and public education about growth trends, impacts of those trends, and development needs in the lower Delaware River Valley.

On October 3, 1957, the Ford Foundation announced approval of the $900,000 grant and Penjerdel Inc. (the Pennsylvania-New Jersey-Delaware group) was founded. Courtney sat on Penjerdel's board for the eleven years until his death, as Penjerdel explored economic patterns, community growth patterns, population trends, government reorganization and cooperation, transportation, sewage disposal, air pollution, park and recreation needs, causes of crime, and the advantages and disadvantages of suburban living and then planned and executed several community information and education ventures.[47] He also hosted a major Penjerdel conference on the Swarthmore campus on June 12, 1968, when five hundred community leaders met to hear addresses by Edmund S. Muskie, chairman of the Senate Subcommittee on Intergovernmental Relations, Robert Wood, undersecretary of the Department of Housing and Urban Development, and Paul N. Ylvisaker, a former Swarthmore professor who was then commissioner of community affairs for New Jersey.[48]

Smith's work with this regional consortium also networked him with other Philadelphia leadership. In 1957 Smith became a manager of the Philadelphia Savings Fund Society (PSFS), a Philadelphia bank founded in 1816 that was closely allied with the city's blue bloods and that had a strong tradition of philanthropic and community activity.[49] He became very active as a PSFS manager and served on several board committees, including a committee to study the geographical extension of savings banks, a committee to study a retirement plan for members of the board of managers, a committee on mutual funds, the nominating committee, and the audit committee.

He was a regular attender at managers' meetings and heavily involved in 1967 when he participated in nearly twenty meetings of the PSFS board and its committees as they planned a significant reorganization.[50] (In that year, the first woman and first African American were nominated and elected to the board.)[51] R. Stewart Rauch Jr., president of PSFS, appreciated Smith's "fairness, consideration of others, [and] determination to find the right solution" and found that Smith's "advice . . . was invariably sound and farsighted."[52]

In September 1968, after Rauch heard of Smith's decision to leave Swarthmore, Rauch and at least two other managers urged Smith to succeed him as president of PSFS. They felt that his skills in personnel relations, community projects, and public welfare were what the bank needed at that point. They emphasized that fine knowledge of banking was not critical for the presidency of PSFS, and that the position would leave time for the "study and writing, educational and foundation affairs" that Courtney obviously enjoyed. Courtney refused the offer, commenting that he was "deeply moved" by their confidence in him, but he was already looking forward to the challenge of the Markle Foundation presidency.[53]

A small regional organization to which he also dedicated time was the Three College Presidents group of Katharine McBride (Byrn Mawr), Hugh Borton (Haverford), and Smith. Meeting monthly beginning in 1959, the presidents worked together to share some faculty, enroll students in special courses, and seek joint funding for programs that no one of the colleges alone could support. From 1955 through 1958, Courtney Smith had had inconclusive discussions with four officers of the Ford Foundation regarding the possibility of a Three College Asian Studies Program.[54] But after Hugh Borton (an Asian specialist) became the new president of Haverford, the negotiations with Ford, which had dragged, took on new life and a collaborative grant application for $136,000 was approved in February 1959.[55] The two-year program was designed "to enable existing faculty members of the three colleges to increase their knowledge and understanding of non-western cultures and to introduce new perspectives into the courses of the existing undergraduate curricula of the three colleges."[56] The grant supported seminars for both faculty and students that were led by visiting Asian scholars and provided funds for books for each library and stipends for additional Asian specialists to give lectures on the campuses.

Courtney enjoyed the comradery of the three academic leaders and attended meetings of the Three College Presidents' group regularly, although he was not always interested in collaborative ventures. He declined proposed projects such as a weekend work camp program and a fine arts program but enjoyed the Asian studies program, which clearly benefitted the three colleges.[57]

Courtney was asked to serve on Johns Hopkins University's Visiting Committee for the Humanities in 1964. Milton Eisenhower was president of Johns Hopkins then and was acquainted with Courtney because his daughter, Ruth, had spent four years at Swarthmore as a member of the class of 1960.[58] Smith served on an eight-member committee that in 1964–66 met with faculty for discussions, consideration of revisions and expansion of the doctoral program, and the development of a post-doctoral center for humanities. Although Courtney finished his term on the visiting committee in 1966, he returned to Hopkins two years later when, as representative of Oxford University (England), he spoke at the 1968 presidential inauguration ceremony for Lincoln Gordon, a fellow Rhodes Scholar.[59]

In the 1960s Smith went to meetings of the Wistar Association, an elite group of Philadelphia intelligentsia who were also members of the venerable American Philosophical Society. Although not a member of either organization, he was invited to attend association events once or twice a year, probably by R. Stewart Rauch or Crawford Greenewalt.[60]

In 1967 Courtney was elected to a two-and-a-half-year term as a board member of the Philadelphia Contributorship, an insurance company founded by Benjamin Franklin. This small and conservative company offered insurance on houses in the Philadelphia area.[61] According to a 1967 article in the *Wall Street Journal,* the company's directors were "influential pillars of Philadelphia's business and professional circles . . . [the Pennsylvania State Insurance Commissioner told the *Journal* that to sit on the contributorship's board] 'is to have arrived.'"[62] Courtney was not uncomfortable in this group since he already knew several board members and officers, including R. Stewart Rauch of PSFS and Morris Duane, who was in the legal combine Duane, Morris and Heckscher, the firm of Claude C. Smith, chair of Swarthmore College's board of managers.[63]

Philadelphia's social issues intrigued Courtney and he continued to invest time and energy in its organizations. He became a board member of the Greater Philadelphia Movement in 1968. It was founded in 1948 to promote better health and living conditions, and the growth of business, industry, and employment in the greater metropolitan area. When Courtney joined its board it was focusing on pressing problems of drug usage, consumer fraud, youth, the judicial system, race relations, transportation, and employment.[64] During the fall of 1968 the movement produced a movie, filmed at Lincoln University, which was intended to "isolate and confront forms of racial hostilities on the part of both Blacks and Whites."[65] On November 14, 1968, Courtney previewed the documentary *Confrontation in Color,* which a psychiatrist described as a "deeply moving and enormously unsettling experience."[66] One wonders what message the film conveyed to Smith, who at that moment had on his desk the initial demands of the Swarthmore Afro-American Students' Society for administrative action in admissions and support of ethnic identity.

President Smith, indeed, was so active in many organizations that he felt he needed to refuse some of the membership invitations that he received in the 1960s. He declined a request to become a member of the Executive Board of the American Association of Independent College and University Presidents because he felt he was being served well enough by activities of other organizations.[67] He also declined the opportunity to serve on the Board of Directors of the new Theater of the Living Arts in Philadelphia.[68]

In spite of such declinations, Courtney carried heavy commitments to the many professional organizations, committees, task forces, and boards, at the same time that he maintained an organized social life typical of his generation. He was a member of the University and Century Clubs in New York City (where he occasionally stayed when he made business and shopping trips to the city) and the Ozone, Sunday Breakfast, and Harvard clubs of Philadelphia, where he gathered with his peers on many occasions.[69]

Golfing became Smith's major avocation while he was at Swarthmore. Although he had begun golfing while working for the Endicotts in 1938, Smith had rarely had an opportunity to pursue that interest during his Harvard, navy, and Princeton years. But with the 1954 invitation to join the Ozone Club (which had also had earlier invited the membership of Swarthmore presidents Frank Aydelotte and John Nason shortly after they became presidents of the college), he got on the links regularly. The Ozone Club was founded in 1901 by twenty-one men who were members of the Arch Street (Quaker) Meeting in Philadelphia; by Smith's time it was made up of approximately forty men, almost all of whom were Quakers and most of whom were leading supporters of Swarthmore. This elite group of Philadelphia men golfed monthly from spring to the fall at various area golf courses and also held a June weekend golf retreat in the Pocono mountains (which wives attended) and an annual meeting and golf retreat in December at Atlantic City. Smith went to an average of three matches a year with this group and usually got to one or both of the yearly retreat weekends.[70]

He also golfed frequently (in most years on twenty or more days) with his administrative staff members Ed Cratsley, Joe Shane, and Bill Prentice and members of the board of managers, especially Claude Smith, Alfred Williams, and Bill Lee. He also golfed, sometimes with Betty joining him, during his summer vacation at Squam Lake in New Hampshire, on business trips to Washington, D.C., and on winter trips to Ponte Vedra Beach.

In 1954 Tom McCabe proposed Courtney's membership in the Sunday Breakfast Club, and he was elected a member that July. The Sunday Breakfast Club, a group of Philadelphia's business, education, and government leaders, met on Wednesday evenings to hear nationally known figures address current issues in American economic and social life. Courtney usually went to the meetings once or twice a year, and he served on the club's Steering Committee from 1961 to 1963.[71] He had lesser commitments to several other leading Philadelphia institutions, such as the Philadelphia Orchestra Association and the Philadelphia Flower Show,[72] and although he got regular invitations to participate in the Harvard Club of Philadelphia events he usually declined them.[73]

In all, Courtney thrived on his affiliation with local, regional, and national organizations. He contacted many people with ease and took thorough notes on their impressions, concerns, and his feedback to them. He drew on his contacts from the network of organizations for the benefit of Swarthmore College and himself, professionally and politically. The colleagues whom he developed through the Harvard overseers, visiting committees, various fellowship programs, and professional groups greatly expanded the network of colleagues who were associated with his work at Princeton and Swarthmore. This extensive web of contacts gave him powerful access to a vast array of people in positions of authority and influence throughout American education, business, and government and enabled him to have credibility in fund-raising and lobbying efforts.

When Swarthmore sought faculty, Courtney often drew on this network, especially those he knew from the Rhodes program, for information about potential candidates and their reputations. While campus guest lecturers usually were men and women of prestige invited by the faculty and students, they were often people whom Courtney already knew and had suggested. Courtney also was able to identify honors program examiners for the departments through his networks.

At critical times in his presidency Smith brought renowned persons into the discussion and debate. During the NDEA disclaimer affidavit controversy, the Centennial Campaign, the Blue Route battle, and when he formed the Commission of Educational Policy to review Swarthmore he specifically called upon his business and Harvard-Rhodes colleagues.

When government educational policy was changing and new programs were being proposed, Courtney regularly turned to the Swarthmore, Princeton, Harvard, and Rhodes alumni who were in positions to communicate with significant politicians and influence legislation. Pennsylvania senator Clarence Bell (Swarthmore '35) frequently sent information on legislative initiatives to Courtney's office. He often consulted State Representative Edward B. Mifflin (Swarthmore '43) about pending legislation. U.S. Congressmen John Brademas (Harvard '49; Rhodes Scholar '49) and Wiley Mayne (Harvard '38) from Iowa were Washington listening posts for Smith's concerns and ideas.[74] The budget director in the Kennedy and Johnson administrations, Kermit Gordon (Swarthmore '38;

Rhodes '38), provided access to the federal government at the executive level and could give good advice in approaching the Ford Foundation, having been an executive associate and director of the Ford program in economic development and administration.[75] Arthur M. Schlesinger Jr. (Harvard '38), one of the senior White House staff with Kennedy, consulted with Courtney at the White House in September 1961. And of course, U.S. Senators Joseph S. Clark (Harvard '23; overseer 1953–59) and John F. Kennedy (Harvard '40; overseer 1957–63) were critical to the disclaimer affidavit debate.

When turning to foundations for funds for Swarthmore Courtney drew on foundation officers Kermit Gordon and Paul Ylvisaker (former Swarthmore professor) at Ford, James Perkins (former Swarthmore vice president) at Carnegie, and Joseph H. Willits (Swarthmore '11, honorary '37) and Chadbourne Gilpatric (Harvard '38) at Rockefeller, and foundation board members such as John Nason (his presidential predecessor), who was on the boards of both the Danforth and Hazen Foundations. With this kind of network Courtney could approach foundations informally and quickly learn which programs were being funded, the concerns of the foundation personnel and board members, and the likelihood of getting their support for Swarthmore initiatives.

With Swarthmore curriculum and programming comfortably in place after the Aydelotte generative and Nason clarifying eras, Courtney was free to work with the larger educational network. With that freedom, he devoted time and energy to the expression of his ideas about liberal arts and American society as a whole. Courtney welcomed the platforms that his network of contacts offered and readily and enthusiastically prepared addresses which spoke to the issues that drove him personally. He spoke about postwar demographic threats to higher education, economic threats to higher education, the benefits of liberal arts education, the admirable qualities of liberal arts graduates, the qualities of excellence in teaching, public alarm about student activism, ways in which individuals and corporations could support liberal arts colleges, and the role of sports in higher education. As American secretary he annually addressed the new classes of Rhodes Scholars departing for study at Oxford. He was an invited speaker for events at Vassar, Earlham, and Guilford colleges, at convocations at Bucknell University and Wilmington College, and at inaugurations for friends assuming college and university presidencies elsewhere, including Carleton, Colby, Johns Hopkins, Wheaton, and West Virginia. He often spoke at Quaker schools' commencements and addressed the June 1960 Friends General Conference and other Quaker events.

In all of his public speaking engagements Courtney sought to influence the audience. He took each opportunity seriously, conscientiously briefing himself about the interests, activities, and concerns of the audiences so that he could speak their language, gain their confidence, confront their assumptions, engage their logic, and transform their ideas and behaviors.

In sum, Smith's investment of time in these networks served educational, political, and expressive functions. Not only did he learn from them, but through them he shared his ideas and, most important, had the opportunity to rally others to the ideas and causes he felt important. The networks gave Courtney Smith a more influential position in the postwar higher education infrastructure than that which the Swarthmore presidency alone could have possibly done.

# 13

## "Nature shaped to advantage": Preserving Campus Viability

Dᴜʀɪɴɢ ʜɪs ᴘʀᴇsɪᴅᴇɴᴄʏ Cᴏᴜʀᴛɴᴇʏ Sᴍɪᴛʜ ʙᴇᴄᴀᴍᴇ ᴀ ɢʀᴇᴀᴛ ᴘʀᴏᴘᴏɴᴇɴᴛ of campus beauty and serenity. He believed that a carefully planned and landscaped campus was "nature shaped to advantage" and should be a constant reminder to constituencies that "the creativity of nature, and the creativity of man . . . are divine qualities."[1] Throughout his time at Swarthmore he defended the status quo regarding landscape matters, but also advocated changes in the built environment that he felt enhanced the campus. In both efforts he drew upon his intellect and communication skills, and encouraged others to catch his vision.

Courtney believed that he was a trustee for all aspects of the college, an attitude that was challenged two years into his presidency, when he learned that the state and federal highway departments had laid plans to cut a new highway through the campus. Designated the "Blue Route" by highway engineers, its path cut deeply into the western portion of the campus.[2] First news of this plan came to Smith in August 1955 when Joseph Shane, college vice president and a Swarthmore resident, heard about the Blue Route from Swarthmore village officials.[3] The Blue Route, which soon was designated a link in the new federal interstate highway system, would move high-speed automobile and truck traffic north and south through the college's properties along the Crum Creek and particularly along its beloved Crum Meadow.

From the time he had arrived at Swarthmore Smith had enjoyed the natural beauty of the campus, which had been maintained in part as an arboretum since 1929 through substantial funding from the Arthur Hoyt Scott Foundation.[4] The foundation was established largely to teach the public about the wide range of ornamental plants that were appropriate for gardens in the Delaware River valley. But it served as well to enhance the sense that the college was dedicated to providing a special environment for students and faculty—an ideal one for thinking and learning. The campus blend of intellectual pursuits and natural beauty was further highlighted in 1942 when alumnus Thomas B. McCabe built the Arthur Hoyt Scott Outdoor Auditorium in a steeply sided cove above the Crum Creek. From that date forward all commencements and a variety of other college events were held among its columnlike oaks, maples, and tulip trees.[5]

Smith, who had grown up in a relatively small and self-contained Iowa town and then had spend much of his adulthood in picturesque, quiet academic enclaves at Harvard, Oxford, and Princeton, clearly felt that the kind of highway development represented by the Blue Route was an assault upon Swarthmore. He had always been enthralled with the Swarthmore campus's beauty, had pride in the campus as a community treasure, and was alarmed by the thought of losing or limiting Swarthmore's quiet and serenity. Smith felt that the visual beauty and the oasislike quality of the campus were critical aspects of the college's stimulating and creative environment.

Soon after he was informed of the Blue Route problem by Shane, Courtney Smith took his first steps against the highway's location in the Crum valley by drawing attention to the alternative "Yellow Route" on the highway planners' drawing boards. Although Smith did not strongly recommend its adoption, he believed that just promoting consideration of the alternative would give him more time to develop his campaign to keep the highway away from the college.

Mild protests, however, proved incapable of slowing the Blue Route juggernaut, which was just one of the many "ambitious designs of state highway engineers" that were epidemic in midcentury urban and suburban America.[6] By January 1957 Smith realized that he had to initiate an active response to the highway threat; he studied the plan with its financial, aesthetic, physical, and governmental parameters. Developing a rebuttal to the existing arguments, he set about to engage the alumni, the administrative staff, and all possible constituencies in the battle, arguing that Swarthmore College's interests should be considered paramount in the planning of the highway.[7] He insisted that the college (and he as its administrator) had to control its own destiny and interests, and not subjugate itself to other powers.

Smith wrote to the Board of Managers in January and the alumni in February to ask for their support. He initiated a series of meetings with Swarthmore Borough officials, the Delaware County Planning Board, Delaware County commissioners, and governor of Pennsylvania, George Leader, during the remainder of that winter and early spring 1957.[8] He tried to carefully articulate concerns to these entities and attempted to build alliances, specifically using the word "we" as he spoke with them about common concerns and anticipated costs.[9] Having lobbied for three months with these bodies, in July 1957 Smith was able to report to the Swarthmore managers that, instead of the Blue Route, the proposed "Yellow Route had been recommended to the Federal Bureau of Public Roads" by Pennsylvania as the preferred track for the future expressway.[10] But the political process was more complicated than Courtney had expected, in part because the nationwide momentum in favor of building express highways was overwhelming.[11]

When the highway's plans reemerged from the federal bureaucracy more than two years later, the Blue Route proposal had been revitalized and once more posed an imminent threat to the college. In July 1960 an entire Board of Managers meeting had to be devoted to studying the Blue Route's potential impact upon the college and the various forces at work.[12] It had become clear that a "powerful political alignment of home owners [was] successful in getting . . . the Federal Bureau of Public Roads [to conduct] further studies of alternative routes," with the result that the Blue Route alignment, which affected fewer private residences than the alternative routes, had emerged from the process as the most viable choice.[13]

Courtney once again had to lobby the political system. He went to Washington, D.C., to meet directly with Rex Whitton, the federal highway administrator in the Bureau of Public Roads, and Clarence D. Martin Jr., undersecretary of commerce. Dean W. C. H. Prentice contacted Kermit Gordon, Swarthmore alumnus and a member of the federal Council of Economic Advisors, for support.[14] Courtney spent substantial energy on lobbying and commented to those outside of the college that the highway had taken almost full-time efforts during the fall of 1961, and (as he related to one colleague) had even become the stuff of his dreams![15]

On December 6, 1961, wishing to gather more political momentum for its cause, the college took the highly unusual step of buying full-page advertisements in the *Philadelphia Inquirer* and the *Philadelphia Bulletin*. Hoping to engage the newspapers' high volume of readership, Swarthmore asked the readers to express sympathy with the college's position and to write David Lawrence, then governor of Pennsylvania, and Rex Whitton at the Bureau of Public Roads to make known their opposition to the Blue Route.[16]

The advertisement outlined Swarthmore's and its president's concerns that the Blue Route would "sacrifice too many other community assets" in addition to those directly related to the college. It argued that the such a route would call for institutional retrenchment, would be shortsighted in terms of other political and cultural concerns for parkland, would not serve the future quality of life, and would place external limitations upon an institution that not only had a long pattern of service, but which would continue to serve the public for many years.

Central to the college's appeal to the public was advertisement's assertion that the Blue Route would take twenty acres of college land that the college had designated for future needs. The college argued that it already was hemmed in on three sides and needed a land reserve to respond to "new fields of learning none of us can even predict." Moreover, in the immediate future the Blue Route would mar the beauty and tranquility of the environment of the college campus with the roar of high-speed traffic on concrete. The natural environment would be irrevocably altered because the highway's design for speed made it impossible to have it "meander through a winding valley or serve as a parkway." It would necessitate "shearing off of hills, the filling in of valleys, and the frequent crossing and re-crossing of the creek," and therefore negatively affect the green space which was so desirable and sought-after not only by the college, but also by the entire community.

The college also attacked the illogic of the Blue Route's impingement on Delaware County's Smedley Park at the same time as other public entities were strongly advocating acquisition of parkland and green spaces. The college reminded the public that "the Delaware County District of the Health and Welfare Council, Inc., has just reported that a doubling of the open space of park and recreation facilities is urgently needed in the next four years if this county is to retain its attractiveness and protect the value of its realty"; "the Governor of Pennsylvania is preparing to ask the 1962 legislature to approve a $70,000,000 bond issue for the purchase of park and recreation lands near Pennsylvania cities in accordance with an open-space program recommended by the State Planning Board"; and that President Kennedy had just told Congress that "land is the most precious resource of the metropolitan area" and open space had to be reserved "to control the rate and character of community development." In sum, the college, describing itself as a tax-exempt entity chartered for the public welfare, argued that for the highway to swallow up a portion of Swarthmore College grounds that the college "opens . . . like a public park" and which it had conserved for the future needs of the society made poor public policy.[17]

Although this extraordinary advertisement brought a flood of supporting letters from alumni and friends, Smith could not afford any pause in his campaign to thwart the Blue Route. Early in 1962 there were public hearings in Delaware County regarding expressway planning. Courtney admiringly reported that Swarthmore College's "participants were in place at the hearing long before it began at 7:30 p.m., and were still there when it ended at 6:47 in the morning, their wives ladling out sandwiches and thermos coffee. Jerry Feldman, Bob Gold and Dave Heider of *The Phoenix* stayed through the night helping in countless ways, after which Jerry went off to his all-day honors laboratory." Smith was very emotional about the hearing, calling it "a cynical performance on the part of the Highway Department," but a moving tableau as he listened during the night to elderly residents "testify to the value of the Crum Creek valley for various trail and nature groups."[18] However, this testimony seemed to make no impact on the bureaucracy: the Blue Route plan remained unchanged and it was sent to the federal officials as the state's recommendation.[19]

Still, the college's appeal to the public seemed to have an effect on the political scene. In his next annual report to the college community President Smith reported that both gubernatorial candidates in Pennsylvania's 1962 election campaign had taken "strong positions against the Blue Route." After the election he met with governor-elect William Scranton to remind him of his pledge and to reiterate Swarthmore's position.[20] Although there was further discussion about modifications to the Blue Route, none were implemented: by mid-1963 Smith recognized that Governor Scranton had not made good on his campaign promise and that the campus was still seriously threatened.

In the fall of 1963 Courtney met with Henry D. Harral, Pennsylvania secretary of highways, and he spoke with Clarence Martin in the federal Department of Commerce.[21] In spring 1964 Courtney spoke with U.S. Senator Joseph Clark, and at the centennial commencement where President Lyndon B. Johnson was present as the featured speaker, Courtney took the opportunity to publicly state his frustrations about the proposed interstate highway.[22] Some faculty were shocked that Smith thought it appropriate to raise a political matter at a celebration, but they knew that his remarks were motivated by the depth of his feelings on the issue.[23]

In May 1965 President Smith testified again at further state highway hearings. He argued that the college's most recent new buildings had been constructed on the front area of the campus that would soon be built up to the "maximum extent desirable"; and he presented the official position of the Association of American Colleges, supported by the Pennsylvania Association of Colleges and Universities, that newly designed express highways too often jeopardized higher education properties.[24] Swarthmore was not the only institution battling the encroachments of new highways intended to provide new outlets for urban areas strangling on heavy traffic, and in fact had been one of the early voices in what one historian has characterized as the "freeway revolts."[25]

After the 1965 hearings and further deliberation, state engineers finally modified the path of the Blue Route in the vicinity of the college. The expressway was moved to the far west side of the Crum Creek valley in order to minimize the noise and visual impact upon the main portion of the college grounds, a design change that saved two-thirds of the acreage that the college expected to lose.[26] It was a partial victory for Smith, but he was never able to see the material result of his nine-year battle: as happened with many interstate highway projects of the Vietnam era, construction through the Crum Valley was delayed for many years.[27]

Many in the college community, even in Smith's time, questioned whether a college president should have put so much time and energy into the Blue Route problem, which seemed distant from core educational matters such as curriculum and faculty development.[28] But for Smith the Blue Route was a concrete example of the kind of ill-considered change that threatened what he valued about Swarthmore, and one that could set dangerous precedents for the future.

Smith certainly believed that the natural and built environments made significant contributions to intellectual and social development at a college. He argued, as we already have seen, that liberal arts education had a critical function in American society and required a special type of environment. Smith knew that Swarthmore's existing campus was integral to his vision, and in addition he anticipated the needs that had to be addressed if it was to serve optimally in the future. The anticipated college-bound "baby-boom" population bulge, the age of the facilities on campus, and the pace with which information and technology were changing indicated that Swarthmore's physical resources needed to be expanded. Nason, the previous president of the college, had outlined the priorities for facilities development, and Smith, who had experience with three other outstanding campuses, quickly recognized that the college lacked appropriate buildings for the future. As early as 1954 he listed the college's outstanding needs as a library, a dining hall, a science building, additional dormitory space, an animal research laboratory, and renovation of several of the more archaic facilities.[29]

At least by 1955, when he began to consider requests for renovations of existing facilities, and throughout the Blue Route period, Courtney put the preservation of the character of the campus and the construction of new facilities high on his administrative agenda.[30] In April 1958 he broke ground for Willets Hall, a dormitory designed to house 180 women, and in July 1958 he broke ground for the science building, funded in part by a 1957 grant from the Longwood Foundation. In order to insure that these first construction projects of his presidency (and the first on campus in a generation) were done efficiently, Courtney recommended that the same contractor build both the science building and the Willets dorm.[31]

As Smith undertook campus construction he usually created a faculty committee to assist in developing plans. For the science building Smith appointed representatives of the chemistry, physics, and mathematics departments to work closely with Vincent Kling, a prominent Philadelphia architect. The committee specified many of the interior components of the buildings, and Kling responded with a pleasing exterior design that complemented other campus features. One of the committee members described the science building: "Four distinct but interconnected units . . . arranged around a central landscaped courtyard . . . providing each department with well-defined quarters while at the same time making for easy intercommunication."[32]

Smith found this committee process a successful means of developing college facilities and continued to follow much the same pattern as he upgraded the remainder of the campus. He continued to use Vincent Kling's architectural firm, which was generating a new style of buildings that the president thought harmonized with the existing fabric of the campus, and he tried to develop relationships with construction firms that he thought met the college's needs.

Smith himself rarely became directly involved in the details of the designs and equipment of the facilities but rather focused on the overall placement of each facility, its usefulness in serving the ideals that he desired for the college, and the aspects of contracts with architects and builders which made those things possible. He most often got involved in the process when he needed to arbitrate disputes between the faculty committees and the architectural and building firms. On those occasions he argued that committee concerns needed to be respected and to receive a positive response. But he also admired Kling's architectural designs and, in spite of faculty criticisms of Kling, retained his commitment to him, trusting that he brought unusual creativity and aesthetic skill to bear on the college's needs. What conflict there was between Smith and Kling inevitably centered on Kling's projections of the costs of the buildings.

In 1962 the Animal Laboratory addition to Martin biological and psychological laboratories was begun.[33] In 1965 Sharples Dining Hall opened and construction of Worth Health Center was started. In 1966 ground was broken for the Dana and Hallowell men's dormitories, and the next year the new and much-needed McCabe Library, with its Friends Historical Library wing, was opened. Finally, in 1967–68 the old library was converted into the new Tarble Social Center for student activities.

Sharples Dining Hall was undoubtedly the most important new building on campus in Smith's eyes. It was designed to bring students together in a setting that would both reinforce traditional social skills and, according to Smith, "stimulate intellectual converse."[34] It had a unifying concept that expressed concretely the belief that "many approaches to education are possible, and need to be protected." "Six deliberately different dining rooms all grouped around a central lounge under steeply pitched roofs" allowed for different eating environments while bringing all students into a single arena.[35] For Courtney, the result was "one of the most impressive college dining halls you will ever see . . . [an] architectural prize already."[36]

In fact, each building design had social purpose and aesthetics in mind, as well as specific functions. Worth was planned to provide students with quiet, self-contained, and supervised on-campus medical care. Tarble was designed to encourage student and faculty interaction. Dana and Hallowell dormitories were designed to cluster rooms for social fellowship and at the same time allow for quiet hallways.

The design and development of the McCabe Library was a true challenge as the college community considered its needs to house books and create a fiscally efficient building that encouraged maximum use. Kling initially designed a building that was approachable from all sides, but it was rejected by the library building committee as a potential management problem. As a result, all functions of the library and its services had to be carefully reassessed. The stack design, carrel, and study space and accessibility to librarian services were critically discussed by library staff and faculty. The effects of carpeting, lighting, furnishings, and organization of the collections were taken into account, and opportunities for future growth and the accommodation of technological devices were considered. Some designs were rejected as ineffective, inefficient, too costly, too complex, or simply vulgar. The committee clearly took its task very seriously. When the new library opened in the fall of 1967 it was acclaimed as an outstanding complement to the academic institution.

By the fall of 1967, the campus's built environment was substantially different and much more developed to meet the college's enrollment and academic needs. It invited both students and faculty to the college with its attractive and comfortable buildings and open and enclosed spaces for recreational activities. The charming nineteeth- and early twentieth-century campus structures were complemented by facilities ready to address the new generation's needs. Smith had modernized the college campus and had preserved its sylvan serenity in pursuit of what he called "an ideal of gracious living."[37] Over two decades later, Thomas A. Gaines in *The Campus as a Work of Art* wrote that in the Smith era "Swarthmore placed its structures carefully to create a number of pleasing spaces . . . [and] avoided the usual campus downfall by building good modern work."[38] Clearly, Smith's strategy had worked for his time and well into the future.

# 14

## Student Activism: "To care about social justice"

DURING HIS PRESIDENCY COURTNEY SMITH ENCOUNTERED STUDENT AC-
tivism at Swarthmore that ranged from expressions of admirably deep
concern about social and political issues to the timeless tensions between
students and administrations on college campuses. Smith's personal view
regarding activism was effectively encapsulated in an essay, "The Academic Community and Social Concerns," that he published in the December 1965 alumni issue of the *Swarthmore College Bulletin.*[1]

Smith began by defining what was the proper role of institutions of
higher education in social change. Arguing that a college's primary function in society is to train the intellect, he proposed that it could do so most
effectively by providing students and faculty "an environment for rea-
soned and honest exploration." (4) For Smith that exploration always led to
an examination of the concerns of society at large. The central passage of
his essay describes his view of the process: "a college's job, drawing on the
contributions of men of intellect and integrity and conscience and good
will, is to determine what *is* social justice, and to help students develop the
capacity to determine in subsequent years what is social justice, and to try
to sensitize students to *care* about social justice, and to produce leaders
who will seek to secure social justice, and to provide within its own walls
an instance of social justice, but not at any moment to be itself a *direct
instrument* for social justice. A college, in short, is the *matrix* of social
justice." (5) Smith went on to determine the coordinates for what he called
"the activist spirit" on campus. He argued that the college as a corporate
body must act on social and political matters in its own interests and
suggested that the students had a role in voicing those interests. He also
emphasized his expectation that members of the college community would
speak out as individual citizens yet would take care in public to distinguish
their views from those of the college.

Finally, Smith considered concrete manifestations of activism itself and
stated that "effective social action must be based on reason, and reason
must be calm and clear-eyed." (7) He called for students to do "what the

public has a right to expect of Swarthmore graduates" (6)—to devote time
to the study of each issue and to the consideration of the consequences of
action. In regard to the latter, Smith urged that action occur in the context
"not only of the compassion that leads us to champion the interests of the
disadvantaged, but the much more difficult compassion for those who are
or seem to be the obstacles in the way of progress." (7) He concluded that
in the combining of intellect and social action Swarthmore could make "a
special contribution to social justice in our time." (8)

Smith certainly had reason to express himself regarding campus activism. During his presidency students took actions or publicly expressed
opinions about the full range of social and political issues in the United
States, including racism, freedom of speech, curricular reform, campus life
and student rights, self-expression and nonconformity, and the role of the
United States in world affairs. Smith's personal views shaped and guided
his responses to each of these areas of student activity.

When Smith assumed Swarthmore's presidency he found that the college already had a strong current of controversy regarding racial and ethnic
discrimination. Students had led in the college's decade-old decision to
end discrimination in admissions, and the college regularly admitted Jews
and a few blacks by Smith's time.[2] Then in 1951 students had begun an
extensive debate about the exclusionary membership policies of the male
fraternities on campus. Despite the objections of their national organizations, by the time Smith took office Swarthmore's fraternities had begun
offering membership to Jews and blacks.[3] Smith voiced his support for
their actions, and supported the fraternities' efforts to reform their na-
tionals and the decisions of three Swarthmore fraternities to become un-
affiliated organizations when that proved impossible.[4]

Another student-related issue of the 1950s was the challenge to intellectual freedom on campuses across the nation. In his inaugural address in
October 1953 President Smith spoke out on behalf of "a tradition of
dissent" at colleges and universities, and later he joined with the students
and faculty to send a petition to Pennsylvania senators Duff and Martin
calling for the censure of Senator Joseph McCarthy, who had become
infamous for his defamatory attacks on academics for their political viewpoints.[5] Later in the 1950s Smith took national leadership in the fight
against the imposition of a disclaimer affidavit on the recipients of National Defense Education Act scholarships and fellowships. He worked
with the students, faculty, and board of managers; recruited other leaders
in higher education to the cause; and eventually testified in Congress in the
ultimately successful campaign to eliminate the oath.[6]

National issues regarding protection of the freedom of speech had local parallels. Quoted in the *New York Times* as saying that American colleges should "resist intellectual bullying and . . . fight the present-day trends that seek to control the spirit of free inquiry on the campuses," Smith forthrightly defended student groups that in the 1950s and 1960s invited such controversial speakers to Swarthmore as William F. Buckley Jr., Gus Hall, Alger Hiss, and Paul Robeson.[7] In 1963 Smith published his views on outside speakers for all alumni to read, declaring that "I am convinced that our policy of permitting students, on their own initiative and on their own assumption of responsibility, to invite any speaker in whom they have a genuine and intelligent interest is right and prudent."[8]

Courtney Smith's view of the students' responsibility for their own dress and behavior was far more critical, however. When he arrived in 1953 Courtney found that he agreed with some members of the board of managers who disliked the decidedly informal dress and appearance of many students. Smith enunciated his long-held perspective in the 1950s in several addresses to the students on what he called "manners and morals." He argued that the college community lived "essentially by mutual trust," and that a necessary component of that trust was the students' agreement to adhere to the standards of behavior and appearance that traditionally governed the college and polite society.[9]

For Smith, a meticulous dresser who shopped at Brooks Brothers and other fine men's shops in New York City for his apparel, and who had dressed well at Harvard despite his limited resources, not the least of the standards to be expected of students was neat clothing. He called on the men, in particular, to take on the "burden of a coat and tie."[10] But the students were unresponsive, and a few years later Smith remarked that he had come to understand that their slovenly appearance had fallen into "a patterned expression of conformity" to a bohemian code.[11]

It is clear that from the beginning of his presidency Smith believed that he needed to be engaged as a constructive critic of students and student activism. As the college moved into the 1960s Smith's commentary on activism continued to center on issues of racial discrimination, government policies, and on-campus expression and behavior, but Smith remarked early in the decade that a new and, for him, disturbing style of confrontation was emerging.[12]

Beginning early in 1962 and throughout the 1962–63 academic year Swarthmoreans joined the Civil Rights movement by regularly participating in sit-ins and marches in Cambridge, Maryland.[13] Led by the Student Nonviolent Coordinating Committee (SNCC), the marches and boycotts in Cambridge were an important training ground for a generation of activists, both black and white.[14] In his annual review of that year Smith commented approvingly on the students' "continuing . . . concern for civil rights, with the concern highlighted in a weekly caravan to Cambridge, Maryland."[15] But the next year brought escalation and different comments.

In November 1963 Swarthmore students from the Swarthmore Political Action Committee (SPAC) were heavily involved in picketing the Chester (Pa.) schools, joining a movement that pressed the local school board to give its predominately black schools, which were overcrowded and deteriorating, the same financial support as those that were predominately white. One of the demonstrations featured civil disobedience—blocking an entrance to a school—and resulted in the arrest of a number of Swarthmore students. The Chester school board ultimately gave in to some of the demands, but in the meantime student demonstrators from Swarthmore were among those blamed for vandalism during the protests. Smith supported the students' right to demonstrate and picket, but also supported a statement from Swarthmore's deans that emphasized (in a reference to civil disobedience) that there are "important differences between socially responsible procedures and those which are violent, or which tend to lead to violence."[16] Students responsible for breaking the law, the deans' statement said, might be subjected to discipline on campus in addition to any action by legal authorities. Students and faculty both vigorously debated this announced policy, but in the end no students were disciplined and neither the college nor the students' deepening involvement in Chester was changed.[17]

By the fall of 1964 student activity in Chester had both moderated and expanded, and at the first Collection that year Smith could say optimistically that he hoped "our [sic] constructive efforts [in Chester] can continue: the tutorial project, the voter registration efforts, the research work on the actual nature of community problems, [and] the Swarthmore-Wade House summer project, which I think was one of the high moments for this college and can serve as a model for many communities throughout the country."[18] In emphasizing the latter project he spoke from personal knowledge, because his daughter, Lee, had been one of the Swarthmore volunteers working in the Swarthmore-Wade Neighborhood House Outward Bound program intended to enhance academic skills of Chester youth.[19] The developments in Chester, which during the picketing appeared to have contained the ingredients of a crisis, turned out, with this new moderation, to be a prime example of how student activism fit Smith's view of a college's role in social concerns.

Early in March 1965 SPAC, now very conscious of racial issues, wrote to Smith asking him to support its request that the college's board of managers sell the college's stock in Chase Manhattan Bank. SPAC had identified divestment as a means of protesting South Africa's apartheid laws, and Chase Manhattan became a focus of SPAC's concern because it had made loans to the South African government. The student council seconded SPAC's request, and Smith took the student initiative seriously, seeking advice from faculty members who had expertise on the history and current situation in South Africa.[20]

Smith also took advantage of his acquaintance with David Rockefeller, Chase Manhattan board chairman, to ask him about the bank's rationale for its loans. Rockefeller justified the bank's investment as promoting economic development that would lead to positive social change.[21] At the April 6, 1965 meeting of the managers Smith explained the students' concerns but told the managers that from the information he had gathered he was sure that "the symbolic act of selling one corporation's stock would in the present instance be misleading and unjust. The corporation which has been singled out has a known reputation for positive influence. It is not clear that withholding of loans to South Africa, on the part of this corporation or others, would combat the ills of apartheid."[22] Smith was persuasive, and after a long discussion that one member characterized as "soul-searching debate" the board took no action on divestiture.[23] The student concerns were shown to have some validity when, a decade later, the Sullivan principles, named for Philadelphia's black activist Leon Sullivan, effectively set anti-apartheid standards for American investment in South Africa.[24]

While Smith at times set limits on student activism, the student newspaper the *Phoenix* was almost impossible for him to regulate. Smith—the advocate of free debate and inquiry—cooperated with the newspaper fully, giving interviews when requested and occasionally contributing an essay to it. Still, he was regularly irritated by its outspoken style and administration bashing. In September 1962 he complained that the *Phoenix* had predictable, politically liberal responses to virtually all issues, on or off campus. He asked pointedly "Has *The Phoenix* become a one-party press?" He also called on the *Phoenix* editors to better check their facts before making "broad jumps" to assertions, and bluntly stated that if they did not they were in fact "engaging in a form of violence." Smith was particularly exercised in 1962 when the *Phoenix* criticized him for spending most of his time in "maintaining the image" of the college (which, in reply, Smith said took "no identifiable time") and in fund-raising (which Smith said took 5 percent of his time).[25] In Smith's view the *Phoenix*'s style changed little in response to his criticisms, and five years later he told the alumni that "*The Phoenix* has never seemed to me to be worthy of this student body."[26]

His critique of the *Phoenix* was a particular example of Smith's concern about what he felt was "the spread of 'doctrinaire' liberalism" on campus. He told the students that he worried that Swarthmore's dominant liberalism could become a "kind of reflex action" that accepted ideas blindly without reflection. "The point is not that Swarthmore is moving to the left or to the right," remarked Smith in an interview, "What I am arguing for is less restricted agendas, more open minds, more dialogue."[27]

Smith's concern about single-viewpoint discussions may be why he never contributed to the overwhelmingly anti-Vietnam War discussion on campus, although he did try to shape national policy regarding the effect of the Vietnam-era draft on higher education and the career paths of students. In 1966 Smith wrote to his friend and Harvard Overseers colleague, Senator Joseph Clark of Pennsylvania, to offer his opinion that "the country will be making a serious mistake if no change is made in existing draft legislation as it affects next year's graduate students." Having worked to attract bright young men and women into academic careers through the Woodrow Wilson and Rhodes programs and as an annual recruiter of new faculty for the campus, Smith was deeply concerned about the "abrupt and severe withdrawal of intellectual talent" that he envisioned.[28] Later in 1966, when the faculty requested that the college's relationship with the Selective Service System be thoroughly reviewed, Smith appointed a committee with representatives from the managers, faculty, administration, and student body. In 1967 that committee recommended supporting the end of student deferments and the college's continued cooperation with the draft system.[29]

Smith did not agree with the egalitarianism implicit in the committee's recommendation, and in 1968 he again expressed his dismay about the effect of the draft on graduate education, telling Congresswoman Edith Green that it was "creating serious shortages in our supply of qualified teachers for higher education."[30] Later, in remarks before the Rhodes scholar class of 1968, which included the future United States president William J. Clinton, Courtney referred to the stress for both students and administrators who had to deal with the difficulty of giving advice on programs of advanced studies while the uncertainties of the military draft were looming over new graduates. His remarks suggested that the recent flux in Selective Service System regulations had left him and other Rhodes administrators frustrated by their inability to negotiate for the new class the unqualified two-year deferments that earlier Rhodes classes had held.[31] But Smith's comments about the draft were among the few he made related to the Vietnam War; as a Quaker president at a Quaker college he may have been content to let his position be assumed.

Overall Courtney Smith had considerable success negotiating between the well-articulated enthusiasms and demands of the students, the doubts and concerns of the faculty and administration, and the general conservatism of the board of managers. His apparent skill in this area over the fifteen years of his presidency had led another college administrator, at the height of student activism in the fall of 1968, to ask for Smith's advice on dealing with anticipated campus disruptions because, "in a recent discussion with . . . a former student at Swarthmore [I heard] of the successes which Swarthmore has had in handling this problem."[32] One assumes that Smith read this letter with a considerable sense of irony, not only because student activism had been a constant concern of his throughout the years, but because at the time he received the letter, one of his most difficult problems in student-administration relationships was brewing. The students were critiquing and directly challenging what they believed were unjust aspects of the Swarthmore admissions process.

(Left to right) Claude Smith (Class of 1914), chairman of the Board of Managers; Thomas McCabe (Class of 1915), chairman of the Presidential Selection Committee; Courtney C. Smith, president-elect; Bill Lee (Class of 1933), president of the Alumni Association, when Smith was appointed Swarthmore's new president, April 7, 1953. Courtesy of Swarthmore College.

Courtney Smith, at Swarthmore College, responding to the announcement of his appointment as president, April 7, 1953. Elizabeth (Betty) Smith looks on from the lower left. Courtesy of Swarthmore College.

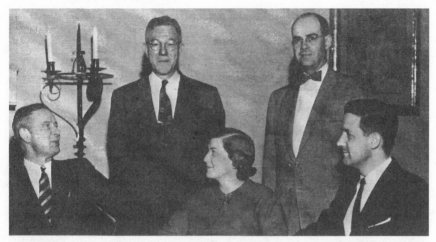

A moment of transition, ca. April 1953. (Left to right) Outgoing President John Nason; Vice-President Joseph Shane; Dean Susan Cobbs; Vice President Edward Cratsley, and President-elect Courtney C. Smith. Courtesy of Swarthmore College.

Claude C. Smith, chairman of the Board of Managers, and Courtney C. Smith, president of Swarthmore College (both on the left), greeting college constituents in Parrish Hall parlor, October 17, 1953, while Smith's daughter Lee glances toward him. Courtesy of Friends Historical Library.

**Smith with alumni in Los Angeles, California, 1956. Courtesy of Friends Historical Library.**

**Smith with Isaac Clothier, and football players Samuel Criswell and Ronald Sutton, ca. 1956. Courtesy of Friends Historical Library.**

Smith conferring with his administrative staff, ca. 1962. Maps of the Swarthmore college campus (rear) and the Blue Route (left) are on the walls. Staff portrayed include (left to right) Gilmore Scott, John Moore (facing away), Joseph Shane, Smith, Edward Cratsley, Susan Cobbs, and William Prentice. Courtesy of Friends Historical Library.

Smith at the Swarthmore railroad station, en route to a meeting, ca. 1964. Courtesy of Elizabeth Smith Ingram.

(Left to right) Smith, Joseph Shane, Susan Cobbs, and John and Gertrude Wistar, with Parrish Hall in the background, early 1964. Courtesy of Friends Historical Library.

Opening the June 1964 Centennial Commencement exercises at Swarthmore College. Smith at center, holding the commencement program and his address, with invited speaker, President of the United States Lyndon B. Johnson, to the left. Courtesy of Friends Historical Library.

Smith working alone, the telephone within reach, ca. 1964. Courtesy of Elizabeth Smith Ingram.

Smith as typically engaged in conversation, one-to-one, ca. 1964. Courtesy of Elizabeth Smith Ingram.

Courtney C. Smith, Swarthmore College president, sometime in the 1960s. Courtesy of Friends Historical Library.

# 15

## Two Decades of Student Life at Swarthmore

As PRESIDENT OF THE COLLEGE SMITH'S DIRECT CONTACT WITH STU-dents was limited. In attempting to manage all the tasks of his presidency, Smith's encounters with students tended to be brief and formal. While other members of the administrative staff occasionally taught classes and were extracurricular advisors, Courtney never taught a class, never acted as an advisor to a student group, and spent limited time in student arenas. He did chat with students while walking from his home to his office in Parrish, regularly attended both men's and women's varsity sports events and Collections, and often went to plays, concerts, and lectures on campus. However, none of those occasions provided time for substantial student interaction or dialogue.

Instead, Courtney relied heavily upon his administrative staff to meet students and to transmit to him their concerns and needs. He regularly inquired about specific students and expected his deans to be able to highlight issues and to advise him about administrative actions in regard to students. Certainly Courtney seems to have consulted one or more of Deans Susan Cobbs, Everett Hunt, W. C. H. Prentice, Robert Barr, Barbara Lange, or his assistant Gilmore Stott on each occasion when a decision was to be made about student life. President Smith did not delegate policy decisions to the deans, but it is clear that he did not make any such decisions without a thorough briefing of the issues and survey of their opinions.

Early each academic year Smith attempted to communicate with stu-dents on issues of mutual importance when he addressed the annual First Collection, a convocation for all Swarthmore students, faculty, and staff, and when he gave formal welcomes to gatherings of the freshmen students and the honors students. At the end of each academic year he reviewed the issues and developments of the year in his commencement address. In turn he tapped into student opinion by reading the *Phoenix* regularly, even though he never expected the *Phoenix* to speak for the larger student body and was quite aware that he had to rely largely upon staff to bring the full range of student opinion to him.

In his early years, Courtney Smith often boasted about the Swarthmore students and their distinctive qualities. He assured incoming freshmen: "we know your capacities; know your test scores; where you stood in your class; [that] some of you have difficulty concentrating; [the] inequality of your preparation; [and] the various kinds of worry and unhappiness (as well as happiness) you bring with you, and we know there is no one here who can't do well here . . . as old hands in this business we're persuaded you're right for Swarthmore and that you will grow here."[1] He bragged to the students, "Swarthmore measures up to the Socratic ideal of offering a continuing conversation of the highest level among faculty and students."[2] Indeed, Courtney did believe that each student would grow in intellect and maturity at Swarthmore and that each student was capable of making wise decisions when presented with all the relevant facts. He also believed that the college had more concern for the total development of the student than many of the institutions whose academic standards rivaled Swarthmore's.[3] He was convinced that with Swarthmore College's concern and students' capacities, Swarthmore students had the potential to be extraordinary persons with valuable leadership skills. Still, Smith knew from an early point in his administration that although he admired the students as individuals, collectively they could act in ways that troubled him. Student governance, he remarked after only two years at Swarthmore, was always "one of the thorniest operating problems" at the college.[4]

One of the early governance issues involved the student-organized folk-music festival. In 1953 when the Smiths arrived at the college there was already an eight-year tradition of holding a spring weekend music festival where college constituents and guests were able to listen and dance to folk music and to engage in discussion with a wide variety of folk artists.[5] With luminaries such as Pete Seeger mixed with lesser but up-and-coming performers, this event was popular and grew throughout the years. It became a nationally recognized forum for folk music, and often included left-wing musicians who were shunned in the McCarthy era (such as Seeger) and politically oriented lyrics that were banned in other venues.[6]

As the special nature of the Swarthmore folk festival became apparent to folk-music devotees, it increasingly drew non-Swarthmorean attendees who spilled into the Swarthmore village. Criticisms from the village and college staff that outsiders were using the campus, and occasionally the village, as a public park and campground led Smith and the administration to cancel the 1956 festival and to evaluate the format for succeeding years. Courtney did not want to have the college sponsor an activity that it could not contain and control, and the organizers even felt that Courtney objected to "the style [of those coming to the festival] as disreputable, distasteful, and menacing. . . . He did not think that men should wear jeans, to say nothing of women wearing them!"[7]

After much discussion by those who wanted the festival to continue, students and their faculty advisors extensively revised festival operating procedures, and in 1957 and later festivals there was access only by pre-sold tickets, which de facto required that a purchaser have a direct Swarthmore connection. In accord with Courtney's desire to eliminate the sources of past criticisms, the reorganized festival was limited in size, contained on campus, and as a result dramatically altered in style.[8]

Smith participated in a general review of student governance in April of 1962 when the *Phoenix* sponsored a colloquium called a "Forum on Rules." The forum was intended to provide open discussion about the concept of student self-rule in the regulation of conduct. Both faculty and students were invited to attend the three evening sessions of the colloquium. Two sessions were devoted to student commentary about the responsibilities of the college and college rules, and the final session was devoted to President Smith's commentary. Although Smith did not attend the first two sessions he did listen to recordings of the sessions in order to · prepare his comments.

When he addressed the forum he was quite clear about his position and his philosophy: he spoke about his role as president of the college and the frameworks in which rules are made and supported. He summarized the college's formal legal obligations, quoted the college charter, and noted his own "formidable" responsibility (and accountability) for student selection, behavior, and safety. He spoke of his responsibilities, as president, for all administrative decisions and his own personal quality of being a "seeker" in the Quaker tradition. About rule making he cautioned that "it is only if we are all seekers . . . that we can work productively on a problem that is not Swarthmore's alone, but the problem of all colleges in 1962." Smith pointed out that his delegation of authority to the Student Affairs Committee (composed of administration, faculty, and student representatives) was intended to facilitate orderly consideration of student rules and behavior.

As he addressed the forum Smith, who was clearly concerned about student perceptions, went on to note that in the nine years of his presidency co-ed visiting hours in fraternity houses were liberalized, open houses permitting men and women to visit each others' dormitories had been restored and then liberalized, student possession of automobiles on campus had been permitted and then liberalized, and the liquor usage of students had been reviewed and was "under a much lengthier review" again. He decried the students' often negative responses to such changes, which were based upon joint student-faculty-administration efforts, and their unfortunate tendency to see rules as the "administration's rules," and to give them less honor and respect than what he felt should be accorded to those created by the community-based process. (He also pointed out that he was "troubled by the 40% [of the student population who report] violating the present liquor regulation.")

Smith argued that "rules have the function of helping us to maintain an orderly society, . . . sometimes represent the distillation of the experience of more experienced and more mature people, . . . and . . . at some point those of us who are held accountable for the community must apply the values we in conscience believe right." He stated that "absolute freedom" cannot be offered in a group, the "balancing" of interests is essential, and the "continuation" of an institution (or group) requires concern for all the diverse parts. He concluded by reiterating his confidence in the Student Affairs Committee as an effective rule-making body with planned diversity of view.[9]

In delivering these remarks Smith was in a sense teaching a history lesson, because many of the students he addressed had little reason to know how the current set of rules had come to be. As the college's beloved history professor Lawrence Lafore commented a few months later, "a student body has no collective memory."[10]

The Student Affairs Committee (SAC), the joint student-faculty-staff body that Smith supported, had worked on a number of very difficult student rules and issues over the years. It had dealt with many concerns about drinking on and particularly off campus. It had considered discrepancies in rule enforcement and expectations for off-campus students. It had responded to questions about increasing automobile usage on campus, the college's "sex rule," pets in dorms, dorm autonomy issues, on-campus corporate and military recruitment, and Collection attendance requirements. SAC had repeatedly deliberated on and reviewed requests to reinstate open houses, which had been terminated in the Nason administration after "a scandalous episode."[11] Meeting after meeting considered the open house question in all its details and implications.

As early as March 1957 President Smith stated that he had no fundamental objection to open houses, but that he believed that open houses were a privilege to be earned and sustained. Characteristically, given his belief in decorum and civility, he argued that the existing accommodations were "woefully inadequate for proper entertaining" and that it was not in good taste to have open houses under those circumstances.[12] But in 1957, despite his concern, SAC approved Sunday afternoon open houses in men's dormitories on terms that included keeping dormitory room doors opened if women were visiting. In 1960, additional Saturday afternoon open houses in the men's dorms were requested and, with the support of the student body, SAC conditionally approved them. In 1966, after two years of trials with evening open houses and much pressure for more visiting in dorms, SAC proposed 7:30 p.m.–12:30 a.m. Saturday open houses with the specific conditions that each dormitory floor or dorm section had to vote its approval, regular proctoring had to be instituted, and rooms with visitors still had to have open doors.[13]

Smith and the administrative staff, believing that a dorm was a "haven, [or] escape," were always cautious and concerned about the rights of those affected by open houses. They specified that noise, disorder, and intimate behavior were to be controlled, and that in order for open houses to continue, they could not infringe upon others' comfort.[14] This relatively conservative and genteel view of the parameters of student life gave authenticity to the remark reputedly made by Smith in the early 1960s that "Swarthmore should be a generation ahead academically, and a generation behind socially."[15]

While regulating specific aspects of student life was of concern to him, Courtney was proud of the range of activities on the campus that provided what he felt were positive outlets for students' energies. In 1959 he proudly shared a list with visiting parents that demonstrated the breadth of student interests: six regular publications, eleven department-organized clubs, nine religious organizations, five regular music groups, four cultural and political groups, seven arts groups, twenty-five sports groups, and thirty student governance committees.[16]

Student Council, one of the groups he listed, managed the budget allocations for student activities and organized the social calendar for the student body, and because it had primarily a coordinating function was normally of far less concern to Smith than major campus events that set precedents (such as the folk festival) or the policy issues of campus rules. He left the supervision of Student Council to its advisors, except when such matters as controversial guest speakers required his support or intervention. On those occasions Smith met with individual council representatives and the council itself to assist in the clarification of issues.

Smith was often personally outraged, disappointed, and even cynical about the student newspaper, *The Phoenix*. Because the newspaper had a wide readership, Smith was particularly concerned about how the editors allowed issues to polarize the campus and how the editors represented him and student life to those off campus who subscribed. He occasionally confronted the editors directly to express his dismay, and sometimes he made his exasperation clear to others, but he always maintained his fundamental support of the students' right to expression. Most of the time Smith had a rather laissez-faire attitude toward the operations of the student newspaper, similar to his relationship to the student council, because in many ways the students contributing to *The Phoenix* were doing what Smith expected of students and he did see its value as a tool to communicate campus happenings and concerns.

When a 1959 issue of *The Phoenix* contained one article about the philosophy department indoctrinating students with atheism and another article making explicit references to sexual matters, Smith received an alarmed letter from an alumna. He told her that no professor in the department of philosophy would indoctrinate students, and he assured her "you have received a false picture . . . the issue was not typical in the reference to sex that you, and I, found offensive, . . . [it was] so out of the pattern that the deans spoke to the editors." Smith went on to say that "it would be unrealistic to expect references to sex never to occur in an undergraduate publication, but I have been impressed by the fact that our students, without faculty censorship, have shown good taste in their publications that exceeds what I am familiar with in most college and university publications. Over and over again I am impressed by the fundamental sanity of this college community, by its concern for the right things, its 'striving for the finest and the best.'"[17]

At various points, however, Smith was publically critical of the *Phoenix*'s journalistic standards and its politicalization of matters. In the fall of 1962, in the midst of a period when the newspaper had a clearly radical point of view, Smith was less proud of the publication and spoke emphatically about his concerns. He argued at a Collection of the college community that college dialogue was not advanced by criticisms made by a *Phoenix* editorial that spoke about president-student distance and lack of contact. He expressed his concern that *The Phoenix* was not advancing dialogue on issues of importance and represented only the overwhelmingly liberal plurality, which was at times doctrinaire.[18] Smith was obviously upset that the less vocal students were not represented by the newspaper, and that, as a result, alumni and parents were being alarmed by the skewed attitudes expressed in the paper.

Student sports were areas of student activity that President Smith enthusiastically and almost without reservation supported. As a student and as a Rhodes Scholar, Courtney had valued and experienced sports as a means to develop character and relationships with others. In high school he had been on a tennis team, at Harvard he played intramural squash and took up golf, and at Oxford he was on a rowing team.[19] He followed professional baseball teams closely and had a long-running wager on each season's pennant-winning teams with his Harvard classmate, William Murphy. By his own account, athletics were his "principal hobby," and he described himself as "an avid reader of the sports pages."[20]

Courtney annually marked his personal calendar for and attended many of both the mens' and women's varsity events on campus, and he supported efforts to develop sports teams and physical education curriculum. He argued that by participating in sports students had the opportunity for "just plain fun," could develop "physical gifts," and might find support for "the mind and, on occasion, the spirit."[21] Swarthmore sports' losing records in the late 1950s and early 1960s disturbed Smith sufficiently that in 1962 he asked the incoming admissions dean to seek students with strong athletic interests and skills, in hopes of raising the level of athleticism and developing more competitive teams.[22]

His personal interest in Swarthmore sports was nowhere better demonstrated than at the college's home football games, when Smith usually appeared just before game time. As he strolled onto the cinder running track around the field, he would stop to greet a few alumni and students; then he often went to the sidelines to wish coach Lew Elverson and some of the players the best of luck. Finally he would amble over to the home team's stands and climb up to a seat in the middle section where, sharing a lap blanket with his wife Betty or daughter Lee on cooler days, he would stoke his pipe and settle in to watch a contest against one of Swarthmore's regional foes.[23]

The decorum and distance President Smith exhibited at football games was metaphorically representative of his general relationship to students. He had a formality and intentionality about himself and had always been particular about his own dress, speech, and social habits.[24] He strongly believed that decorum was essential if one was to be taken seriously and to be influential: "Courtly Courtney" was his reputation with the students.

Perhaps because of this transcendent commitment to decorum Courtney's relationship with students was more conflicted than his relationships with other constituencies. Although he idealized students' capacity to learn and recognized Swarthmore students' potential, in the 1960s he was increasingly frustrated by the many shortsighted desires students expressed and the simplicity of their arguments. And the students, in turn, recognized President Smith's outstanding rhetorical and ethical qualities and often felt that they were being manipulated by his logical arguments and confined by his rigid adherence to a predetermined set of standards.

Nagged by concerns about his relationship to students, in the fall of 1966 Courtney decided that he wanted to give students more opportunity to speak with him about whatever matters were on their minds. He began weekly office hours for students and announced that his intent was to initiate dialogue and encourage informal discussion, "not [to have] a press conference to be reported in *The Phoenix*."[25] In the first year of office hours he met with forty-four different students and meticulously took notes on the content of the conversations and his impressions of the student concerns. They spoke to him individually and on some occasions in small groups about existing campus rules, their career dilemmas, complaints about campus affairs, social activism, annoyance about the nature of some of the Swarthmore College Corporation's investment holdings, and visions for the college's development. In several instances, students came in merely to meet him and become acquainted. He noted his pleasure at meeting those who stopped in, and he often encouraged individual students to follow up on their ideas by offering suggestions for further action that he felt would be constructive and productive. He was disturbed, however, by the occasional office hour when the students he met exhibited "sloppy thinking" and "irrational discussion."[26]

Many students, even those very active in campus matters, never knew Courtney Smith as an individual. They knew him as an almost mythical authority figure who while spoken about frequently was seen only occasionally. Those students who did get to know President Smith because of their campus leadership roles or because they sought personal dialogues with him found that he was a father figure who responded to them in a gentle but interrogative fashion, and asserted his own viewpoints in order to direct their behavior.[27] He was friendly but formidable; he could reach out but remained at arm's length; he respected students' ideas, but he believed that they sometimes had erroneous notions that he could correct by persuasion.[28] Students recognized Courtney Smith's persuasive powers and often felt vulnerable. In the early 1960s Courtney spoke with Jed Rakoff, then student council president, about a Student Council plan to challenge the Open House rules, and Rakoff found himself convinced to change his position on the matter and to reverse his vote in the next session of the Council.[29]

In the spring of 1967, another student described an office hour visit with President Smith that was equally powerful. A plan for a new campus road that would cut into the edge of the Crum woods was the topic of discussion. After the meeting the student wrote to Smith: "I had been informed by many people that I should be most wary as I would find you a very persuasive speaker. I was informed that I would leave the open hour with the feeling that everything is under control, that the administration knew what it was doing. This is the impression I left the meeting with, at least in part. I cannot yet say whether I was convinced by the facts or was smooth talked into it. . . . The students seem to feel the administration is being quite dictatorial about some matters (ranging from sex and drinking to the wearing of socks) and that the administration is trying to put something over on the students."[30]

Although students who dealt with President Smith directly felt his care and respect, his authoritative style gave some credence to those who were inclined to see him as crudely manipulative. When anti–Vietnam War sentiment was rising to a crescendo, Smith was described in *The Phoenix* as a functionary of capitalists who were on the Board of Managers who had "hired a President to pacify the militant opposition. . . . He appeals to reason: 'rise above class, ethnic, generational and personal interests. Keep the peace and keep talking; obey the rules and don't run together like a mob.'"[31]

The 1967 edition of the Hamburg Show, an annual springtime satirical review written and performed by students, effectively capsulized the ambiguity felt about Smith. In that year President Smith was a central figure in the play, and his character, "Courtney," was a Jesus-like figure, son of Aydelotte. Judas, the protagonist, in a revealing soliloquy, reflected on why he wished to eliminate Courtney from the scene: "The system is evil, evil is bad, what is bad must be destroyed. Courtney is part of the system, therefore Courtney must be evil. Hold it—I've seen him, he ain't bad, he talks nice, dresses nice—nope we gotta get rid of him—there's alot to think about . . . such a sweet face, such shiny sandals, ooh and such impeccable sackcloth . . . he isn't really wrong often; but then people who speak only in analytic statements aren't wrong too often."[32]

With this kind of overt tension, student governance was indeed a thorny business for Courtney, as it was for most college presidents and administrators during the 1960s. Students who were energized by President Kennedy's call for youth leadership, angered by Vietnam War developments, and moved by racial and women's rights movements were much more argumentative and skeptical about institutional leadership. They were questioning authority at every turn.[33] Students had changed dramatically throughout Smith's presidency and so did his relationship with them. In the 1950s and early 1960s students were less anxious about rights and authority and appreciated the protection that Smith's powerful persuasion, of others afforded them; in the mid- and late-1960s students were very suspicious of authority in general and then tended to resent Smith's powers of persuasion which they felt asked them to subvert their needs to the more powerful "establishment," as well as to the "traditional" culture.

Robert Cross, who succeeded Courtney as president of Swarthmore, agreed with his predecessor "that the questions of student life are some of the most troubling, because they are the most unresolved ones that Swarthmore, and for that matter, most other colleges have to face."[34]

# 16
## Personal Things

the Personal things, never of less moment to me, sometimes don't get
expressed.

DURING HIS SWARTHMORE PRESIDENCY, PERSONAL LIFE FOR COURTNEY
Smith—time for community, friends, family, and his personal needs—
was heavily circumscribed by his professional responsibilities and seldom
mentioned in his records. His appointment book was always full of professional meetings, events, and commitments. His multiple responsibilities as
president, Rhodes secretary, and board member (the Markle Foundation
and the Harvard Overseers being the most demanding) left few free hours
in a week or even an average month.

At Swarthmore, moreover, times of true relaxation for Smith were few.
There were many invitations to cocktail and dinner parties, both on campus and in the village, but whatever light moments they may have contained, they were never casual affairs for the Smiths. Instead they tended to
be purposed discussions of the events and concerns of the community or
occasions to meet and greet not only friends, but also representatives of
the college's various constituencies, such as alumni, Quakers, potential
donors, or parents of current or future students.

Events at the president's house at Swarthmore did not allow for many
informal encounters, either. It was large, with an ever-present staff, and
was altogether "a very forbidding sort of place" for outsiders.[1] Children
could be uncomfortable visiting the Smith household because it appeared
so formal, and indeed most of the family activities occurred on the second
floor, out of the view of visitors.

Dinners at the Smiths's residence were always assisted by household
staff and had a routine way about them. Forty-five minutes were allocated
for the dinner, and throughout, the discourse was intentional, with both
adults and children discussing current events and debating the issues of the
day.

Visitors often heightened the sense of challenging conversation. Indeed,
the Smith children long remembered occasions when their dinner included

dignitaries visiting the campus in order to give lectures and talks, such Justice Hugo Black, Senator Hubert Humphrey, Senator Paul H. Douglas, E. T. Williams (an official of the Rhodes Trust), Lord and Lady Elton, and artists Andrew and Jamie Wyeth. Others who had dinner at the house were Nobel prize-winning chemist Harold Urey, journalist Seymour Harris, art historian Erwin Panofsky, Cold War strategist Dean Acheson, biophysicist Leo Szilard, cyberneticist Norbert Wiener, sociologist Gunnar Myrdal, and economist Kermit Gordon.[2] Frequently these dinner guests stayed overnight and were hosted again in the morning at breakfast.

This style of household life could be alternately exhilarating and anxious for the children as well as for their parents. Betty and Courtney understood the scrutiny that the family received; Betty in particular tried to find ways to protect the children from it. Her husband seemed more resigned to the pressures, and once included in a draft of a talk some remarks that show he was capable of a certain ironic perspective on the narrow range of expectations for his family: "All [a college President] has to do . . . is to have a wife who is attractive yet doesn't look like Miss Rheingold of 1953, who is intelligent, yet doesn't go on fact-finding junkets, who likes to have people in her home, yet is not a Pearl Mesta, who likes to help people, yet doesn't sound like Dorothy Dix. All he has to do, in addition, is to have several bouncing, radiant children who say just the right thing at just the right time."[3]

Betty was perhaps better prepared than Courtney for this environment. She had grown up in a family with some community connections and an upper-class social life: social pressures were not new to her. Although she had attended intellectually demanding Smith College and been a high achiever on her own, she took on the role of mother, spouse, and hostess with grace and diligence. She was a highly organized woman who cared for the three children, kept in touch with friends and family—in short, a homemaker—who also was an accomplished pianist and an avid reader, and who sewed, drew, painted, and demonstrated creativity in many ways.[4]

Betty always had an active life outside of the household. She became a Girl Scout leader and was asked to undertake increasing responsibilities in the local Girl Scout network until she found that the demands, including training new troop leaders, were too much in conflict with her other cherished roles.[5] She often traveled with Courtney and socialized frequently with his network of associates, all the while caring for him in subtle ways and protecting their private time and space as much as she could.

As the president's wife, Betty was nearly constantly engaged in hosting and preparing for college events. She instructed and supervised the president's house staff, arranged dinner parties, entertained house guests, and took on other leadership roles that were expected of the woman in the president's house. In addition, Betty was the *de jure* head of the Campus Club, a Swarthmore College organization that met bimonthly throughout the year to network spouses of faculty and administration. On occasion she also was called upon to host official events in the absence of her husband. For example, she was the hostess for the foreign Fulbright Scholar's conference held at Swarthmore while Courtney spoke at Sidwell Friends School in 1954, and she organized a dinner party for the spouses of the administrators who were at the Rehoboth Conference in 1966.[6]

While Betty Smith's skills and abilities were universally recognized as contributions to the life of the college—some regarded them as "essential"—members of the community had widely differing assessments of her personality.[7] Some Swarthmoreans saw her as formal, reserved, and unresponsive to their concerns. Others often found her witty, outspoken, direct, and even, at times, insightfully acerbic. Still others thought that Betty added an "extraordinary elegance" to college events, and some found her considerate and offering "places to connect" when Courtney's conversation was overly intense.[8]

These different perceptions of Betty can be related at least in part to the degree of understanding that people had about her substantial deafness that was particularly acute in her right ear. Many Swarthmoreans were unaware of this long-term, inherited condition and did not know it was the reason for her limited or waning attention to conversations, particularly in groups.

No matter how crowded their calendar of social engagements, Betty and Courtney found time to be with their children. Courtney's commitments to them are evident from his meticulous notes in his appointment books. He went to Craig's school events, took him to Phillies games, visited with him at Harvard, and encouraged Craig to play golf with him. He visited with Craig and Peggy (neé Remington) after they were married in 1967. Courtney also went to his daughter Lee's class dinner and concert and birthday celebrations; encouraged her work with Chester youth when she was a Swarthmore College student and assisted in hosting Lee's fellow Chester counselors; was supportive of her fiancé's post-graduate study at Oxford University; and corresponded with her the year she was teaching in Banbury, England. When at Squam, Lee and her father shared quiet conversation in the early morning when they went swimming before breakfast. There was less time for recreation with the youngest child, Dabney, who grew up during the more demanding later years of his presidency. She attended The George School in Bucks County, Pennsylvania (less than fifty miles from Swarthmore) until 1966, lived in Italy for a year, then went to Barnard College in New York City. Courtney had lunch with her on his regular trips to New York for Markle Foundation meetings.[9]

Within the family Courtney displayed a sense of humor and often dealt wryly with potentially awkward situations. He could disarm his children's' visiting friends by jesting with them, and he could poke fun at himself. Once he designed an addition to a bird feeder in an attempt to foil the squirrels who feasted on it, and when he saw that in a few days they had mastered a way to outwit it, he jocularly claimed that his efforts had created a new breed of squirrel. He could respond quick-wittedly when annoyed, writing poetry about the potential ill fate of a library book one of his daughters had left out in the weather, and he could poke fun at himself, once commenting whimsically on the disparity in Betty's favor between his and Betty's high school and college achievements, particularly in athletics. Courtney also initiated a system of "orts," or Ortega points (named for José Ortega y Gasset), which he frequently assigned to family members for efforts beyond the call of duty.[10] This fanciful encouragement of efforts, ideas, and what he considered noble acts added a tone of encouragement and levity to family travel and vacations.[11]

Courtney combined his work with recreation on some occasions. He golfed with the Ozone Club, some of whose members were significant college alumni or on the board of managers. He also scheduled short visits with family when he made business trips to the Midwest, Boston, and Washington, D.C. For example, he visited his oldest brother, Murray, who was working for Commonwealth Edison, when he was on a trip to Chicago in 1954 and saw Murray's son, "Smitty," in Boston on several occasions in the late 1950s.[12] When he was in Washington to meet with government officials, he usually visited his brother Carleton, a regional vice president of NBC and RCA.[13]

Courtney's sister, Florence, and her husband, Bryce Van Syoc, whom she married in 1943, kept up their relationship with the Smiths by visiting wherever Courtney and Betty lived. In the Swarthmore years they often arrived during the Christmas holidays, when Bryce, an English professor (who taught at University of Michigan and later at Southern Illinois University) had a break from teaching and Swarthmore's campus life was quieter. Myrtle Smith, Courtney and Florence's mother, then lived near the Van Syocs and often came to Swarthmore with them to have an extended visit with her son and his family. During the visits Betty was the primary hostess for her fiercely independent, elderly mother-in-law, Mrs. Smith, who loved to play canasta and needed some assistance due to a stroke and her own hearing impairment. In 1966 Myrtle moved east to live in the northern suburbs of Washington, D.C. where she was near Courtney's older brother, Carleton.[14]

When Courtney and Betty lived in Princeton and Swarthmore they visited Betty's parents, the Proctors, for a few days at a time. Typically they saw the Proctors in Boston at Thanksgiving time and at the Proctors' country house at Marblehead Neck (Mass.) during the summer. Betty and Courtney seemed to enjoy those visits, and from all accounts the Proctors were very proud and enthusiastic about Courtney and his work, even though he was a professional academic and not a businessman.

Getting away from work and the house was always the most relaxing way for the Smith family to find recreation and renewal. About 1950 the family began vacationing regularly at Squam Lake, New Hampshire, where the family relaxed, enjoyed outdoor sports, caught its breath, and prepared for the upcoming year. Squam Lake, a large but quiet body of water in central New Hampshire, was ringed by family compounds.[15] Betty's maternal uncle, a Bowden, had bought a sixty-acre property with a long shoreline about 1900 for a summer residence and had built a complex, including a huge, lovely house, that accommodated family, staff, and accompanying horses. Later two other houses were built for the extended Bowden family. The Smiths stayed in the second-oldest house during their visits. In the Princeton years the family had no staff, but during the Swarthmore years their butler and cook from Swarthmore College accompanied them. Betty's parents, the Proctors, often visited for several days.

Although the days at Squam constituted a family retreat and vacation there was a pattern to the days. Courtney regularly read throughout the morning, then corresponded on Rhodes matters, caught up on academic affairs, and entertained certain Swarthmore personnel and staff. The Prentices, Decrouezes, Moores, Barrs, George and Dorothy Becker, and Susan Cobbs were hosted there for several days at a time.[16] The family and guests went swimming, canoeing, and hiking, held family tennis tournaments, played golf and poker, water-skied, took out the sunfish-class sailboat, read, and took occasional indoor naps on the much fought-over chaise lounge.[17]

Overseas travel, though infrequent, seems to have provided the greatest opportunity for family bonding. In June 1953, just before Courtney took on the presidency of Swarthmore, the Smiths sailed to England on the *Mauritania* so that Courtney, now that he was the American Rhodes secretary, could develop a stronger relationship with the Rhodes officials in Oxford. The family lived at Standlake, outside of Oxford, for three months while Courtney worked at the Rhodes House in Oxford each day. They lived in a thatched roof house with low, narrow doorways and an extraordinarily big garden. The Smith children enjoyed playing with the village children and broke the local code by doing so without regard to class. That summer was the coronation festival for Queen Elizabeth, and for Standlake's celebration Betty dressed the children as American colonists! To conclude this cross-cultural experience the family took a two-week tour of France and Switzerland, and then returned to the United States (appropriately enough) on the *Queen Elizabeth*.[18]

In 1961, after having been at Swarthmore for seven years, Courtney and Betty took the family to Europe for a more extensive tour. They obviously enjoyed promoting the personal growth and development of character that came from such travel and probably were motivated to some degree by memories of the importance of European travel during their formative years and young adulthood. The family left New York on the *Queen Mary* on June 28, then took a three-month automobile tour throughout Western Europe.

Courtney insisted that everyone had ideas and should contribute to the development of the trip, permitting no one to sit "like a bump on a log." At the same time he acknowledged that each family member had special interests, which he denominated as "fatal flaws," and he tried to accommodate each of them. Courtney's fatal flaw was seeing universities, Craig's were cathedrals and museums, Betty's were houses, castles, and mansions, Lee's were the local scenery and outdoor paths, and Dabney's were chair lifts. They managed to indulge everyone's interests before finishing the auto tour and returning to the United States from Cherbourg, again on the *Queen Elizabeth*.[19] Courtney remarked to a friend that this trip "couldn't have been better."[20]

In the fall of 1965, with all of the Smith children out of the household or at boarding school, Courtney and Betty took a five-month sabbatical to travel in Europe and Egypt. They spent six weeks at Grindelwald, Switzerland, then flew to Athens, sailed to the Isle of Rhodes, and finally stopped at Cairo, Egypt (where their children, Craig, Dabney, and Lee, and Lee's boyfriend, Greg Ingram, joined them for the Christmas holidays). Afterward they went on to Taormina, Sicily, for two months, then sailed from Naples to New York City. Courtney described this sabbatical as a wonderful, happy, and highly meaningful sojourn with his wife.[21]

Late in his career Smith found another opportunity for retreat and recreation at Ponte Vedra Beach, a community near Jacksonville, Florida, known for its golf, pools, and tennis. After an initial visit in 1959, Smith and Betty began taking a winter week there regularly beginning in 1963.[22]

In his classic study of the American executive of the 1950s, *The Organization Man,* William H. Whyte Jr., argued that for an institutional leader of Smith's generation there was "between work and the rest of his life a unity" that never permitted him to fully exclude the demands of his job from what was intended to be leisure.[23] Clearly, Courtney Smith was well aware of his need for recreation and family time and scheduled it regularly in spite of his heavy administrative and professional commitments. But as Whyte's observation suggests, these respites were never pure relaxation; even at Squam Lake or while on sabbatical in Europe he had books to read or, more frequently, letters and speeches to write. While Smith took the opportunities of planned leisure to have deeper, more personal connections with co-workers and to have extended, more carefree engagement with his family, the demands of his presidency and his other roles as an academic leader were never far away.

# 17
## Administration of a College

W HEN SMITH CAME TO SWARTHMORE HE INHERITED AN ADMINISTRATIVE team assembled primarily by his immediate predecessor, John Nason: Registrar John Moore, Deans Susan Cobbs and Everett Hunt, and Vice Presidents Edward Cratsley and Joseph Shane.[1] John Moore had been at the college since 1943 when he had come as an associate professor in philosophy. Everett Hunt had come in 1925 during Aydelotte's presidency to teach public speaking, and he had become acting dean of men in 1932.[2] Susan Cobbs arrived in 1945 as dean of women and taught classics. Joseph Shane had come from the George School, a Quaker preparatory school of Hicksite origins, in 1950 to work with public relations, fund-raising, and alumni.[3] Together, this team had a broad understanding of the college, its constituencies, and its dilemmas. They were a solid source of information during the early years of the Smith administration, and indeed Courtney trusted their advice and drew heavily upon them throughout his tenure.

Dean Cobbs and Vice President Shane were consistently his closest advisors, and also those most likely to deflect criticism of Smith, Shane when it came from alumni and Cobbs when it came from faculty. In turn, Smith gave them his full support and relied on them without hesitation when he was away from the campus. At the end of each summer vacation, for example, he immediately turned to them for updates on the status of the college.

Although the triumvirate of Cobbs as dean, Shane as alumni officer, and Cratsley as administrator of financial matters was in place throughout Smith's presidency, there were changes in other major offices during his tenure. The first major change occurred in 1955 when dean of men Everett Hunt retired, possibly because (as many thought) Hunt never fully became part of Smith's inner circle. However, there is no documentary evidence of conflict between them, and the book Hunt published a few years later, *The Revolt of the College Intellectual,* a semi-autobiographical memoir of his experiences with Swarthmore students, shows no evidence of ill feeling.[4]

In any case, Smith filled Hunt's deanship with William (Bill) C. H. Prentice, a faculty member who was highly recommended by former president John Nason. Prentice, a 1937 Rhodes scholar whom Smith had known from Oxford days, had come to Swarthmore to teach psychology in 1947. Prentice served as dean of men for seven years until he left in 1962 to become president of Wheaton College in Massachusetts.[5] Robert Barr was recruited by Courtney in 1957 to work under Prentice as assistant dean of men, and upon Prentice's resignation moved into the dean of men position. Barr was a 1956 Swarthmore graduate who had been both president of the Student Council and president of the Intra-fraternity Council in his senior year and served on several college committees as the student representative. After his graduation he had served briefly in the military and in the personnel office of ESSO (Standard Oil Company of New Jersey). Barr, easily the youngest member of the team, seemed to grasp student concerns and interests more easily than the other deans. He and his family became close friends of the Smiths, and Courtney and Betty Smith were virtual "foster grandparents" to the Barr children. Robert Barr and his family even spent time with the Smiths during their summer vacations at Squam Lake.[6] Indeed, Barr was so committed to the Smith administration that he remained in the deanship throughout Smith's tenure.

In 1956, faced with increasing professional responsibilities (such as service with the Harvard Board of Overseers, the Eisenhower Exchange Fellowships, and the Markle Foundation), Courtney began a series of appointments of former Rhodes scholars as administrative assistants who were to help him manage the Rhodes program as well as some college affairs. Even though Courtney was able to rely on Elsa Jenkins, who had run the Rhodes secretary's office full-time under Aydelotte and was a very able manager of all aspects of the program, there was Rhodes fieldwork and travel which she could not do in the course of managing the day-to-day operations for Smith.[7]

The first administrative assistant whom Courtney Smith appointed was Prosser Gifford, who had just completed his law studies at Harvard. In 1956 Gifford became both assistant to the president and assistant to the American secretary of the Rhodes program. He stayed only two years and then went on to Yale University for doctoral studies.[8] Courtney enjoyed this relationship and became the godfather to the Giffords' second daughter. Gifford was succeeded in this role by Aldon Duane Bell (assistant to the president and assistant to the American secretary of the Rhodes Scholar Program, 1958–60[9]) and then Richard W. Pfaff (assistant to the president and assistant to the American secretary of the Rhodes Scholar Program, 1960–62). Although these appointments were brief Smith took a personal interest in his young assistants' careers. He and Betty not only remained friendly with the Giffords but also attended Pfaff's ordination ceremony at Christ Church of Ramapo (N.J.) in 1966.[10]

In 1962 when both Bill Prentice and Dick Pfaff resigned Courtney decided it was an opportune moment to create a new administrative structure. Gilmore Stott ( Rhodes 1938), who had been an assistant dean of men since 1950 when he was brought to Swarthmore by John Nason, was appointed administrative assistant to the president with "duties of greater responsibility" and received the new title of deputy American secretary of the Rhodes Scholarships. Susan Cobbs, who had been dean of women from the Nason era, was appointed to the new position of "dean," with "academic responsibilities" and oversight of the offices of the dean of men, the dean of women, and the registrar.

Smith's new design created more permanent administrative positions but also maintained a simplicity of authority and communication for himself by requiring that most of the administrative staff report to him through Dean Cobbs. Barbara Lange, who had taught dramatics at the college since 1949 and had become assistant dean of women in 1961, was appointed dean of women in 1962. Bob Barr, who had been Prentice's assistant for five years, was appointed dean of men. This reorganization permitted the same triumvirate of Cobbs, Cratsley, and Shane to report to him despite the expansion.[11]

The key component of this reorganization was Courtney's decision to create a single coordinated admissions office, separate from the offices of the deans of men and women. John C. Hoy was appointed the first dean of admissions for all students in 1962. He had been working in admissions at Lake Forest College (Ill.), where he had successfully recruited black students for the school. Hoy understood that Smith expected him to increase student body diversity by seeking out more minority students and better athletes and to enliven the alumni's engagement in student recruitment. At Swarthmore Hoy helped to shape the new dean of admissions role, worked on the initial phases of the Rockefeller Foundation grant for strengthening the college's ability "to discover talented Negro and other minority group students," and served in the role for two years before he moved on to become dean of admissions at Wesleyan University in 1964.[12] Frederick A. Hargadon, who came to Swarthmore as a lecturer in political science in 1963, succeeded Hoy as dean of admissions in 1964 and continued work begun by Hoy. Hargadon served for the remainder of the Smith presidency, through the tumultuous 1968–69 academic year, and then left to become dean of admissions at Stanford University.

Smith, who was thorough, deliberative, and organized, used his administrative staff as consultants and expected them to respond to all sorts of questions and issues and to keep him informed about concerns arising within the college. He regularly circulated memos and dictated task and assignment notes to himself and others while out of the office. He asserted his needs for information and solicited staff commentary on proposals that came to him. He routinely asked for feedback from all administrators before considering changes in policy or making any decisions that might set precedents. He generally informed them of his activities and dilemmas, so that they could intercede with data, advice, and insights they might have. He took all administrative advice seriously and in turn, gained their respect. The "team in Parrish Hall" worked smoothly under Smith's firm, principled, and conscientious approach, which was implemented with a "velvet glove" composed of gentle suggestions and a genuine concern for each issue.[13]

Courtney certainly relied on his administrators for specific expertise. Courtney believed that Shane, who had responsibility for publicity and fund-raising, truly had his fingers on the pulse of the alumni and normally relied on his judgment in alumni matters.[14] He asked Shane to scout for major donors for particular needs, to reflect on giving trends and what might enhance giving, to devise new formats for communication with alumni, and to help him find ways in which to cultivate specific alumni. Smith knew Shane understood the hearts and minds of Swarthmore's most important constituencies, its alumni and Quakers in the Philadelphia region. Much of Smith and Shane's bimonthly golf outings was devoted to a dialogue about the college and its future. Shane encouraged Smith to speak to many groups, and indeed Courtney knew that it was likely that Shane would encourage his speaking when invited. Courtney, when bombarded with requests to speak at commencements and other events in 1955, quipped to Shane: "I am turning down speeches right and left . . . and in many instances have not asked your advice because you only tell me to do all of them!"[15]

Susan Cobbs was the administrator who had Smith's deepest level of trust. She had been at Swarthmore since 1945, and although she was a half-generation older that Smith, she seems to have been the staff person who most closely identified her views with his. She was, on many occasions, the person who ran proposals up the flagpole to see who saluted and was the staff member who most readily shared with Smith personal observations about how the faculty was responding to important issues. Susan Cobbs knew Courtney's style, values, and perspective intimately, and she and the Smiths socialized more frequently than other administrators over dinner and cocktails at each other's homes.[16]

Cobbs was given increasing responsibility throughout the Smith administration. As dean of women, Cobbs focused her attention on women's admissions and student life; as dean she had broader responsibilities for the effective functioning of the college. As faculty and administrators reflected upon her role at Swarthmore, there was consensus that Susan Cobbs was a particularly loyal and respected source of support to the president during his administration. In many ways, she "functioned as a provost before there was a provost," and she was appreciated for her extraordinary common sense.[17] Because she assumed Smith's value system and understood his priorities, she could be counted upon to take his principles into consideration as she dealt with sensitive matters. On one occasion, for example, Courtney asked her to speak to a professor whose nominee for an honorary degree was being vehemently opposed by a member of the board of managers. She clarified the professor's rationale for the nomination without offending him and gave Courtney the ammunition he needed to overrule the manager's objection.[18]

Ed Cratsley was Smith's nickel-and-dime man. He knew virtually every detail about the college's operations and was the administrator who reviewed all budgetary matters. Courtney routinely told both administrators and faculty to check their proposals with Cratsley, knowing that Cratsley was both very good and very conservative fiscally.[19] Courtney was not the only person who made this assessment of Cratsley's qualities. In 1964 a Rockefeller Foundation officer who met with Cratsley noted that he "made an excellent impression in his view of the proper role of the relationship between a financial comptroller and the educational offices of an institution." Cratsley had shared his perspective that the function of a financial officer is to "work with the individuals primarily concerned with academic affairs so that the best interests of the academic can be carried through." He viewed "the role of the financial officer essentially as one who can make the best use of the resources rather than [act] as a policeman blowing a whistle." Cratsley reported that he made "the bulk of the financial decisions with the academic ones being settled via the President. The President and Department Chairmen discuss overall staff numbers and it remains to Cratsley and the Chairmen to work out exact financial details."[20] It was this sort of recognition of Cratsley's qualities and his success in such institutional negotiations that made him the logical person to serve as acting president during Smith's 1965–66 sabbatical.

The senior administrative team of Shane, Cratsley, and Cobbs worked like a well-oiled machine throughout the Smith years. They kept the college functioning when Smith's attention was diverted by such matters as the NDEA disclaimer affidavit fight, the Centennial fund-raising campaign, the on-again, off-again struggle against the Blue Route expressway, and his five-month sabbatical (October 1965–February 1966).

Smith's tendency to work in detail, regarding nothing as unimportant, sometimes became tedious to others. He was known to some faculty as "dirty-desk Courtney" because reports and proposals went to him but seemed never to return.[21] One cause of the slow process of decision making was his commitment to sending drafts of his presidential reports, letters, and other documents to administrative staff in order to get their thoughts and comments. He felt that his decisions and the outcomes were significantly improved by receiving such preliminary feedback. Staff learned to take his requests seriously and responded with precision and critical insight: John Moore, for instance once warned about a comment being "not quite right . . . or quite fair" to a particular committee, and Gilmore Stott, in another instance, warned that a comment was "probably right though . . . [it sounded] too strong."[22] Joe Shane regularly gave strong advice on how Smith should deal with outside groups. However, Dean Hunt, early on, and, increasingly, department chairs found his deliberative style excessively slow and thought that his interest in detail indicated that he might rather do the whole job for them.[23]

During Courtney's sabbatical of 1965–66 he had the first occasion in many years to deeply and reflectively read about issues and dilemmas in higher education. When he returned to campus he asked Gilmore Stott to arrange for an administrative staff retreat to deal with some of the issues he had contemplated. Stott scheduled the retreat for Rehoboth Beach (Del.) during the final week of June 1966,[24] and Courtney gave the staff fifty-two questions, which he referred to as "52 Riddles of the Sphinx," for the retreat discussion.[25]

Coincidentally, in May of 1966 several faculty members sent a collaborative letter to Courtney Smith: Monroe Beardsley, Charles Gilbert, Samuel Hynes, Helen North, Dean Peabody, Hedley Rhys, and David Smith warned their president that the college had an impending crisis, a crisis in faculty recruitment and satisfaction, particularly in the increasingly specialized disciplines. They suggested "a deep and radical consideration of the college and its future, with no questions out of order and no holds barred." While they emphasized that retention of faculty was critical and, among other things, required a more flexible leave and research policy, they also argued that students merited both more intensive teaching and greater flexibility of program, and that the college as a whole needed to assess its viability for the coming decades when higher education would be more competitive in attracting both faculty and students.[26]

Smith responded to the letter by summoning all seven signatories to his office and opened the meeting by stating to the group that he had hoped for something like a full assessment of the college. He told them "the letter gave me a sense of elation, [I thought] this is it; this could be basic." He welcomed their proposal for a thorough, no-holds-barred review because, he said, so much recent academic reform had been "tinkering." Discussion then turned immediately to how the evaluation could be done, and there was discussion of the composition of the review body: "outsiders" were suggested by the faculty; but "insiders" were suggested by Courtney, who felt that insiders would put most energy into an assessment of the college.

Courtney, who had served on review committees of the Harvard Board of Overseers, quickly took charge of the planning process. He framed the central problem as "how to draw heavily on outsiders, but have [the] design, conduct, [and] conclusions of [the] study done from within."[27] He then focused on how the task force should be composed, when and how time would be found for the study, how it might be funded, and whether it could be related to the studies of library needs and student life that were already anticipated. As one professor later commented, this letter had not gotten clogged up on the second floor of Parrish Hall, in Courtney's office, as many faculty thought other initiatives had.[28]

A month after the letter had come to his desk, Courtney was already announcing to the college community the shape of the coming initiative. He wrote a collegewide memorandum: "A Commission on Educational Policy is being established to design and conduct a thoroughgoing study of our entire academic program. The Commission, made up of faculty members from within the College and experts from outside the College, will seek to draw everyone in the community into the consideration . . . the Commission will review the role of an independent liberal arts college at a time when there have been marked improvements in secondary school education and when the needs of our society lead so many students to go on from college to graduate and professional schools. . . . In the same spirit a special committee will also be established to consider the function and operation of the library in a liberal arts college." Smith also announced that "a joint committee made up of members of the Board of Managers, the faculty, the administration, and the student body [will] consider the College's responsibilities beyond the provision of an academic program . . . it will not consider specific social issues or regulations, but will decide instead if there are, or are not, guiding principles that need to be seen as forming the foundation of social life on the campus."[29] Courtney supplied Charles (Chuck) Gilbert and several other people who were interested in the campus study with an annotated list of books and journals that he thought might be useful. It included *An Adventure in Education* (a book about the Aydelotte years at Swarthmore), *The American College, The College and the Student,* and *Examining in Harvard College.*[30]

The Rehoboth administrative staff conference (Barr, Cobbs, Cratsley, Hargadon, Lange, Moore, Stott, and Smith) in June now took on a greater sense of importance. The staff discussed the responsibilities of the college for the full development of the students, staff-student relationships and goals, Quaker impacts upon the college mission, student unrest, student diversity and its effects, the increasing sense of power struggles within the campus community, admissions issues and dynamics, changes in student interests and character, changes in loyalty and identity of faculty, faculty and housing alternatives, counseling options and guidance alternatives regarding academic problems, presidential associations with students, student participation in college governance, morality of students and its impact upon the college's reputation, the increasing burden of administrative work, the frightening rate of federal program growth and its need for attention and response, factors impacting the size of the college, and needs for facility renovation and expansion.[31]

Later, while on his August vacation at Squam Lake (N.H.), Smith worked out the details of appointments to the commission and two committees, making extensive notes about candidates for the positions.[32] In the end Robert Sproull (vice president for academic affairs at Cornell University), Kermit Gordon (vice president of the Brookings Institution, a Swarthmore alumnus, and a Smith Rhodes classmate), Winnifred Poland Pierce (a Swarthmore alumna), and Swarthmore professors (Beardsley, Field, Gilbert, Heald, and Hynes) were chosen for the Commission on Educational Policy (CEP), and political science professor Chuck Gilbert agreed to chair the commission.

By September 19, 1966, Courtney was able to publish a list of members of the CEP and of the library committee and project a partial membership for the student life committee. Within a few days the work began, and the CEP members solicited "expressions of faculty concerns," promised that hearings would begin soon, and asked for detailed comments on a two-page list of "subjects for study."[33] By the end of October the student life committee members were announced, and funding for the three studies had been assured by the Danforth Foundation.[34] Throughout that fall there were numerous meetings, and in November the Smiths' home even lodged the off-campus members of the commission who were there for two days.[35]

All three review bodies gathered commentary, published preliminary findings, went through deliberations, and presented final reports about administrative issues by the late summer of 1967. Although Courtney was not engaged directly in the review process, the chairs of the commissions requested his input, and he closely followed the proceedings.[36] A faculty committee suggested that the CEP and student life committee findings and recommendations be published and thoroughly discussed by the college community during 1967–68. Smith readily agreed, believing that Swarthmore could then move into implementation of changes in 1968–69.[37]

In December 1967 there was a concentrated student review and discussion of the newly published "red book" containing the CEP, library, and student life reports. Known as "Superweek," all classes and seminars were suspended and the students published a special newspaper to cover the various daily discussions and events. Student recommendations of all sorts were then sent to the faculty.

From February through May of 1968 the faculty turned its concentrated attention to discussion and action on the commission's and committees' recommendations. Courtney, who chaired and facilitated the faculty meetings, said it was "a moving experience . . . to see, in this day, a high-powered faculty with strong research interests spending hours and hours conscientiously and sensitively considering every aspect of a college's academic program."[38]

Smith probably was not quite so enthusiastic about all of the contents of the actual CEP report. Regarding administration, the report noted that "Swarthmore has a tradition of strong presidential authority. . . . Working as it does against the deterioration of quality that often follows diffusion of responsibility, we believe that it has served the College well and should be preserved." Nonetheless, the Commission believed that there were "deficiencies . . . of information flow," and that faculty who addressed "reasonable requests" to the administration had "some difficulty in finding out to whom they should be addressed, have been evaded, or refused, or fulfilled grudgingly or slowly." The Commission opined that increases in college business in recent years had overburdened the administration, and that there had been no compensation for it by instituting the "important corporate form of middle management."[39] In recommendation number 153, the Commission proposed as its chief remedy for this situation "That the new administrative position of Provost be established. The Provost is to serve as the President's chief adviser in academic affairs, and as the representative of the faculty in matters of its professional concern."[40] The suggested duties of the provost included assisting the president with long-range academic planning, evaluating faculty performance and promoting the faculty's professional growth, and chairing a new Council on Educational Policy charged with continuing the consideration of fundamental issues that the Commission itself had addressed in the previous year.[41]

There is no doubt that this recommendation expanded the power of the faculty and de facto reduced the power of the president. Some observers thought that Smith took this as a gentle slap in the face, but as a slap nonetheless; others thought that the CEP simply recognized the realities of higher education administration in an era of greater government regulation, faculty, and student demands for power sharing, and diminished respect for authority in general. In any case, it was clear that the power of Swarthmore's president would be significantly circumscribed in the future.[42]

The CEP study and recommendations received positive feedback from alumni and many American educational leaders regarding its thoroughness and honesty, and Courtney Smith got credit for his role in the entire initiative. At the start he had displayed outward equanimity in response to what could have been perceived as a personally critical letter from members of the faculty; he had fairly and energetically established a systematic review process; and in the end he had accepted without reservation all of the CEP's recommendations, including those on change in the administration of the college, which some faculty and staff believed he disagreed with substantially.[43] Many, in fact, thought that the anticipated changes in the college's structure were a primary reason why Courtney announced his intention to step down from the Swarthmore presidency a short two months later. He never said so, but he may have taken the adoption of the CEP recommendations as in part a wish for change.

# 18

## The Final Year

THE FINAL REPORTS OF THE COMMISSION ON EDUCATIONAL POLICY (CEP) and its parallel bodies, the Special Committee on Library Policy and the Special Committee on Student Life, were timely when they were published and distributed to every student, faculty, and staff member in November 1967. American education and the country were in transition. The culture was confronted with dramatic scientific changes and needs for coping with increasingly complex information and had begun to question its traditional means of establishing and maintaining authority. The CEP identified these as problems that needed to be addressed directly within the small liberal arts college and made dozens of recommendations for change at Swarthmore. The *Critique of the College,* the 461–page volume containing the three bodies' final reports, detailed Swarthmore's strengths but made recommendations that followed the increasingly strong trend within America to have more lateral organizational structures with more consumer input.[1]

The CEP recommended improved institutional research and evaluation, better information flow between the administration and the faculty, and substantial faculty involvement in long-range planning for the college. The CEP also found that there was a sense among the faculty that its increased needs for staff service were not adequately met, and that "departments had become laws unto themselves" with little awareness and coordination of curriculum patterns.[2] To provide more support for faculty in such areas as professional development and grant seeking, they recommended that department chairs be relieved of some teaching responsibility in order to have more time to assist their own faculty, and that the college create an office that would keep abreast of opportunities for research funding.

The trend of the CEP's recommendations was to remove much of the president's responsibility for overseeing the faculty and coordinating the curriculum. Although the CEP's report was careful not to make ad hominem comments regarding Smith's strong leadership style or his role in creating the existing patterns of governance, the members of the commis-

171

sion argued that the overall growth of the college, the demands of modern scholarship, and the need for greater flexibility in the curriculum had made it imperative that decision making be less centralized. While stating that it favored the continuation of Swarthmore's tradition of a strong president, the CEP in fact pushed the administrative structure of the college in a direction familiar to higher education in succeeding decades—toward a decided division between the fiscal and operational authority of the administration on the one hand, and the curricular and educational policy-making functions of the faculty on the other.[3]

The report of the Student Life Committee was not nearly so far-reaching, perhaps because everyone recognized that the rapid changes in student behavior that were underway in the latter 1960s could not be harnessed by alterations in rules and procedures.[4] The committee instead called for a renewed emphasis on the Quaker traditions of "seriousness of purpose, concern, non-materialism, equality, tolerance, social service, and meditation," values that the committee believed were already held by substantial numbers of the college community. The committee also argued for continuing the maintenance of a campus-centered social life and promotion of strong interrelationships between students, faculty, and the administration. Its modest initiatives were to recommend mandatory appointments of students to governing bodies that dealt with student affairs and to suggest that rigid responses to violating the existing prohibitions on sex, alcohol, and drugs should be tempered.[5]

This tempering was fastened on by the news media, which drew out the statement that "The Committee recommends that the present sex rule be rescinded," but omitted mentioning the recommended revision ("The College does not condone or permit the use of college facilities to engage in sexual intercourse"). The newspapers turned these statements into headlines proclaiming that Swarthmore had dropped its prohibition of sex on campus. Smith was chagrined to find that this media proclamation was the major way in which alumni and other friends of the college learned of proposed student life changes at Swarthmore.[6]

The third report, that of the Special Committee on Library Policy, focused on developing and assuring the students' library skills, providing better access to librarians' expertise, improving the process for selecting and purchasing materials that would support all academic and extracurricular activities on campus, and establishing a permanent advisory committee on the library.[7] The new McCabe Library, which had just opened in the fall of 1967, made it feasible and appropriate to implement these long-needed changes in library services.

The reports of the three committees quickly became the subject of student, faculty, staff, and manager discussions. The students were given the first week of December 1967 to discuss the reports in what became known as "Superweek." Group discussions were set up that accounted for each students' affiliation with the multiple constituencies affected by the reports. All students were encouraged to attend dormitory section meetings for input related to the student life recommendations and "major" meetings for input related to the curricular recommendations. There were also panel discussions to present both faculty and student views on general topics, including the college's relationship with students and the Quaker tradition. Ad hoc meetings were held on virtually any topic that drew a few students together. Summaries of the many discussions at these events were dutifully reported in a student newspaper established just for the occasion called *The Egg,* which was edited with sufficient sense of whimsy to each day publish a bit of humor—"The Egg Yolk."[8]

In February 1968, as the second semester opened, the faculty began to consider the CEP's 165 recommendations and the Special Committee on Library Policy's 26 recommendations. (Faculty consideration of the student life recommendations were deferred until they were reviewed by the standing Student Affairs Committee.) President Smith chaired the weekly two-and-one-half-to-three-hour meetings in which the faculty systematically reviewed and voted upon each recommendation, forwarding those they approved to the Board of Managers for final action. He ran a tight ship in these meetings, limiting debate to set periods of time and specifying the work that had to be accomplished in each session.[9] The result of this careful consideration, in Smith's view, was a set of changes, "complex and qualified, but . . . interrelated and derived from a set of consistent principles."[10]

In his commencement remarks in June 1968 Smith commented in general on the process of institutional review that had been put in motion two years before. He declared that the recommendations had been based on an examination of "everything from the ground up," and that adopting them meant "a Swarthmore that will be new in striking ways." He called the changes "another giant step" in the college's history, similar to the new directions of the Aydelotte era forty years earlier, and commented approvingly that the college community had "agreed on the changes not because they compromise or take some middle course, but because they are faithful to two things: they see clearly the larger scene of education and training of which Swarthmore education is only a part; and they find our place in this larger scene in terms of what we ourselves want ourselves to be." He seemed relieved to note that "the extent of the agreement is impressive, since academic aspects of the *Critique* [i.e., the CEP report] were drawn up with substantial help from the younger alumni, are liked by our students (no small achievement!), have been debated and refined by our Faculty, and heartily approved by our Board of Managers." Smith summarized the process by calling it "wearing but exhilarating."[11]

Although in his commencement remarks Smith proudly drew the curtain on the review process itself and viewed it as providing some confirmation that the campus dialogue he desired continued to flourish, he also was compelled to identify three serious and potentially intractable problems facing the college: responses to the Vietnam War, racial injustice in American society, and the phenomenon of campus disturbances.

Looming most dramatically were "the long shadows cast by the problems of the [Vietnam] war," which engaged students and faculty in political action and had forced on the graduating seniors (both men and women) agonizing responses to the military draft. Smith noted that students were involved in organized opposition to the war, and that it was his personal belief that "men's method for adjudication of their own affairs [by] war is by nature a wrong method, because it cannot be followed without cutting short the full course of individual spirits, each with its absolute worth, and each deserving of time and opportunity to work out its destiny."[12]

Courtney knew very well the disturbing effects of war on young people. The beginning of World War II in 1939 had interfered with his Rhodes Scholarship studies and in 1968, as secretary of the American Rhodes Scholar office he was deeply engaged with draft boards, having to alert newly selected Rhodes Scholars, among them the future president of the United States, William J. Clinton, about the disturbing effects of the escalating war on their educational plans.

He noted that "problems of racial injustice" were other pressing matters for higher education. The recent assassination of Martin Luther King Jr. had recently heightened national concerns about racial issues, and the activism of the college's new Swarthmore Afro-American Students' Society (SASS) made racial understanding a matter for campus discussion. Smith ventured a personal observation that the deterioration of race relations nationally and the rise of a distinct black identity on campus made him wonder "whether inside Swarthmore we were not in fact *getting used to* less dialogue, rather than more, between the races." With concern he stated that "there were moments of edginess on these matters during the year, reminding us that our only immunity at Swarthmore inheres in the lively continuance of our community's reasonableness."[13]

And finally he reflected briefly on the rapidly growing phenomenon of disturbances on college and university campuses, a problem that Swarthmore had to that point not experienced. Noting that there were divisive issues on Swarthmore's campus, and that "many colleges have either swept these issues under the rug or taken them to the barricades," Smith called for adherence to the Quaker tradition of "reasoning 'coldly out of a warm perception,'" and concluded that he hoped "that one college can demonstrate that when men of good will are willing to keep counting to ten, and believing in and appealing to the good in one another, something viable and inspiriting can come from it, something that will indeed draw out the best in all of us."[14]

Smith could speak about these trends assertively because he was not only monitoring trends and changes on Swarthmore's campus, but he also was networked with many university professors and presidents, was continuing to read many professional journals and newspapers, was working closely with Philadelphia-area businessmen, and during 1967–68 was leading the Markle Foundation's search for a new program orientation.

The Markle Foundation, a New York City organization of which Smith had been a trustee of since 1953, had for twenty years provided research stipends for promising young M.D.s in the expectation of improving the level of medical research in the United States. Growing federal support of medical research had made this program less significant, and in 1966 the foundation's trustees had constituted a committee to look into how the organization's resources could be more effectively utilized for the improvement of human welfare. Smith accepted the chairmanship of the committee and took his responsibility seriously. By June 1968 (the time of his annual commencement address) he had interviewed a wide range of American leaders of education, government, and industry and had given considerable thought to the problem of what a middle-sized foundation with a small staff could do to make an impact if it directed its resources toward one of the more pressing problems facing American society. He and his committee had come to focus on three problems that needed to be addressed, each of which would be a marked departure for the foundation: (1) pollution of the environment, (2) problems of higher education, especially governance and administration, and (3) urban and minority problems, "with emphasis on medicine of, by and for, the Negro."[15]

In July, having been persuaded that he would have the opportunity to lead the foundation into one of these new areas, Smith announced his intention to leave Swarthmore in the summer of 1969 to become Markle's president. The authority with which Smith directed the study of future directions for the foundation had made him a natural candidate for its leadership when John Russell, who had been president since 1946, decided to retire.[16]

Many of the faculty and staff reacted with surprise to Smith's announcement and shared with him their sense of bereavement and grief. In his resignation announcement to the faculty and staff Smith noted his appreciation of the support that he had had at Swarthmore but also the high hopes he had for the college under "new leadership and fresh energies."[17] The July 17, 1968, *New York Times* announced to the world Courtney's career plans and his intention to head the foundation which had to that point focused its resources on supporting medical research and education.[18] Smith told others that he was enthusiastic and inspired by the new tasks and challenges which the Markle role would offer him, as well as by "the absolute free hand" that he would have in shaping the foundation's program.[19]

Smith continued to serve in several Philadelphia-area organizations throughout the spring and summer of 1968. He was active with Penjerdel, the Greater Philadelphia Movement, and the Philadelphia Savings Fund Society (PSFS). In June he hosted a Penjerdel conference at Swarthmore.[20] On the twenty-second of July he accepted a position on the board of directors of the Greater Philadelphia Movement, an organization in which he had been active for several years, and which was concerned with racism, civic leadership, and business and economic development.[21] He was also actively engaged with PSFS, which was strategically working on community projects and public welfare, to the extent that he was offered its presidency in September 1968, a frankly stated attempt by the PSFS board to keep him in the Philadelphia area rather than have him depart for New York. But he turned down that offer, not only because it would have meant reneging on his commitment to the Markle Foundation, but also because he knew that PSFS's central activity, banking, would not hold his interest in the long run.[22]

In the fall of 1968, after announcing his intended departure, he returned his attention to leading Swarthmore College. He spoke to the incoming freshmen about the differences of opinions that the students would find on campus, the attempts to seek the good in each person, the sense of community within the college, and the college's instinct to utilize and appeal to Quaker values in times of crisis. Then at the first Collection President Smith, who was very aware of unrest and disruption on other campuses, encouraged the entire student body to utilize the CEP recommendations. He reminded the community that the college through the CEP process of analysis and discussion already had begun to move toward more flexibility in decision making, and he emphasized that the college had not been and would not need to be shaped by demands.[23]

One of the more pressing issues that Courtney foresaw calling for future discussion and flexibility was a review of the Swarthmore admissions program for Negro students. The college had to prepare a report on the program in order to apply for an extension of its Rockefeller Foundation grant providing scholarships for minority students, and Frederick Hargadon, the dean of admissions and author of the report, also took the opportunity to take what he called a "hard nosed" look at evidence of the program's results in order to consider how to develop a more effective minority admissions program in the future.[24] Because the black students on campus—almost all of whom had come to Swarthmore through the program—had been asked by Courtney to give their views on the black admissions process, the report was distributed to each of them, as well as to the Admissions Policy Committee.[25] Early in October the committee endorsed Hargadon's report as providing valuable data and statistics for its fall deliberations on the subject and decided to make the report available to the whole college community by placing copies of it in the college library.

The reaction of the majority of black students to public access to the report, as represented by the membership of the Swarthmore Afro-American Students Society (SASS), was negative.[26] At two places in the report Hargadon accused SASS of making the work of the admissions office more difficult by promoting a separatist ethic among the black students, creating "a deterrent to attracting some Negro students to enroll here." He also remarked that the "militant separatism of many of the Negro students" made them opposed to any interracial dating, a stance which he thought decidedly limited the social possibilities for the small number of black students.[27]

At a meeting of the Admissions Policy Committee on October 14, to which all black students were invited, a SASS spokesman declared the organization's outrage at the tone of the report and according to a member of the committee made "a direct personal attack on Dean Hargadon." After the statement most of the black students left the meeting, refusing to further contribute to the discussion. The committee reiterated its endorsement of the report as a factual basis for the discussion but agreed to remove the report from the library because SASS had argued that the report's statistical tables (which looked at such variables as family incomes, parents' occupations, and student grades) dealt with such a small sample that personal data for particular students could be identified.[28] SASS then issued a set of demands as preconditions for further cooperation with the Admissions Policy Committee, including that the Hargadon report be rewritten jointly by SASS and the committee; that the college form a Black Interests Committee to "insure that Swarthmore in the future will be sensitive to the interests of Black people"; that the college "actively recruit, subject to our [SASS's] review, a high-level Black administrator"; and that SASS work directly with Hargadon and the committee to develop a new strategy for recruiting black students.[29]

This confrontational situation was the opposite of what Smith had hoped would be the tenor of campus life in the fall of 1968. In an essay published in the October 1968 issue of the *Swarthmore College Bulletin* (revised from remarks made on Alumni Day in June) Smith had expressed unqualified enthusiasm for the college's "intensive as well as comprehensive" self-study of the past two years and emphasized its participatory character. He praised the students' commitment to the so-called Super-week of the past December when "there were meetings of students in dormitory sections, and joint sessions of men's and women's dormitory sections; meetings of department majors, and of majors with faculty members in their departments; and there were panel discussions with students, faculty members, and administrators participating." He noted that "no one was required to stay on campus during this week, but almost no one left."

Smith went on to describe how the *Critique of a College* was successfully reviewed by "four discussion groups of faculty members, administrators, and students," the latter chosen partly by the student body and partly by Smith; and then was considered, recommendation by recommendation, by the faculty and the Board of Managers. Smith was gratified to report that by October all of the recommendations of the CEP and the Special Committee on Library Policy had been acted on. He described the results as providing greatly increased flexibility in the curriculum, with opportunities for individuality and diversity yet the possibility of depth. In the honors program there would be "less high-class prepping, [and] more tough inquiry." In the sciences "more opportunities will be provided for independent, research-oriented laboratory work . . . encouraging as much self-education as [students] can handle." The freshman year would be made less oppressive by recording all final grades as "pass or fail," even though grades would be given during the semester for papers and exams. Smith concluded that "we are moving as quickly as possible to implement our new program, and the spirit of the undertaking has so infected us that already much that can be put into effect by departments is under way."

Smith observed, however, that "the report of the Special Committee on Student Life still lies ahead of us" and would be considered in the 1968–69 academic year by a regular organ of campus government, the Student Affairs Committee, which would be augmented for this occasion by six additional faculty members and by twelve students appointed by the Student Council. Smith concluded that "the question of the College's responsibilities beyond providing an academic program will, therefore, have to be our first order of business in the fall."[30]

Unfortunately, the deliberative process that Smith expected to characterize the year was overwhelmed by the unexpected conflict that began over the Hargadon report. The conflict was based in part on the beginning of full-fledged participation in the affairs of the college community by the black students and by SASS, the body that represented the majority of them. Never before had an ethnic or cultural group at Swarthmore demanded to have a continuing and independent voice in the campus polity—a stance in obvious conflict with the college's traditional consensus-seeking style, a style to which Smith was committed.

The African-American students had brought to Swarthmore a different view of American life and culture than the typical Swarthmore student, even if the black students themselves were largely from the same privileged, largely middle-class backgrounds of most other students. The entering African-American students came to Swarthmore in the aftermath of the rising expectations of the Civil Rights movement and knew the dissonance of racism in American culture first-hand. Many found that they could not, or out of conscience would not, casually meld with the white academic elite culture that Swarthmore represented. Like fellow African-American students at institutions such as Vassar, Penn, Princeton, and Berkeley, they felt compelled to organize in order to put forward such issues as the creation of black studies courses and programs, promotion of black admissions, and the founding of institutions that would nurture black culture. The rapidity by which these issues changed from requests and proposals to demands was to some degree a product of the heightened black militancy throughout the United States in the late 1960s, but in historical hindsight this change in approach seems largely a reaction to the black students' finding that their initial claims for self-actualization were met with indifference or incomprehension.[31] Certainly most white Americans, including those who were in charge of higher education, and many of whom were descended from ethnic groups that had substantially blended with American culture, found it difficult to understand the point of view of those whose American-ness always had been shaped by the continuous experiences of racism.

It is clear that Smith and others in his administration had believed that almost all of the black students who came to Swarthmore through the Rockefeller scholarships could be assimilated into the student body without any programmatic efforts, and Smith believed personally that the black students did not want to be identified as "special."[32] But it was becoming apparent that what the majority of the black students wanted instead was recognition and self-identity while remaining an integral part of the college community, a condition more difficult to achieve. The process of working out this new relationship was complicated by the mood and style of the black students: as one inside observer put it, "Swarthmore's black students were lonely and angry . . . lonely because there were fewer than fifty of them in a white student body of a thousand . . . and angry because anger was the uniform of the time."[33]

To Smith—and to virtually every other administrator at the time—the situation was unique and almost intractable. He responded to SASS's demands regarding the Hargadon report by maintaining his faith in the usual machinery of the college bureaucracy, a machinery whose workings were currently questioned by both students and faculty, but which appeared to be working smoothly in the area of producing a black studies curriculum.[34] Smith left revision of the Hargadon report and development of new ways to recruit black students to the Admissions Policy Committee, and on December 18 it produced a new report with eight recommendations. These focused on finding ways to increase black enrollment at the college, including admitting so-called risk students (who "fall just below our normal admissions standards") and improving the college's response "to those particular needs, both academic and social, deemed to be uniquely theirs by the Negro students already enrolled in the College."[35]

But this report, labored over for two months, continued to express the style that blocked communication between the Admissions Policy Committee, the dean of admissions and SASS. Most obviously, it continued to use the term "negro," a term acceptable to social scientists such as Hargadon, who regularly taught a political science course, at a time when "black" was in vogue and already had been used as the preferred term in the title and report of the Black Studies Committee.[36] The admissions report completely avoided any reference to SASS's demands and actions and made only one oblique reference to SASS as one of the organizations on campus that should be consulted in order to identify "those 'felt needs' deemed by Negro students to be uniquely theirs."[37] The dean of admissions certainly believed that SASS had forfeited its consultative role by (in his view) refusing to engage in productive dialogue, but his report also demonstrated that he, and the Admissions Policy Committee that he chaired, accorded little respect to SASS and its views.[38]

SASS now decided that it had to force the issue on the admissions policy. During the college's Christmas break SASS's president, Clinton Etheridge, presented Smith a series of revised demands regarding Swarthmore's commitment to blacks, including enhanced recruiting of both regular and risk students, an overall increase in the number of black students admitted, the creation of support programs for black students, and the hiring of an African American as assistant dean of admissions for minority students, "subject to consultation with SASS." The dean of admissions also stood accused of "undermining the integrity of SASS and black students on this campus" by his public statements, and SASS demanded his removal from office. The entire document was framed by the arresting declaration that "if you fail to issue a clear, unequivocal public acceptance of these non-negotiable demands by noon, Tuesday, January 7, 1969, the Black students and SASS will be forced to do whatever is necessary to obtain acceptance of same."[39] Anyone who read that immediately recognized it as a threat to take some kind of "direct action" of the type that at the moment was quite visible on American campuses: in October 1968 radicals at the Berkeley campus of the University of California had seized a building to protest the low rate of black admissions there, and in November 1968 black students at San Francisco State College had led first the student body, and then the faculty, to strike in support of their demands.[40]

Smith immediately called Etheridge and asked him to return to campus to meet to discuss the letter, but Etheridge refused to do so without other members of SASS present. Smith then agreed to set a meeting on the morning of January 6, the day all students returned to campus, but told Etheridge that in the meantime he would distribute SASS's letter, as well as his own comments on it, to all members of the college community. On December 31 he did so.

In addition to summarizing the actions of the college and SASS regarding black admissions policy in the last three months, Smith stated firmly to all that "this college has never and must never be governed by demands or moved by threats." He also pointed out that "the President does not have the authority to act alone on basic policy matters," and that he therefore would not act in the unilateral fashion that the demands assumed. Smith announced that the SASS demands would form "the first order of business" at the faculty meeting on the afternoon of January 7, and at the same time he asked SASS "to recast their letter and accompanying document in the form of proposals which can be discussed by all students and go to the Faculty and Board of Managers for full and unprejudiced consideration, along with the report of the Admissions Policy Committee."[41]

Smith knew that tensions were high as the students and faculty reassembled for the last few days of the first semester on January 6. Smith and Gilmore Stott, his assistant, met with fifteen members of SASS that morning, and Smith expressed "his strong personal hope for an increase in the number of black students and faculty members and administrators at the college, the need to create a viable healthy black student population, and the nature of his belief in the importance of self-definition." The SASS representatives repeated their demands, "insisting that President Smith make a strong statement to the Faculty calling for the College to accept and implement SASS's demands." Essentially the two parties had reiterated their existing positions.[42] That same day Smith went to a meeting of the new Council on Educational Policy, which was to take up the Black Studies Curriculum Committee's proposals; but Smith instead reported on the impasse with SASS. The council, which was composed of students, faculty, and administrators, "expressed sympathy for the sense of urgency felt by SASS and recognized the need to deal with the problems of black admissions as quickly as is consistent with democratic and rational methods." Smith concluded by speaking broadly of "the responsibility of academic institutions to provide a model for rational decision-making," and said that "he could not in conscience do what SASS demanded of him—recommend that the faculty act only on the SASS demands."[43]

The faculty in its meeting of January 7 did not take specific action on the demands, but did adopt them as its agenda for framing its discussion in later meetings and passed a resolution (based on one it had received from the Student Council) stating that "We favor a substantial increase in the number of black students. We favor immediate interim steps to increase the number of black students. We favor immediate interim steps to increase the number of black students in the class of 1973 (including the admission of 'risk' students). We recognize the need for a more viable life for black students here (including the appointment of black administrators and counselors)."[44] The faculty also invited the membership of SASS to its next meeting, or to meet at any time SASS would designate.

The Student Council responded by thanking the faculty for its actions but used the term "crisis" to describe the situation for the first time. It also upped the ante by contending that it was "equally imperative" that there be "immediate implementation" of the "SASS demand which calls for student participation—particularly black student participation—in the decision-making process."[45] Thus the issue of student power in general became intertwined, as it had become on other campuses, with the issue of black student power.[46]

SASS in the meantime issued a hastily prepared three-page commentary on race relations at Swarthmore which pointed out that no blacks had been allowed at the college until the 1940s, and which argued that the college now suffered from a "white liberal mind set on race relations." In a rambling but passionate argument, SASS called for the college to overcome the underlying racism of American society and to "advance racial equality," concluding that "we hope that President Smith and Swarthmore College will not turn their backs on the greater [sic] crisis of this century."[47]

On January 8 SASS staged a demonstration on the plaza in front of the dining hall in order to inform students of their grievances. That evening a group of students went to the home of Robert Barr, dean of men, and told him that "some direct action was being considered and they believed it would be for Thursday [the next day]."[48]

In its view having exhausted all approaches and having justified its position, just after noon on January 9 SASS began a sit-in in the Admissions Office in Parrish Hall. Entering the office in the lunch hour, they asked the remaining staff to leave, covered the windows, and chained all of the doors. They issued a statement that they had "suspended the customary admissions process of Swarthmore College. This decision-making process has persistently denied black people basic self-representation and must now be drastically changed to reflect a participatory democracy." SASS also expanded its demands to require that the college make public "a complete identification and description of [its] decision-making organs . . . on every level," and that blacks be part of the process at each level. And in a demand similar to those of other student actions of the 1960s, SASS demanded that "no disciplinary action whatsoever be taken against black people, both students and employees, who have participated in this direct action."[49]

SASS held a press conference in the Commons Room of Parrish Hall on the same day, read its statement, and answered a few questions. After SASS completed its remarks, the floor was taken by representatives of the student council, who urged that the student body give full consideration to SASS's demands. A majority of the student body responded by convening that evening in Clothier Hall: they voted to endorse the SASS demands as proposals to be considered by the faculty, and to ask the faculty to postpone the impending end-of-semester examinations for two days so that the student body could give further consideration to the current crisis.[50] The SASS demands thus had commanded the attention of one of the college's constituencies.

In response to these developments Smith, as chair of the faculty, called it into almost daily sessions to consider both SASS's demands and college policies, and the faculty began to enact a series of recommendations and resolutions regarding minority admissions. The bulk of the white students continued to convene mass meetings to hear reports and presentations from both the faculty and SASS, and to formulate their own resolutions of support, compromise, and agreement. Campus routines had been displaced by "the crisis."

Suddenly Swarthmore and its president were in the public eye and the press was on campus daily. Philadelphia press coverage was generally unsympathetic to what were immediately labeled "militants—members of the Swarthmore Afro-American Students Society." A nationally syndicated column by Drew Pearson, a Swarthmore alumnus, described SASS's action as radical and conspiratorial at worst and as completely misguided at best.[51] The president's office began receiving a deluge of letters from alumni, many of whom expressed support for the college whatever the current problems, but others demonstrated resentment of SASS's action and attitudes: typical of the latter was the comment of a prominent figure who called SASS members "ingrates" who did not appreciate "the traditional friendliness of the Quakers to colored people."[52] Another wrote to say "as a Friend, I believe in compromise—but not this time."[53] Smith was thus made aware that he would have to respond to the outrage and dismay of a substantial number of alumni.

In this whirlwind Smith made few public statements except to plead for calm, orderly debate and the adherence to the Quakerly behavior of mutual respect and careful deliberation that he had advocated throughout his presidency. He was neither attacked nor maligned by any of the parties, and it appears that appreciation of his qualities grew in some quarters.[54] Within the college community Smith remained firmly in charge, rejecting any plan for outside police action to force an end to the sit-in, even though two members of the college administration approached Swarthmore borough and state police to discuss what action could be taken if the college called for it.[55] At the same time Smith refused to negotiate with SASS on the basis of "demands"; but he did make it clear that he thought SASS's general concerns were legitimate and could be reviewed and acted on with deliberate speed.

The strain on Smith of managing the demands and expectations of contentious college constituencies was substantial. The depth of his personal distress was clear when he spoke to the faculty and students assembled in Clothier Hall during the afternoon of Monday, January 13, at a point when he believed that the cumulative actions of the faculty had framed a comprehensive response to SASS's demands. Smith lamented that "we have lost something precious at Swarthmore—the feeling that force and disruptiveness are just not our way," and expressed his hope that "maybe we can see to it that this one time is only the exception that proves the rule."[56] Noting that he had chaired faculty meetings every day for the last five days, and for more than fourteen hours the previous day, he told the assembly that he believed that "our entire College community [has considered] conscientiously and imaginatively the best way to achieve what I believed to be the underlying concerns of SASS." The student body rose and applauded his remarks.[57]

By the evening of January 13, however, it became clear that Smith's hope for agreement was a chimera because although SASS regarded some of the faculty's actions as acceptable responses to its demands, it refused to accept all of them. SASS was particularly insistent that two new bodies that would have black representatives, a Black Interests Committee and the Ad Hoc Black Admissions Committee, have the authority to act on their own, and not be simply advisory.[58] Smith was forced once again to call for "clarification from SASS of its position."

On January 14 he asked several faculty members to meet with SASS and intended to call a meeting of the faculty "as soon as this Committee is satisfied that it fully understands SASS's position."[59] That day and January 15 the faculty committee met with SASS and hammered out clarifications of the faculty actions that were acceptable to both parties and which were to be presented to the faculty for agreement on January 16.[60] Smith in the meantime tended to some Markle Foundation business and sent his regrets to Wheaton College that he could not attend his first trustees' meeting a few days away.[61] About this time he stopped to talk with Nancy Bekavac, a senior and recognized student leader, who asked him how he was coping with the situation. He told her that he thought of the Anglo-Saxon poem "The Seafarer," about a sailor "with the waves breaking over him, who still insists that's where he wants to be."[62]

On the morning of January 16, 1969, at about 9 a.m., after walking to his office from the president's house, President Smith felt sick, and he asked his secretary to call the college physician, Morris A. Bowie, who happened to be at the Worth Health Center on campus rather than at his office in Bryn Mawr.[63] Bowie arrived at the president's office at 9:42 a.m. As Bowie was conducting an examination Smith slumped forward unconscious in his chair and two minutes later stopped breathing. Artificial respiration failed, and Bowie pronounced Courtney C. Smith dead at 9:58 a.m. A postmortem examination conducted the same day but never made public showed that his heart had suffered a hemorrhage of the right coronary artery, and that he had "severe artherosclerosis of both coronary arteries . . . the calibre of both coronary arteries was considerably reduced in diameter so that only a small probe could be put through them."[64] Unknown to all, and least of all to himself, Smith had been living with serious heart disease for some time.

Smith's death was announced to the college community at a hastily called all-college convocation in Clothier Hall at 11 a.m. Afterward the student body stumbled out of the auditorium into a sunny, unusually mild winter day, and "instinctively several hundred of them gathered on the lawn of Parrish Hall, standing in silent vigil. As the group dispersed, some remained sitting on the cold lawn."[65] In the afternoon SASS chose to end its sit-in, releasing at the same time a statement that "we sincerely believe that the death of any human being, whether he be the good President of a college or a black person trapped in our country's ghettoes, is a tragedy." The student council president, Ellen Schall, issued a press release that called "for sorrow, not for bitterness" as the college mourned. The faculty's memorial resolution described him as a man who "gave himself unsparingly to the defense of reason in a time of passion."[66]

Personal reactions to Smith's death often were powerful and poignant. Professor Peter van de Kamp, the college's internationally known astronomer, expressed outrage. One student heard him exclaim repeatedly, "they killed him."[67] Two weeks later, while showing some of his personal collection of silent-film comedies (known affectionately by the students as "Chaplin seminars"), van de Kamp read a polemic in which he emphasized that "any student, or group of students, or any faculty member, or others who issue demands, or carry out, support, or condone any action which interferes with the functioning of the College do not belong here. They were admitted to, or joined, Swarthmore, but obviously do not understand the spirit and meaning of Swarthmore."[68] The *New York Times,* commenting on recent campus upheavals, editorialized that "the death of Dr. Courtney C. Smith, in the face of disruptive action by a small group clamoring for more black power, appallingly underscores the price extorted by these policies of excess."[69] Claudio Spies of the music department dedicated a performance of one of his compositions at Carnegie Hall to the fallen president.[70] Some alumni expressed the opinion that Smith was "a martyr to the cause of peace between the races," and others thought he was the victim of what one writer called "savage killers in action."[71] One senior student expressed the opinion that "we all must have a small sensation of guilt," and another student said simply "it's like I lost a good friend."[72]

At the campus's Quaker-style memorial service on January 20 Smith was eulogized by his colleagues and friends.[73] The chair of the board of managers, Robert Browning, called Smith's death "untimely and unnecessary" and said that "he did more for us here at Swarthmore than we could ever do for ourselves. He was a man dedicated to excellence and insisted on achievement." Professor of political science Roland Pennock, who had been a confidant of Smith throughout his administration, described him as "a man who hungered after righteousness" and "who never knew bitterness or hatred."[74] After the memorial service Smith's ashes were taken to the cemetery in Winterset, Iowa, his birthplace, and interred there on April 23.[75]

The college as a community recovered its routines rather quickly after the events of January, but a fundamental change had occurred in the college's self-perception. The board of managers appointed Vice President Cratsley (who had served as chief administrator during Smith's 1965–66 sabbatical) the acting president. He called for all parties to make a commitment to "communication and understanding" and announced that the college would soon undertake the "analytical and evaluative examination of our structure, communications, and decision making arrangements" that SASS had called for and the faculty had agreed to.[76] Dean Susan Cobbs spoke for many when she remarked pessimistically that "we used to think that we could talk our way through any crisis; now we realize we've failed."[77] In truth the college slowly began to find a means of decision making that stood between its former tradition of consensus seeking through dialogue and the power sharing required to reconcile the sometimes incongruent interests of groups with differing self-identities.

In the spring of 1969 some of the cause of the winter's tension was relieved when the college announced that the upcoming freshman class would have thirty-one blacks, exceeding the goal set by both SASS and the faculty. Later the presidential nominating committee (which had been at work since the fall after Smith announced his resignation) agreed on a new president-elect—former Swarthmore history professor Robert Cross, a choice that seemed to indicate that the college would experience continuity rather than a dramatic change of direction. Cross led the college into its first years of what he soon began to call "a multiracial institution."[78]

# Conclusion

THE SUDDEN AND SEEMINGLY PREMATURE END OF COURTNEY SMITH'S life—a life so full of accomplishment and promising yet more—makes a full assessment of him both necessary and difficult. The circumstances and meaning of the ending have carried so much weight that appreciation of the rest of his life has been diminished. Yet the foregoing study shows both how rich, varied, and significant Smith's life and career were, and that he struck a path through nearly two decades of academic leadership that we would do well to consider and emulate.

Courtney Smith was a leading member of the higher education elite of the 1950s and 1960s, a generation that was in one context called "the best and the brightest" of the cold war era.[1] Smith's training and experience—degrees from Harvard, a Phi Beta Kappa key, a year at Oxford, military experience, some seasoning in the professorate, and foundation or other nonprofit connections—were those that marked and propelled many into leadership of academic and governmental institutions at midcentury. James A. Perkins, for example, a former vice president of Swarthmore College, had a career with strong parallels to Smith's.[2] When John F. Kennedy was assembling his cabinet, Perkins (who was then an officer of two Carnegie philanthropies) came up so often in discussions that Kennedy is reported to have said, "Who the hell is this Perkins?"[3]

Smith escaped being on everyone's "A list," as Perkins was, because in a subtle but critical way, he chose to swim against the tide by not just taking the presidency of Swarthmore, but also by taking it on, essentially, as his life's work. By choosing to meld his career with a small, historically pacifist institution, passionately committed to liberal education and with a tradition of political activism, Smith unfitted himself for any post of major significance. He had come of age professionally in the post–World War II era, when the nation was increasingly dedicated to the creation of what Eisenhower called the "industrial-military complex," and in education dedicated to the notion of the "multiversity," an institution focused on research and postgraduate programs.[4] If the presidency of Swarthmore was prestigious and vested with a certain moral authority, clearly in the 1950s and 1960s it did not have the attributes of a stepping-stone to power.

Arguably, nonetheless, the sum of Smith's years at Swarthmore yields a quite considerable legacy for the history of American education, and for American history generally. There are two areas of his life and career, personal values and leadership, which stand particular examination, both for a better understanding of his times, and—because of the timeless need to reflect on lives that seem well-lived—for a better understanding of our own.

Smith deeply influenced Swarthmore College by sustaining three central values throughout his presidency: a commitment to egalitarian discourse in every aspect of the college's life; a belief that the selection and production of an intellectual elite is important for the preservation and furtherance of culture; and a personal faith in the dignity of each human being that he conveyed to everyone, even those who opposed him. Moreover, Smith saw discourse as the shared value that bound together the students, faculty, and administration. He thought that humane, measured, searching interchange in the classroom was a means to understanding; outside of the classroom he thought it to be the basis for civics and cultural criticism.

Smith deplored the limits to personal expression when he encountered virulent racism in the navy; he spoke up against the dampening effect of McCarthyism in American politics and education in the early 1950s; and he was appalled by the excesses of campus radicals in the 1960s. In each case he believed that either restoration or implementation of thoughtful dialogue would fruitfully bring ideas to bear on problems. He favored passionate argument but believed that each party to a debate had to be open, in the Quaker fashion, to the rays of light that emanated from truth. For Smith, intellectual blindness was the fundamental sin that divided those who were truly students, educators, or leaders from those who merely professed to be.

More positively, Smith understood egalitarian dialogue, as epitomized in the liberal arts tradition, to play a role well beyond higher education: he thought it was a crucial underpinning of modern democratic society.[5] His doctorate in seventeenth-century English literature must have made him aware of the centrality of public discourse to the awakening of democratic ideals,[6] and he never wavered from a view that citizenship requires engagement with the moving issues of the times. Smith's understanding resonates with the approach of recent scholars who regard citizens' commitment to activity in organizations dedicated to the commonweal as the difference between a society that sustains a democratic polity and one that does not.[7] Smith would have agreed with the recent argument that "through its role in fostering social mobility and the belief in a society open to talents, American higher education legitimates the social and political system, and thus is a central element in the society as it is nowhere else."[8]

Still, although a firm believer in political democracy, Smith was unabashedly elitist in his understanding of how the proper moral and intellectual leadership of modern society is created. He believed that natural processes in an egalitarian society led inexorably to the identification of young men and women whose intelligence and character made them fit to be trained for leadership. That training should be composed of the strongest possible challenge to each person's ability to investigate, create, express, and defend ideas—not just to absorb and recite them. In addition, he wanted learning to take place in an environment where personal commitment to the improvement of society was held out as an ideal, but was at the same time a potential reality; one's ideals had to have sufficient grasp of the practical and the concrete so that they could be acted on. Smith thought that if one did not come to grips with the realities of life, intellectual pursuits could be exciting and absorbing but were ultimately of little value to the building of individual character.

It was in fact character, which led to a sense of self-worth and the reinforcement of essential human dignity, that Courtney Smith searched for in every personal encounter. He always identified his encounter with a person's authenticity and strength of internal values as central to his assessment of each individual, whether conducting interviews with disgruntled African-American sailors at Pensacola, meeting potential professorial appointees at Swarthmore, or making speeches. Perhaps it was his fatal flaw that he wanted a Swarthmore education to promote, or strengthen, character and send forth people into the world that, in ofttimes quiet but sometimes in public ways, stood for human dignity.

Certainly just the normal travails of any twentieth-century college president would try this set of values, but it was Courtney Smith's fate to attempt to sustain them through the turbulence of the latter 1960s. It was there that his qualities of leadership—sustaining his values as guideposts while leading a conglomerate of staff, students, faculty, trustees, and alumni through the storm—were severely tested and proved equal to the task. Largely because of Smith's leadership, manifested in both his actions and his style, Swarthmore escaped the damaging disruptions experienced at so many leading American institutions of higher education. Faced with the severest test, his response was self-sacrificial, a word that may be used in this case without any appeal to metaphor.

Smith's style of leadership was based on a strong belief in himself, a quality that was visible as early as his high-school years in Iowa, and which some of those who knew him later thought bordered on arrogance. Coupling this self-confidence to an ability to articulate a vision of institutional growth and direction that others could grasp and to a reservoir of drive and ambition, Smith was a formidable leader. He was able to rally others to his causes but would stand alone or for unpopular ones when necessary. He understood his constituencies (from his Harvard and Rhodes networks to the Swarthmore alumni to the ever-changing campus milieu) and seldom failed to stir their loyalty when he needed it. Whatever personal criticisms may have been leveled against him—certainly his strong beliefs and his classically intellectual conversational style made some people dislike him—the historical record reveals an exceedingly high level of support for him as a president and leader.

We can better evaluate Smith by comparison of his actions and leadership in his last years at Swarthmore with other presidencies and institutions during upheavals that occurred elsewhere in the latter 1960s. In the wake of the growing body of historical criticisms of many others who were academic leaders in that time it seems possible to make this judgment without looking through either elegiac or rose-colored glasses. In particular, recent critics seem to have focused on three elements of academic leadership in the 1960s that shaped the effectiveness of responses to the problems on campus: density of communication within the institution; top-down understanding of the issues involved; and ability to recur to a sense of educational mission that overrides particularities.[9]

The positive effect of a high density of communication was apparent at the University of Michigan, for example. Despite a well-organized body of radical activists there, serious disruptions were avoided because of strong channels of communication between all the parties involved. Intimacy of student-faculty relationships, fostered by faculty using their homes for seminars and advisers' meetings and reinforced by students living in the same small city as the administration and faculty seemed to be the key ingredient. In contrast, San Francisco State College came near to complete disintegration because the students and faculty had little relationship outside of the classroom. There were few channels for defusing escalating tensions because there had been little basis for establishing personal trust between various strata of the institution.[10]

At Swarthmore there was a tradition, already in place when Smith arrived, of close student-faculty-administration relationships. Almost all classes were small, many were held in professors' homes, and several administrators taught at least one class a year: these dynamics enabled people at different points in the social structure to know that they had contacts at various points across the institution. Smith, who placed a high value on dialogue and community, strongly supported the continued development of interrelationships among the staff and faculty. He personally interviewed all candidates for positions, seeking to hire staff who would fit into the close-knit Swarthmore community. He maintained personal contact with a fairly broad spectrum of existing faculty, including both senior and middle-range professors, and he personally chaired all of the faculty meetings. While Smith did not have a reputation for casual comraderie, he certainly was known to take seriously anyone who broached an important subject with him, and faculty knew he would be supportive of them.

While overseeing all facets of the college, Smith typically maintained a certain distance from students. But from the beginning of his presidency he established relationships with student leaders and attended a range of extracurricular activities. He respected student involvement in governance, early on defending student participation in admissions committees, and when something seemed to veer out of control, such as the Folk Festival, he found a way to take charge without crushing student authority. Toward the end of his tenure he established office hours, patiently listening to complaints, dreams, ideas, and arguments, trying to better understand the motivations of the revolution in student lifestyle and attitudes.

Thus Smith and others in his administration, such as Deans Barr and Stott and Vice President Shane, had reputations for sympathy with student concerns, even if they did not agree with them; and many of the faculty were deeply involved with organizations and activities that students also were committed to, from political action to social action. This top-down understanding of student interests meant that there was a built-in constituency in the faculty and administration that gave some credence to even the wildest claims or demands of students. Access to the administration was possible. When the Swarthmore African-American Students Society's "non-negotiable demands" were put on the table in the fall of 1968, they were neither rejected nor belittled, even by those like Smith who were appalled by the tactic. Similarly, while SASS and many students were exasperated by the pace and style of academic dialogue as practiced by their elders, the generality of the student body never got to the point of feeling that "the system" at the college was totally unresponsive or impenetrable.

Equally important was that Smith's high regard by the campus community was based significantly on his consistent and regular articulation of the college's mission. To every audience he made his point that the college was pursuing excellence in education by bringing together an elite body of students and faculty in an environment that fostered personal self-examination, academic challenge, and expectations of a future life well-lived. In his personal life he exemplified the same expectations that he had of the college: he stood up for his beliefs and Swarthmore's traditions in various political and other venues, and he encouraged and supported student and faculty commitments to lives of meaning through professional development and social action. In all circumstances, even extreme ones, Smith's administrative style and personal history gave him respect.

Epilogue

On a Saturday evening in October 1999, in a Presbyterian church in Greenwich, Connecticut, an enthusiastic and diverse audience that included several prospective Swarthmore College freshmen as well as a number of alumni heard a spiritually uplifting and musically spellbinding concert by the Swarthmore College Alumni Gospel Choir. The twenty-two member choir represented thirty-five years of the college's history, in a concrete way recapitulating the years since that first significant cohort of African-American students had walked into Swarthmore's classrooms and dormitories in 1964.

The event that night in Greenwich in many ways would have been familiar to Courtney C. Smith. Had he been in the audience (at age eighty-two) he probably would have recalled his World War II service as a race-relations officer and might have reflected on the evidence of a half-century of change represented by staging a celebration of African-American spirituality in a prestigious white suburb. At the same time, he surely would have understood the reference to a continuing racial divide when a visiting African-American Baptist minister concluded the evening by remarking that the occasion was an extraordinary collaborative effort between white and African-American institutions.

But Courtney Smith probably would have focused primarily on the choir of African-American alumni, gathered from a range of professions and Atlantic seaboard cities and giving a virtuoso performance after only a few hours of practice together. He would have been secretly pleased to read a notice in the evening's program that a national magazine recently had ranked Swarthmore as the best liberal arts college in the United States. And he would have had no difficulty with the program's accompanying description of the college as a place where "challenge to dogma, independence, tolerance for dissent, and an inquisitive intensity are cultivated. Free expression is highly valued, and there is room to be wrong or right as long as the intention is serious. Those who teach and those who learn share a common purpose."

Courtney Smith would have been proud that in the view of those alumni the legacy that he had tried to preserve at Swarthmore lives on.

# Interviews Conducted by the Authors

We thank the following persons for their time and comments for this Courtney C. Smith biography, and for permission to cite their remarks. We were able to arrange personal interviews with most of them; those names are found in bold print. Others listed were equally generous with their time and spoke to us at length by telephone. Given the age of Smith's peers at the time of the interviews, several of those interviewed are since deceased.

By permission of the interviewees, most of the interviews were recorded on audio tape, and some were transcribed fully or in part. The remainder of the interviews are preserved in the notes of the authors. All interview records are in the possession of the authors.

Family:

**Ingram, Elizabeth (Lee) Smith—daughter—March 8, 1991, April 2, 1995**

**Smith, C. Craig, Jr.—son—February 12, 1993**

**Van Syoc, Florence Smith—sister—December 23, 1991**

Harvard:

**Lasker, Morris—class of 1938—October 15, 1994**

Mayne, Wiley—class of 1938—April 4, 1996

**Murphy, William M. (and Harriet Murphy)—class of 1938— October 22, 1994**

Sorlien, Robert Parker—class of 1938—September 14, 1994

Strider, Robert E. L., II—class of 1939—July 14, 1999

Rhodes Scholar Associates:

Hector, Louis—class of 1938—January 13, 1994, January 28, 1994

**Hester, James M.—administrative staff—January 16, 1995**

Stahr, Elvis J., Jr.—class of 1936—January 16, 1995

**Stott, Gilmore—administrative staff—February 10, 1996**

**Weismiller, Edward R.—class of 1938—November 11, 1994**

195

Princeton Colleagues:

Goheen, Robert F.—Woodrow Wilson Fellowship Program successor to CCS—October 11, 1994

Ludwig, Richard—faculty—April 14, 1996

Perkins, James A.—faculty—September 27, 1994

Swarthmore Contemporaries:

**Avery, George—faculty—August 6, 1991**

**Barnard, Boyd—class of 1917, Board of Managers—November 16, 1991**

**Barr, Robert—administrative staff—May 7, 1993**

**Browning, Robert M.,—Board of Managers, 1958–74, chair, 1966–71—October 31, 1999,** November 29, 1999

**Clarke, Eleanor S.—Board of Managers—May 10, 1991**

**Cross, Robert (and Ruth Cunningham Brown)—faculty and succeeding president—November 12, 1994**

**Dukakis, Michael—student, class of 1955—October 9, 1994**

**Field, James—faculty—April 30, 1993**

**Gifford, Prosser—administrative staff—May 3, 1989, November 11, 1994**

**Gilbert, Charles E.—faculty and administrative staff—February 10, 1996**

**Graves, Michael and Cheryl Browne Graves—students, class of 1969—May 27, 1999**

Hoy, John C.—Dean of Admissions, 1962–64—February 11, 1999

**Hynes, Samuel L.—faculty—May 7, 1994**

**Legesse, Asmaron—faculty—July 24, 1993**

**Moore, John (and Margaret Moore)—administrative staff—November 16, 1991**

**Pagliaro, Harold—faculty—August 9, 1991**

**Peele, Paul E.—student, class of 1969—October 10, 1994**

**Pennock, J. Roland—faculty—February 21, 1992**

**Rakoff, Jed S.—student, class of 1963—March 12, 1993**

**Shane, Mrs. Joseph (Terry)—spouse of administrative staff—August 6, 1991**

**Smith, David—faculty—August 7, 1991**

**Stone, Jeremy J. (and B. J. Stone)—students, class of 1957—January 15, 1995**

**Stott, Gilmore—administrative staff—February 10, 1996**

**Wright, Harrison M.—faculty—May 8, 1993**

Others:

Endicott, Bradford M.—tutee of Courtney C. Smith—September 17, 1997

**Hayden, Nancy Smith—daughter of Claude C. Smith, chairman of the Board of Managers, 1952–66—April 5, 1997**

Kerr, Clark—Swarthmore College Board of Managers; university administrator—August 28, 1995

McCabe, James—son of Thomas McCabe, member of Swarthmore Board of Managers; family friend—September 12, 1995

**Nason, John W. (and Elizabeth M. K. Nason)—preceding Swarthmore College president—February 20, 1992**

Pusey, Nathan—Harvard University president—November 9, 1995

**Rockefeller, David—Harvard University Board of Overseers—December 4, 1992**

**Smith, Richard—son of Claude C. Smith, chairman of the Board of Managers, 1952–66—April 5, 1997**

# Notes

## Abbreviations

CCS personal papers      Courtney C. Smith Personal Papers, in possession of Elizabeth Smith Ingram, Chevy Chase, Maryland.

CCS presidential papers      Courtney C. Smith Presidential Papers, Friends Historical Library, Swarthmore, Pennsylvania.

## Chapter 1. Childhood

1. Federal Writers' Project, *Iowa: A Guide to the Hawkeye State* (New York: Viking Press, 1938), pp. 26–31, 41–60, 65–83, 228.

2. In addition to other sources on Smith family history, the authors are grateful to Elizabeth Smith Ingram for providing them a transcript of an interview with Courtney C. Smith's sister, Florence Smith Van Syoc: "Oral History of the Samuel Craig Smith/Myrtle Dabney Smith Family," typescript dated October 6, 1990 (hereafter "Oral History").

3. "Madison County, Iowa, at a Glance," *Time,* June 12, 1995, p. 19.

4. W. S. Cooper to CCS, January 14, 1939, Rhodes Scholar "Folder, Box I, CCS personal papers. In all footnotes Courtney C. Smith will be abbreviated as CCS.

5. W. S. Cooper to CCS, January 14, 1939, "Rhodes Scholar" Folder, Box I, CCS personal papers; E. R. Zeller, "Official Service Commended," *Winterset Madisonian,* January 27, 1915; Edward M. Smith to CCS, 8 February [1930], personal folder, box H, CCS personal papers.

6. All family records give the date of Samuel Craig Smith's death as December 26, 1929. Recent correspondence from the Madison County Genealogical Society documents a death date of December 28, 1929: Donna Golightly to Darwin H. Stapleton, 21 November 1991, in authors' files.

7. W. S. Cooper to CCS, January 14, 1939, "Rhodes Scholar" folder, box I, CCS personal papers.

8. Florence Smith Van Syoc interview, December 23, 1991, in authors' files. Sam and Myrtle were buried in Winterset Cemetery, where Courtney also was buried.

9. Federal Writers' Project, *Iowa,* pp. 65–76, 397–98, 404–5, 521. The preserved covered bridges of Madison County provided the idyllic setting and a title for Robert Waller's best-selling book, *The Bridges of Madison County* (New York: Warner, 1992).

10. Van Syoc interview; Murray D. Smith et al. to Myrtle D. Smith, December 24, 1969, box G, CCS personal papers.

11. Myrtle D. Smith to Elizabeth P. Smith, March 8, 1969, box H, CCS personal papers; Edward M. Smith to CCS, April 27, 1933, high school folder, box I, CCS personal papers.

12. Van Syoc interview; Myrtle D. Smith to Elizabeth P. Smith, March 8, 1969, "personal" folder, box H, CCS personal papers.

13. Della Mae Leinard Spurgin to the Editor of the Madisonian, *Winterset Madisonian,* May 21, 1969; CCS to Florence and Carlton Smith, March 16, 1927, first tan album, box H, CCS personal papers.

14. CCS to Murray and Helen Smith, January 5, 1929, and CCS to Murray and Helen Smith, May 15, 1929, both in first tan album, box H, CCS personal papers.

15. Myrtle D. Smith to Elizabeth P. Smith [1969], personal folder, box H, CCS personal papers; Myrtle D. Smith to Elizabeth P. Smith, February 25, 1969, folder S, box G, CCS personal papers.

16. Samuel C. Smith to CCS, Monday eve [December 1929], "personal" folder, box H, CCS personal papers.

17. CCS to Murray and Helen Smith, February 21, 1930 and March 1, 1930, first tan album, box H, CCS personal papers; CCS to Murray D. Smith, April 20, 1930, album C, box H, CCS personal papers.

18. Myrtle D. Smith to Elizabeth P. Smith, March 8, 1969, "personal" folder, box H, CCS personal papers.

19. Van Syoc interview.

20. Federal Writers' Project, *Iowa,* p. 234.

21. Myrtle D. Smith to Elizabeth P. Smith, March 8, 1969, "personal" folder, box H, CCS personal papers; Van Syoc interview.

22. Van Syoc interview.

23. "Courtney Smith Wins Honors at Roosevelt," n.d., newspaper clipping, "H.S." folder, Box I, CCS personal papers.

24. C. C. Carothers to Myrtle Smith, April 4, 1933, "H.S." folder, box I, CCS Personal Papers.

25. Myrtle D. Smith to Elizabeth P. Smith, March 8, 1969, "personal" folder, box H, CCS personal papers.

26. "Scholarships Are Awarded to Joseph Silver and Courtney Smith," "Courtney Smith Wins Honors at Roosevelt," "Courtney Smith Wins First Place in Speaking Contest," "State Champions," n.d., unidentified clippings, "H.S." folder, box I, CCS personal papers; CCS to Committee on the Selection of the Rhodes Scholars for the State of Iowa [November 1937], "Rhodes Scholars" folder, box I, CCS personal papers; Myrtle D. Smith to Elizabeth P. Smith, March 8, 1969, "personal" folder, box H, CCS personal papers.

27. CCS to Murray and Helen Smith, May 1, 1933, first tan album, box H, CCS personal papers.

28. *The Annual Roundup, 1934* (Des Moines: Roosevelt High School, 1934), p. 52.

29. "Notes on the President," *Swarthmore College Bulletin,* 50 (1953): 4.

30. S. O. Goodman, "C.D. Smith Named to High RCA Post," *Washington Post,* 4 June 1960, p. C9.

31. CCS to the Committee on the Selection of Rhodes Scholars for the State of Iowa [November 1937], "Rhodes Scholar" folder, box I, CCS personal papers; Van Syoc interview; W. S. Cooper to CCS, March 6, 1934, "H.S." folder, box I, CCS personal papers.

32. CCS to Florence D. Smith, June 25, 1934, "H.S." folder, box I, CCS personal papers.

33. CCS to Florence D. Smith, July 11, 1934, "H.S." folder, box I, CCS personal papers; Myrtle D. Smith to Elizabeth P. Smith [1969], "personal" folder, box H, CCS personal papers.

## CHAPTER 2. HARVARD, OXFORD, AND MARRIAGE

1. William "Bill" M. Murphy remembered Courtney's great enthusiasm for being at Harvard. William M. Murphy interview, October 22, 1994, in authors' files.

2. Marcia Graham Synnott, *The Half-Opened Door: Discrimination and Admissions at Harvard, Yale, and Princeton, 1900–1970* (Westport, Conn.: Greenwood Press, 1979), p. 115. The division between the more wealthy prep school freshmen and the working scholarship students at Harvard could be brutal. CCS's classmate, Arthur M. Schlesinger Jr., noted that Choate graduate and future president John F. Kennedy, in his freshmen year at Harvard in 1936–37, was careful to keep "apart from the greaseballs in the Harvard Student Union": Arthur M. Schlesinger Jr., *A Thousand Days: John F. Kennedy in the White House* (Boston: Houghton Mifflin, 1965), p. 82.

3. Morris Lasker interview, October 15, 1994; Murphy interview and Wiley Mayne interview, April 4, 1996, in authors' files.

4. Morris Lasker interview, October 15, 1994; and Murphy interview, in authors' files; CCS resume notes, summer 1944, "Navy Veterans Administration" folder, box I, CCS personal papers; CCS to Leonard Rosenfeld, September 28, 1959, "correspondence" folder, box D, CCS personal papers.

5. Synnott, *The Half-Opened Door*, pp. 91, 111–14, 118, 121, 207; *Education, Bricks and Mortar: Harvard Buildings and their Contribution to the Advancement of Learning* (Cambridge: Harvard University, 1949), pp. 20–27, 76–77. Other American educational institutions had similar Jewish quotas: James O. Freedman, "Ghosts of the Past: Anti-Semitism at Elite Colleges," *The Chronicle of Higher Education*, December 1, 2000, pp. B7–B10.

6. William M. Murphy, *David Worcester, 1907–1947: A Memorial* (Clinton, N.Y.: Hamilton College, 1948), pp. 14–15.

7. Murphy interview.

8. Van Syoc interview; John Ashmead to Elizabeth P. Smith, January 18, 1969, folder A, box G, CCS personal papers; Jean and Win Pettingell to Elizabeth P. Smith, January 25, 1969, folder P, box G, CCS personal papers; William D. Murphy to Darwin and Donna Stapleton, August 14, 1994, in authors' files.

9. Courtney Smith's father was reportedly "very meticulous about his appearance, always": "Oral History of the Samuel Craig Smith/Myrtle Dabney Smith Family," typescript dated October 6, 1990.

10. CCS, "Milton's *Of Education* and Other Puritan Tracts on Education, 1600–1660," "Harvard Undergraduate 1934–38" folder, box I, CCS personal papers.

11. CCS to the Committee on the Selection of the Rhodes Scholars for the State of Iowa [November 1937], "Rhodes Scholar" folder, box I, CCS personal papers. Copies of two of his undergraduate essays, "Milton's *Of Education* and Other Puritan Tracts on Education, 1600–1660" and "Tears of Eternity: A Study of the Poetry of A. E. Housman," are in box I of his personal papers.

12. William M. Murphy interview, October 22, 1994, in authors' files.

13. CCS to the Committee on the Selection of the Rhodes Scholars for the State of Iowa [November 1937], "Rhodes Scholar" folder, box I, CCS personal papers.

14. Lasker interview and Murphy interview.

15. Lasker interview; Murphy interview; Wiley Mayne interview, April 3, 1996, in authors' files; *Biographical Directory of the United States Congress, 1774–1989*, S.V. "Mayne, Wiley" (Washington: Government Printing Office, 1989), p. 1443.

16. Lasker interview; Murphy interview; Robert Parker Sorlien interview, September 14, 1994, in authors' files.

17. Murphy interview.

18. CCS notes, "1st Collection, 27 September 1962" folder, box B, CCS personal papers.

19. Van Syoc interview.

20. Van Syoc interview; CCS to the Committee on the Selection of the Rhodes Scholars for the State of Iowa [November 1937], Rhodes Scholar folder, box I, CCS personal papers.

21. CCS notes for the U.S. Navy, summer 1944, "Navy Veterans Administration" folder, box I, CCS Personal Papers.

22. Van Syoc interview.

23. CCS to Myrtle Smith, June 18, 1938, "Harvard Undergraduate—1934–38" folder, box I, CCS personal papers; Van Syoc interview.

24. Van Syoc interview.

25. *Who Was Who in America,* vol. 3, *1951–60* (Chicago: Marquis Who's Who, 1960), pp. 260–61.

26. CCS to Murray and Helen Smith [May 1938], C album, box H, CCS personal papers (quote); Bradford M. Endicott interview, September 17, 1997, in authors' files.

27. Endicott interview.

28. Ibid.

29. Bradford M. Endicott interview, September 17, 1997, in authors' files; CCS to Murray and Helen Smith, [May 1938], album C, box H, CCS personal papers. A portion of the estate and the house were given to the Massachusetts Institute of Technology in the early 1950s to create the MIT Endicott Conference Center.

30. CCS to Murray and Helen Smith [May 1938], album C, box H, CCS personal papers; H. Wendell Endicott to Sidney J. Weinberg, April 21, 1942, "Navy Veterans Administration" folder, box I, CCS personal papers.

31. Giles B. Gunn, *F. O. Matthiessen: The Critical Achievement* (Seattle: University of Washington Press, 1975), pp. 6, 11.

32. *The Rhodes Trust and the Rhodes House* (Oxford: Oxuniprint, 1992), pp. 3–5; J. G. Darwin, "A World University," in *The History of the University of Oxford,* vol. 8, *The Twentieth Century,* ed. Brian Harrison (Oxford: Clarendon Press, 1994), pp. 610–19.

33. Van Syoc interview.

34. CCS to the Committee on the Selection of the Rhodes Scholars for the State of Iowa [November 1937], "Rhodes Scholar" folder, box I, CCS personal papers.

35. "Rhodes Scholars in Varied Fields," *New York Times,* December 26, 1937.

36. Minutes of the Swarthmore College Corporation, October 4, 1938, Friends Historical Library, Swarthmore, Penn..

37. CCS to "All of You," October 20, [1938], album C, box H, CCS personal papers.

38. Ibid.

39. Quoted in Dennis J. Hutchinson, *The Man Who Once Was Whizzer White: A Portrait of Justice Byron R. White* (New York: Free Press, 1998), p. 131.

40. "Notification of Acceptance as a Probationer-Student for the Degree of Bachelor of Letters," October 23, 1939; "Notification of Admission as a Full Student for the Degree of Bachelor of Letters," February 4, 1939, "Rhodes Scholar" folder, box I, CCS personal papers; CCS, draft of curriculum vita, March 17, 1947, "Princeton" folder, box H, CCS personal papers.

41. CCS to "All of You," October 20, [1938], album C, box H, CCS personal papers; CCS biographical notes [1944], "Navy Veterans Administration" folder, box I, CCS personal papers; Hutchinson, *Whizzer White,* p. 128.

42. Van Syoc interview.

43. Frank Aydelotte, Office of the American Secretary of the Rhodes Scholarship Trust, to CCS, September 13, 1939, "Rhodes Scholar" folder, box I, CCS personal papers.

44. CCS memorandum book, 1943, unmarked envelope, box I, CCS personal papers; Van Syoc interview.

45. "Miss Proctor Wed to Mr. C. C. Smith," newspaper clipping, "personal" folder, box H, CCS personal papers.

46. Ibid.

47. Photograph which appeared in the *Boston Herald,* October 22, 1939.

48. "Poem by Edward R. Weismiller for CCS and EPS," dated October 12, 1939, gold envelope, "personal" folder, box H, CCS personal papers.

49. John W. Nason to CCS, September 18, 1939, with CCS notes on reverse, "Rhodes Scholarship—Oxford—1938–39" folder, box I, CCS personal papers.

50. Van Syoc interview; CCS to Murray D. Smith, February 9, 1940, album C, box H, CCS personal papers.

51. Rollins (1889–1958) and Munn (1890–1967) were professors of English literature. Rollins's research and publication received support from a special humanities fund at Harvard: "Report on Grants Made by the General Education Board for the Support of the Humanities, 1929–30," and related documents in the same folder, folder 6514, box 616, series 1.4, General Education Board Archives, Rockefeller Archive Center, Sleepy Hollow, New York.

52. Al Damon to Elizabeth P. Smith, January 25, 1969, folder D, box G, CCS personal papers.

53. Murphy interview.

54. "Academic and Professional Record," September 1, 1943, "Smith, Courtney C., 1943–1953" folder, series 3, Faculty Personnel Files, Papers of the Department of English, Princeton University Archives, Princeton, New Jersey.

## CHAPTER 3. IN THE NAVY

1. James B. Munn to Officer in Charge of Naval Procurement, October 18, 1943, "Navy Veterans Administration" envelope (hereafter NVA envelope), box I, CCS Personal Papers.

2. December 24, 1943, CCS appointment diary 1943, box H, CCS personal papers. Player cigarettes had a naval motif on the package.

3. October 25, 1943 and November 26, 1943, CCS appointment diary 1943, box H, CCS personal papers; CCS to Frank R. Sullivan, April 9, 1955, Harvard Board of Overseers 1954–58 folder, box C, CCS personal papers.

4. CCS biographical notes, [fall 1943], NVA envelope, CCS personal papers.

5. Officer Qualifications Questionnaire, February 8, 1945, NVA envelope, box I, CCS personal papers.

6. Paul Stillwell, ed., *The Golden Thirteen: Recollections of the First Black Naval Officers* (Annapolis, Md.: Naval Institute Press, 1993), pp. xv–xxii; John Celardo, "Shifting Seas: Racial Integration in the United States Navy, 1941–1945," *Prologue: Quarterly of the National Archives* 23 (fall 1991): 230–35; "Notes Taken at Conference with Regard to Negro Personnel, First Session 0945, 26 October 1943," in *Portfolio for Officers in the Negro Personnel Program* (Hampton, Va.: U.S. Naval Training School, 1944).

7. Celardo, "Shifting Seas," 230–231.

8. Stillwell, *The Golden Thirteen,* pp. 89, 128, 153–54.

9. Edwin H. Downes to the Chief of Naval Personnel, February 25, 1944, in *Portfolio For Officers in the Negro Personnel Program* (Hampton, Va.: U.S. Naval Training School, 1944).

10. Ibid.

11. Captain H. B. Grow to Commander E. H. Downes, January 31, 1944, in *Portfolio for Officers in the Negro Personnel Program* [1944], box I, CCS personal papers.

12. CCS to Chief of Naval Personnel, July 3, 1945, unmarked envelope, box I, CCS personal papers.

13. CCS, "Statement of Mission, Tasks and Standards of Performance," August 29, 1944, unmarked envelope, box I, CCS personal papers.

14. Minutes, Commanding Officer's Honor Committee, August 11, 1944; Memorandum to CCS, January 20, 1945; CCS memorandum, June 22, 1945; FSB to CCS, [July 1945]; all in unmarked envelope, box I, CCS personal papers.

15. CCS, "Report of the NAS Liaison Officer for Colored Personnel on ******, William R.," April 9, 1945, unmarked envelope, box I, CCS personal papers.

16. G. H. Ellis, "Problems Facing the Boys in the Bowling Alley and Their Reasons," January 26, 1945, and attached CCS notes, n.d., box I, CCS personal papers.

17. CCS memorandum, [1945], unmarked envelope, box I, CCS personal papers.

18. H. B. Grow to S. Hayes, February 11, 1944; H. B. Grow memorandum, July 29, 1944, both in unmarked envelope, box I, CCS personal papers.

19. CCS, "Democracy's Yardstick: The Negro in the Navy," [1946], box I, CCS personal papers.

20. FSB to CCS, [July 1945], with CCS notes dated July 7, 1945, unmarked envelope, box I, CCS personal papers.

21. "R. L. F. Sikes, 88; Congressman Led Military Committee," *New York Times,* September 30, 1994.

22. "Sikes Is Told Racial Mixing Charges False," *Pensacola News,* April 18, 1944; "Sikes Is Probing Reports of Mixing of Races at Station," *Pensacola Journal,* April 24, 1944.

23. CCS, "Democracy's Yardstick: The Negro in the Navy," [1946], box I, CCS personal papers.

24. CCS notes, "Exec to Relief," December 6, 1945, box I, CCS personal papers. The Honor Committee had been set up by Captain Grow, commanding officer, Naval Air Station, Pensacola, Florida, prior to CCS's arrival, and CCS advised the committee throughout his tenure there.

25. *Gosport* (Newspaper of Naval Air Training Bases, Pensacola, Florida), August 24, 1945, copy in unmarked envelope, box I, CCS personal papers.

26. CCS, "The Third Quarterly Installment of the History of the Liaison Officer for Negro Personnel, 1 July 1945 to 2 September 1945," unmarked envelope, box I, CCS personal papers; CCS to James B. Munn, November 28, 1945, box I, CCS personal papers.

27. CCS to James B. Munn, November 28, 1945, box I, CCS personal papers.

28. George W. Cowan to CCS, July 17, 1946, NVA folder, box I, CCS personal papers; *Gulf Health and Welfare Council, Pensacola, Florida* (Pensacola, Fa.: Hayes Printing Co., 1946), copy in NVA folder, box I, CCS personal papers.

29. "Notice of Separation from the U.S. Naval Service," April 30, 1946, NVA folder, box I, CCS personal papers; honorable discharge certificate, December 28, 1953, NVA folder, box I, CCS personal papers.

## Chapter 4. Return to Education

1. CCS to George W. Cowan, [July 1946], draft, Navy Veterans Administration envelope, box I, CCS personal papers; G. H. Gerould to CCS, March 15, 1946, "Princeton"

204     DIGNITY, DISCOURSE, AND DESTINY

folder, box H, CCS personal papers; "Smith, Courtney C., 1943–1953" folder [hereafter Smith folder, PUA], series 3, Papers of the Department of English, Princeton University Archives, Princeton, New Jersey.

2. See Nathan M. Pusey, *American Higher Education, 1945–1970: A Personal Report* (Cambridge: Harvard University Press, 1978), pp. 9–10, on the anticipation of veterans in 1945–46.

3. G. E. Bentley to Hyder E. Rollins, December 7, 1945, copy with note from Rollins to CCS, December 10, 1945, "Princeton" folder, box H, CCS personal papers.

4. Alexander Leitch, *A Princeton Companion* (Princeton, N.J.: Princeton University Press, 1978), pp. 138–39.

5. Appointment record ("Form X"), March 29, 1946, Smith folder, PUA.

6. CCS to Rev. John Bodo, June 8, 1953, in "CCS—Personal 6/6–8 1953," box 71, CCS presidential papers; Richard M. Ludwig interview, April 14, 1996, in authors' files.

7. Claude C. Smith, "Frank Aydelotte—In Memoriam," Ozone Annual Meeting, December 6, 1957, Ozone Club Minute Book, 1958–60, box 3, Ozone Club Records, Friends Historical Library, Swarthmore, Pa.

8. CCS appointment diary 1946, August 29, 1946, Box H, CCS personal papers; Frances Blanshard, *Frank Aydelotte of Swarthmore* (Middletown, Conn.: Wesleyan University Press, 1970), pp. 133–35, 239, 241, 292–95, 382; Leitch, *A Princeton Companion,* p. 271.

9. Alexander Leitch to CCS, April 18, 1946, April 17, 1947, "Princeton" folder, box H, CCS personal papers; CCS appointment diary 1948, July 1, 1948, box H, CCS personal papers.

10. CCS, "The Seventeenth-Century Drolleries," *Harvard Library Bulletin* 6 (winter 1952): 40–51; CCS memorandum, May 6, 1949, "Princeton" folder, box H, CCS personal papers; CCS Curriculum Vitae, March 17, 1947, September 27, 1949, December 2, 1949, Princeton folder, box H, CCS personal papers.

11. Faculty Minutes, February 21, 1949, series 1, Papers of the English Department, Princeton University Archives (hereafter PUA), Princeton, New Jersey.

12. The "key course" comment is on Smith's departmental review for 1950, signed by the department chairman: Smith folder, PUA.

13. Princeton University Catalogue, *Undergraduate Issue, 1950–1951* (Princeton, N.J.: Princeton University, 1950), p. 202.

14. Minutes of the Rockefeller Foundation Trustees, June 16, 1944 and November 16, 1945; David H. Stevens interview of Harold W. Dodds, March 13, 1944; and David H. Stevens interview of Willard Thorp, March 3, 1943, all in folder 3499, box 405, series 200, RG 1.2, Rockefeller Foundation Archives (hereafter RFA), Rockefeller Archive Center, Sleepy Hollow, N.Y.

15. Princeton University Catalogue, *Undergraduate Issue, 1949–1950* (Princeton, N.J.: Princeton University, 1949), pp. 285, 287.

16. CCS appointment diaries 1943–1950, box H, CCS personal papers; CCS Curriculum Vita, December 2, 1949, Princeton folder, box H, CCS personal papers; Willard Thorp to CCS, June 6, 1950, Princeton folder, box H, CCS personal papers; Leitch, *A Princeton Companion,* pp. 20–21.

17. Richard M. Ludwig interview.

18. Leitch, *A Princeton Companion,* pp. 374–75.

19. "The Idea of a Good Preceptorial," c. 1950, "Princeton" file, box H, CCS Personal Papers.

20. *Princeton Herald,* May 9, 1951; *Announcing the Bicentennial Preceptorships Made Possible by Annual Giving* (Princeton, NJ: Princeton University, [1950]).

21. Coit to CCS, 22 May [1952], "Princeton" folder, box H, CCS personal papers; Floyd A. Couch Jr. to Elizabeth P. Smith, January 23, 1969, folder C, box G, CCS personal papers; John E. Hughes to Elizabeth P. Smith, October 5, 1969, folder H, box G, CCS personal papers; Warren H. Simmons Jr. to Elizabeth P. Smith, February 12, 1969, folder S, box G, CCS personal papers; "Courtney Smith," [winter 1953], "Selection of a President 1953" folder, box 69, CCS presidential papers.

22. "Courtney Smith," [winter 1953], "Selection of a President 1953" folder, box 69, CCS presidential papers; Ludwig interview.

23. "Courtney Smith," [winter 1953], "Selection of a President" 1953 folder, box 69, CCS presidential papers. The English department chair noted, within two years of Smith's arrival at Princeton, that "Men in charge of upperclass courses frequently ask specifically to have him as preceptor": department recommendation, January 29, 1948, Smith folder, PUA.

24. Alexander Leitch to CCS, April 18, 1946, April 17, 1947, "Princeton" folder, box H, CCS personal papers; "Announcing the Bicentennial Preceptorships Made Possible by Annual Giving."

25. CCS to Donald A. Stauffer, May 19, 1947, draft, "Princeton" folder, box H, CCS personal papers; Leitch, *A Princeton Companion,* p. 168.

26. CCS to James Thorpe, May 10, 1953, draft, "Woodrow Wilson Fellowship" folder, box H, CCS personal papers.

27. CCS appointment diaries 1946–48, 1950–52, box H, CCS personal papers; Blanshard, *Frank Aydelotte,* pp. 171–72, 382; David Wright, "His Feet Are in the Real World [Gilmore Stott]," *Swarthmore College Bulletin* 95 (March 1998): 17–19.

28. "Aydelotte to Retire from Rhodes Office," *Princeton Herald,* July 30, 1952; Blanshard, *Frank Aydelotte,* p. 390.

29. Hugh S. Taylor to Members of the Association of Graduate Schools, February 11, 1953, "Princeton" folder, box H, CCS personal papers; Blanshard, *Frank Aydelotte,* p. 390.

30. "Courtney Smith" [winter 1953], "Selection of a President 1953" folder, box 69, CCS presidential papers.

31. Ibid.; CCS appointment diary 1950, June 13, 1950—June 26, 1950, box H, CCS personal papers; *Decennial Report, Harvard College Class of 1938* (Cambridge: Class of 1938, 1948), p. 430.

32. "Courtney Smith" [winter 1953], "Selection of a President 1953" folder, box 69, CCS presidential papers.

## CHAPTER 5. THE WOODROW WILSON PROGRAM YEARS

1. Alexander Leitch, *A Princeton Companion* (Princeton, N.J.: Princeton University Press, 1978), p. 343.

2. Whitney J. Oates, "Princeton's Woodrow Wilson Fellowship Program in its Fifth Year," *School and Society* 73 (1951): 216.

3. Hugh S. Taylor to Members of the Association of Graduate Schools, February 11, 1952, Princeton folder, box H, CCS personal papers.

4. Ibid.

5. CCS to L. F. Kimball, January 3, 1953, folder 2615, box 253, series 1.2, General Education Board Archives (hereafter GEBA), Rockefeller Archive Center, Sleepy Hollow, N.Y.; Princeton University Press Release, April 26, 1953, folder 2618, box 254, series 1.2, GEBA; CCS to Hugh S. Taylor, August 31, 1953, "Woodrow Wilson Fellowship" folder, box H, CCS personal papers.

6. Standard histories of the early years of the Woodrow Wilson Fellowship Program have been used as references and will be quoted and referred to throughout this chapter. They are Oates, "Princeton's Woodrow Wilson Fellowship Program in Its Fifth Year," 215–18; [Whitney J. Oates and Courtney C. Smith], "Brief History of the Woodrow Wilson Fellowship Program from 1950–1952," in Hugh S. Taylor to L. F. Kimball, November 21, 1952, folder 2614, box 253, series 1.2, GEBA; Courtney C. Smith, "The National Woodrow Wilson Fellowship Program," *Association of American Colleges Bulletin* 34 (March 1953): 68–69; Courtney C. Smith, "The Forecast for Tomorrow: An Account of the National Woodrow Wilson Fellowship Program", *The Cooperative Bureau for Teachers Newsletter* [October 1952]: 8–10, copy in "Woodrow Wilson Fellowship" folder, box H, CCS personal papers.

7. Smith, "The Forecast for Tomorrow," pp. 8–10; CCS to James B. Munn, November 28, 1945, draft, box I, CCS personal papers.

8. CCS memorandum to Members of Regional Selection Committees, November 4, 1952, quoted in CCS to Gerald George, July 31, 1968, "Woodrow Wilson Fellowship" folder, box H, CCS personal papers.

9. Harold Dodds to Dean Rusk, January 21, 1953, folder 2615, box 253, series 1.2, GEBA, CCS memorandum to R. F. Goheen, August 10, 1953, Woodrow Wilson folder, box H, CCS personal papers.

10. Princeton University Press release, April 26, 1953, folder 2618, box 254, series 1.2, GEBA.

11. Hugh Taylor to the Association of American Universities, October 7, 1953, folder 2618, box 254, series 1.2, GEBA.

12. Frederick Rudolph, *The American College and University: A History* (reprint, Athens, Ga.: University of Georgia Press, 1990), pp. 430–34.

13. Leitch, *A Princeton Companion* pp. 82–83; see Ellen Lagemann, *The Politics of Knowledge: The Carnegie Corporation, Philanthropy and Public Policy* (Chicago: University of Chicago Press, 1992).

14. CCS memorandum of conversation with Hugh Taylor, November 20, 1952, "Woodrow Wilson Fellowship" folder, box H, CCS personal papers.

15. General Education Board, *Annual Report 1951* (New York: General Education Board, 1952), pp. 40–41; General Education Board, *Annual Report 1952* (New York: General Education Board, 1953), pp. 29–34; Minutes, Trustees of the General Education Board, December 4, 1952, folder 2614, box 253, series 1.2, GEBA; Robert W. July diary entry, July 10, 1952, folder 2614, box 253, series 1.2, GEBA. See Raymond B. Fosdick, *Adventure in Giving: The Story of the General Education Board* (New York: Harper and Row, 1962).

16. Robert W. July memorandum, June 7, 1950; Fellowship conference memorandum, May 5, 1951; EFD interview of Whitney J. Oates, December 29, 1951; all in folder 2614, box 253, series 1.2, GEBA.

17. General Education Board, *Annual Report 1951,* p. ix; *Who Was Who in America* (Chicago: Marquis Who's Who, 1986), p. 112.

18. L. F. Kimball diary entry, November 10, 1952, folder 2614, box 253, series 1.2, GEBA; CCS memorandum of discussion with Kimball, November 19, 1952, "Woodrow Wilson Fellowship" folder, box H, CCS personal papers.

19. L. F. Kimball diary entry, November 10, 1952, folder 2614, box 253, series 1.2, GEBA.

20. General Education Board, *Annual Report 1953* (New York: General Education Board, 1954), pp. 3–4, 24, 43; Minute of the Trustees of the General Education Board,

December 4, 1952, folder 2614, Dean Rusk to Harold W. Dodds, January 26, 1953, folder 2615, both in box 253, series 1.2, GEBA; Hugh S. Taylor to CCS, December 12, 1953, "Inauguration—CCS letters re 1953–54" folder, box 45, CCS presidential papers.

21. Robert W. July diary entry, December 29, 1952, folder 2614; CCS to L. F. Kimball, January 3, 1953, folder 2615, both in box 253, series 1.2, GEBA.

22. CCS to Gerald George, July 31, 1968, "Woodrow Wilson Fellowship" folder, box H, CCS personal papers.

23. CCS to Hugh S. Taylor, August 31, 1953, Woodrow Wilson file, box H, CCS personal papers; Robert W. July diary entry, December 29, 1952, folder 2614, box 253, series 1.2, GEBA.

24. Rodman W. Paul to CCS, August 21, 1953, "Inauguration CCS Letters, 1953–54" folder, box 45, CCS presidential papers.

## Chapter 6. Swarthmore College at Mid-Century

1. Richard J. Walton, *Swarthmore College: An Informal History* (Swarthmore, Pa.: Swarthmore College, 1989), pp. 1–13.

2. Walton, *Swarthmore College,* pp. 15–29.

3. Abraham Flexner, *I Remember: The Autobiography of Abraham Flexner* (New York: Simon and Schuster, 1940), p. 322; Frank Aydelotte, untitled essay in *The Function of a College* (n.p.: Frederic S. Bell, 1933), p. 13.

4. Walton, *Swarthmore College,* p. 33.

5. For a negative view of the consequences of the changes wrought by Aydelotte, see E. Digby Baltzell, *Puritan Boston and Quaker Philadelphia* (New York: Free Press, 1979), pp. 511–13.

6. Frances Blanshard, *Frank Aydelotte of Swarthmore* (Middletown, Conn.: Wesleyan University Press, 1970), pp. 217, 218, 264–76; John Nason interview, February 20, 1992.

7. Flexner, *I Remember, pp. 322–23;* Raymond B. Fosdick, *Adventure in Giving: The Story of the General Education Board* (New York: Harper & Row, 1962).

8. Walton, *Swarthmore College,* pp. 41–43.

9. Blanshard, *Frank Aydelotte of Swarthmore,* p. 152; Frederick Rudolph, *The American College and University: A History* (Athens, Ga.: University of Georgia Press, 1990), pp. 456–57.

10. Walton, *Swarthmore College,* p. 49; John Nason interview, February 20, 1992, in authors' files.

11. Nason interview.

12. "Board of Managers Names John W. Nason as Swarthmore's Eighth President," *The Garnet Letter* 4 (July 1940): 2–3; Brand Blanshard, "Two Swarthmore Presidents, II: John Nason," *Friends Intelligencer* 97 (October 26, 1940): 687–89; *Who's Who in America, 1990–91* (Wilmette, Ill.: Marquis Who's Who, 1990), 2:2392.

13. Nason interview; Walton, *Swarthmore College,* p. 49.

14. Warren Weaver diary entry, April 19, 1946, box 68, RG 12.1, Rockefeller Foundation Archives, Rockefeller Archive Center, Sleepy Hollow, N.Y.

15. Nason interview.

16. Ibid.

17. Everett Lee Hunt, The *Revolt of the College Intellectual* (Chicago: Aldine, 1963), p. 102.

18. Quoted in Walton, *Swarthmore College,* pp. 57–58.

19. Nathan M. Pusey, *American Higher Education, 1945–1970: A Personal Report* (Cambridge, MA: Harvard University Press, 1978), p. 11.

20. Walton, *Swarthmore College,* p. 50.

21. Walton, *Swarthmore College,* pp. 50, 57, 60–61.

22. Swarthmore Chapter of Delta Upsilon to Arad Riggs, 14 March 1951, "Delta Upsilon Fraternity" folder, box 31, CCS presidential papers.

23. John Nason to Claude C. Smith, November 29, 1952, in minutes of the Swarthmore College Corporation, December 2, 1952, Friends Historical Library, Swarthmore, Pa.

## Chapter 7. Swarthmore Looks for Courtney

1. Claude C. Smith to George Becker, December 9, 1952, "Selection of President 1952–53" folder, box 69, CCS presidential papers; Thomas B. McCabe, "Mr. Smith Comes to Swarthmore," *Swarthmore College Bulletin* 50 (May 1953): 4.

2. *Who's Who in America, 1976–77* (Chicago: Marquis Who's Who, 1976), 2:2072.

3. On deliberation and committee work within the Society of Friends see *Faith and Practice,* rev. ed. (Philadelphia: Philadelphia Yearly Meeting, 1972), p. 18.

4. George Becker, "Committee Narrows Field of Potential Presidents," *Phoenix,* March 3, 1953.

5. December 16, 1952, Minutes, Committee to Select a New President, "Selection of President 1952–53" folder, box 69, CCS presidential papers.

6. "Names Suggested for the Presidency of Swarthmore College, 1953," "Selection of the President 1952–53" folder, box 69, CCS presidential papers.

7. Frances Blanshard, *Frank Aydelotte of Swarthmore* (Middletown, Conn.: Wesleyan University Press, 1970), p. 294; Boyd Barnard interview, November 16, 1991, in authors' files.

8. "Courtney Smith," "Selection of a President 1953" folder, box 69, CCS presidential papers. According to Claude C. Smith, Aydelotte was not the first person to nominate Courtney C. Smith: Claude C. Smith to CCS, May 27, 1953, "Inauguration—Courtney Smith 1953" folder, box 45, CCS presidential papers.

9. Blanshard, *Frank Aydelotte of Swarthmore,* pp. 171–72.

10. Barnard interview.

11. February 6, 1953, Minutes, Committee to Select a New President, "Selection of a President 1952–53" folder, box 69, CCS presidential papers.

12. Roland Pennock interview, February 21, 1992, in authors' files.

13. "Courtney Smith," "Selection of a President, 1953" folder, box 69, CCS presidential papers.

14. Ibid.

15. February 23, 1953, March 16, 1953, Minutes, Committee to Select a New President, "Selection of a President, 1952–53" folder, box 69, CCS presidential papers.

16. Clair Wilcox, [Agenda for] Monday March 23 [1953], "Swarthmore" folder, box D, CCS personal papers.

17. Minutes, April 7, 1953, Swarthmore College Corporation, Friends Historical Library, Swarthmore, Pa.; McCabe, "Mr. Smith Comes to Swarthmore," pp. 1–4.

18. Minutes, April 7, 1953, Swarthmore College Corporation; McCabe, "Mr. Smith Comes to Swarthmore," pp. 1–4.

19. CCS memorandum for April 7th, 1953, "Swarthmore" folder, box D, CCS personal papers; April 7, 1953, CCS appointment diary 1953, box H, CCS personal papers.

20. "Board OK's Courtney Smith, Rhodes Head, As President: English Professor at Princeton to Assume Duties Next Autumn," *Phoenix,* April 7, 1953; McCabe, "Mr. Smith Comes to Swarthmore," 3–4.

21. Board of Manager's minutes, quoted in Janet G. Bourne to Charles Thatcher, September 17, 1953, "Courtney Smith" folder, box D, CCS personal papers.

22. April 9–10, 1953, CCS appointment diary, box H, CCS personal papers.

23. *Newark Sunday News,* April 12, 1953; "Future-Minded New President," *Philadelphia Sunday Bulletin,* April 12, 1953.

24. CCS to Chadbourne Gilpatric, May 25, 1953, "Personal—1953 (5/25–28)" folder, box 71, CCS presidential papers.

25. CCS to Margaret B. Anderson (Mrs. Harry G. Barnes), June 8, 1953, "Courtney Smith—Personal (6/6–8/53)" folder, box 71, CCS presidential papers; Lee Smith Ingram interview, April 2, 1995, in authors' files.

26. April 24, 1953, May 5, 1953, CCS appointment diary 1953, box H, CCS personal papers; Blanshard, *Frank Aydelotte of Swarthmore,* pp. 390–92.

27. July 14–August 9, 1953, CCS appointment diary 1953, CCS personal papers; CCS to Robert Goheen, June 8, 1953, "Courtney Smith—Personal, 6/6–8/1953" folder, box 71, CCS presidential papers.

## Chapter 8. Inauguration

1. John W. Nason to CCS, August 31, 1953, "Swarthmore" folder, box D, CCS personal papers.

2. "Inauguration—Courtney Smith—letters re 1953–54" folder, box 45, CCS personal papers.

3. December 3, 1952, Minutes, Swarthmore College Corporation, Friends Historical Library, Swarthmore, Pa.; John and Margaret Moore interview, November 16, 1991, in authors' files.

4. Terri Shane interview, August 6, 1991, in authors' files; John and Margaret Moore interview.

5. August 30, to September 24, 1953, CCS appointment diary 1953, box H, CCS personal papers.

6. CCS notes on talk to Class Agents, [September 1953], "Class Agents" folder, box A, CCS personal papers; September 9, 1953, CCS appointment diary 1953, box H, CCS personal papers.

7. CCS address to First Faculty meeting, September 23, 1953, "First Faculty Meeting" folder, box A, CCS personal papers.

8. CCS notes for Collection, October 1, 1953, "Collection intros etc." folder, box A, CCS personal papers.

9. CCS to A. L. Pittinger, [late October 1953], "Inauguration—Courtney Smith—Letters re 1953–54" folder, box 45, CCS presidential papers.

10. CCS to Edmund Dews, [late October 1953], "Inauguration—Courtney Smith—Letters re 1953–54," box 45, CCS presidential papers.

11. CCS to W. Wendell Endicott, February 19, 1954, "Inauguration CCS letters 1953–54," box 45, CCS presidential papers.

12. *The Inauguration of Courtney Craig Smith as Ninth President of Swarthmore College, October 17, 1953,* (Swarthmore, Pa.: Swarthmore College, 1953); "Courtney Smith Is Inaugurated at Swarthmore," *Philadelphia Sunday Bulletin,* October 18, 1953; "Swarthmore Gets Its Ninth President," *New York Times,* October 18, 1953.

13. "Swarthmore Gets Its Ninth President."

14. See the discussion of McCarthyism at Harvard in Kai Bird, *The Color of Truth: McGeorge Bundy and William Bundy, Brothers in Arms* (New York: Simon and Schuster, 1998), pp. 122–33.

15. "Courtney Craig Smith, Inaugural Address," *The Inauguration of Courtney Craig Smith,* pp. 4–18.

16. CCS, address to alumni dinner, [October 17, 1953], "Alumni Dinner" folder, box A, CCS personal papers; *The Inauguration of Courtney Craig Smith,* p. 1.

17. Clarence H. Faust, "Specialization and the Liberal Arts in Higher Education," pp. 1–6, Ernest O. Melby, "Looking Forward in Higher Education," pp. 23–28, Charles J. Turck, "College Responsibilities in Moral and Spiritual Values," pp. 205–10, Royce S. Pitkin, "What Is the State of Freedom in Education?" pp. 303–6, all in G. Kerry Smith, ed., *Current Issues in Higher Education* (Washington, D.C.: Association for Higher Education, 1954); Douglas T. Miller and Marion Nowak, *The Fifties: The Way We Really Were* (Garden City, N.Y.: Doubleday, 1977), pp. 220–47.

18. Royce S. Pitkin, "What Is the State of Freedom in Education?" in *Current Issues in Higher Education,* pp. 303–6.

19. Smith's address was generally well received by students: "Student Reports on the Inaugural Address of President Courtney Craig Smith," spring 1954, "Inauguration CCS, letters 1953–54" folder, box 45, CCS presidential papers.

CHAPTER 9. THE CASE FOR THE LIBERAL ARTS COLLEGE

Our title is taken from CCS, "The Case for the Liberal Arts College as a Separate Institutional Entity," "Regional Orientation Program for New Faculty, 30 September 1960" folder, box B, CCS personal papers.

1. Bruce A. Kimball, *Orators and Philosophers: A History of the Idea of Liberal Education* (New York: College Entrance Examination Board, 1995), pp. xii–xiii, 190–91, 237. A convenient summary of Hutchins's views may be found in Robert Maynard Hutchins, *The Higher Learning in America* (New Haven: Yale University Press, 1936), especially chapter 4.

2. CCS to Committee on the Selection of Rhodes Scholars for the State of Iowa, [November 1937], "Rhodes Scholar" folder, box I, CCS personal papers.

3. CCS to Florence, Carleton, Murray, and Myrtle D. Smith, October 20, 1938, album C, box H, CCS personal papers.

4. CCS to Murray D. Smith, February 9, 1940, album C, box H, CCS personal papers.

5. Interviews with William Murphy, October 22, 1994, Edward Weismiller, November 11, 1994, and Morris Lasker, October 15, 1994, in authors' files.

6. CCS to James B. Munn, November 28, 1945 [draft], box I, CCS personal papers; CCS curriculum vita, March 17, 1947, CCS memorandum regarding discussion with Willard Thorp, May 6, 1949, CCS curriculum vita, December 2, 1949, with revision of fall 1950, "Princeton" folder, box H, CCS personal papers.

7. CCS, notes on precepts and classes in Blue Book, n.d., "Princeton" folder, box H, CCS personal papers; Alexander Leitch, *A Princeton Companion* (Princeton, N.J.: Princeton University Press, 1978), pp. 374–75; CCS to Donald A. Stauffer, February 15, 1947 [draft], "Princeton" folder, box H, CCS personal papers.

8. Floyd A. Couch Jr. to Elizabeth P. Smith, January 23, 1969, folder C, box G, CCS personal papers.

9. *Princeton Herald,* May 9, 1951; *Announcing the Bicentennial Preceptorships Made Possible by Annual Giving* (Princeton, N.J.: Princeton University, 1950), copy in box H, CCS personal papers.

10. "Princeton's Men of the Week," *Town Topics,* April 13–19, 1952, p. 1, copy in "Princeton" folder, box H, CCS personal papers.

11. CCS curriculum vita of December 2, 1949, amended fall 1950, "Princeton" folder, box H, CCS personal papers.

12. *Princeton Herald,* May 9, 1951; Leitch, *A Princeton Companion* pp. 20–21; Harold Dodds to CCS, January 12, 1950, and Willard Thorp to CCS, June 6, 1950, "Princeton" folder, box H, CCS personal papers.

13. President's Commission on Higher Education, *Higher Education for American Democracy* (Washington, D.C.: Government Printing Office, 1947), 1:10.

14. CCS, "Market Value and Real Value," in *Free Enterprise in Education: Remarks at the Fifteenth Annual Forum on Education of the Tuition Plan at Hotel Ambassador in New York, February 9, 1955* (New York: The Tuition Plan, 1955), p. 18.

15. CCS, "Market Value and Real Value," p. 19.

16. Ibid., pp. 22–23.

17. *New York Herald Tribune,* February 13, 1955. CCS's remarks were featured in the article regarding the panel.

18. CCS, "Market Value and Real Value," p. 24.

19. CCS, "The Educator's Dream—Vision or Nightmare?" February 21, 1956, box C, CCS personal papers; CCS, "The Case for the Liberal Arts College as a Separate Institutional Entity," "Regional Orientation Program for New Faculty, 30 September 1960" folder, box B, CCS personal papers; CCS, *The Liberal Arts College,* Voice of America Forum Lectures (Washington, D.C.: Voice of America, 1960); CCS, "The Dialogue," *Swarthmore College Bulletin* 60 (May 1963): 1–13.

20. Ray Stannard Baker and William Dodd, eds., *Selected Literary and Political Papers and Addresses of Woodrow Wilson.* 3 vols. (New York: Grosset and Dunlop, 1925–27), 1:55–57, quoted by CCS in remarks, "Regional Orientation Program for New Faculty, 30 Sept [19]60" folder, box B, CCS personal papers.

21. CCS, "The Dialogue," p. 6.

22. Ibid.

23. Ibid., p. 7.

24. CCS to James B. Munn, November 28, 1945, box I, CCS personal papers; CCS to Charles E. Gilbert, July 11, 1966, "Commission on Educational Policy 1966 (1–9)," box 28, CCS presidential papers; Lee Smith Ingram, interview, April 2, 1995, in authors' files.

25. Jacques Barzun, *The House of Intellect* (New York: Harper and Brothers, 1959), p. 27.

26. Ibid., p. 96.

27. Our reading of Ortega y Gasset has benefitted from the analyses in Robert McClintock, *Man and His Circumstances: Ortega as Educator* (New York: Teachers College Press, 1971), and Rockwell Gray, *The Imperative of Modernity: An Intellectual Biography of José Ortega y Gasset* (Berkeley and Los Angeles: University of California Press, 1989). For a recent argument on behalf of liberal education that derives from Ortega y Gasset, see Henry Rosovsky, *The University: An Owner's Manual* (New York: W. W. Norton, 1990), chap. 6.

28. José Ortega y Gasset, *Mission of the University,* ed. and trans. Howard Lee Nostrand (New Brunswick, N.J.: Transaction Publishers, 1992), p. 60.

29. Ibid., pp. 28–29.

30. Ibid., pp. 28, 32, 69.

31. Ibid., pp. 49–50.

32. Ibid., p. 81.

33. Thomas Bender, perhaps the foremost commentator on the history of American intellectual life, states that after 1950 "academics sought some distance from civics . . . they were openly or implicitly drawn to the model of science as a vision of professional maturity." Further he argues that the new structures of postwar federal funding "encouraged a focus on the model of science, an emphasis on method, and a narrowness of reference in social studies and humanistic scholarship." Thomas Bender, "Politics, Intellect, and the American University, 1945–1995," in ed. Thomas Bender and Carl E. Schorske, *American Academic Culture in Transformation: Fifty Years, Four Disciplines,* (Princeton, N.J.: Princeton University Press, 1998), pp. 22, 26.

34. Irving E. Dayton to authors, June 10, 1992, in authors' files.

## CHAPTER 10. FACULTY

1. Faculty Salary Comparison, April 1954, "Alumni Council Breakfast at Shane's, June 5, 1954" folder, box A, CCS personal papers.

2. CCS address to the Foxhowe Association, "Foxhowe—July 18, 1954" folder, box A, CCS personal papers.

3. Benjamin Fine, "Education in Review: Liberal Arts Colleges Take Stock of Their Present Status and Future Needs," *New York Times,* January 17, 1954, sec. 4, p. 9.

4. Benjamin Fine, "Jammed Colleges Will Open Today," *New York Times,* September 20, 1954, p. 19.

5. "N.Y.U. to Raise Faculty's Pay by Increasing Tuition Next Year," *New York Times,* December 17, 1954, pp. 1, 34.

6. Leonard Buder, "Study of Schools Stresses Low Pay," *New York Times,* October 25, 1955, p. 24.

7. Benjamin Fine, "Sharp Rise Asked in Professor Pay," *New York Times,* March 8, 1956, p. 26.

8. Jay Walz, "Presidential Study Warns of Growing College Crisis," *New York Times,* August 11, 1957, pp. 1, 54.

9. Crawford H. Greenewalt to CCS, October 18, 1956, "Greenewalt Committee" folder, box 41, CCS presidential papers; CCS to Crawford H. Greenewalt, October 23, 1956, "Greenewalt Committee" folder, box 41, CCS presidential papers.

10. Jay Walz, "Presidential Study," p. 54; Crawford H. Greenewalt to CCS, August 8, 1957, "Greenewalt Committee" folder, box 41, CCS presidential papers.

11. "Faculty Salaries, 1957–58," *Higher Education* (Washington, D.C.) 14 (March 1958): 109.

12. Swarthmore College Corporation minutes, October 2, 1956, Friends Historical Library, Swarthmore, Pa.; CCS, Annual Report for 1955–56, "Annual Report 1955–56—December 4, 1956" folder, box A, CCS personal papers.

13. Benjamin Fine, "U.S. Aid Is Asked on Scholarships," *New York Times,* January 24, 1957, p. 30.

14. CCS, Report of the President for the Year 1956–1957," *Swarthmore College Bulletin* 5 (April 1958): 19; CCS to W. E. Stevenson, president of Oberlin College, November 7, 1957, "Swarthmore College and Church" folder, "1947–57" box, "Subject Files" series, "Administrative Files" subgroup, papers of William E. Stevenson, Archives of Oberlin College, Oberlin, Ohio.

15. Minutes, April 2, 1957, October 1, 1957, Swarthmore College Corporation, Friends Historical Library, Swarthmore, Pa.; "Swarthmore College Salary Boost Ups Professors' Pay to $14,000," *Boston Traveler,* July 1, 1957, p. 17.

16. CCS's marginal note on "Mean Salaries for 1958–59," "Salaries 1954–58" folder, box 66, CCS presidential papers.

17. Minutes, October 1, 1957, Swarthmore College Corporation, Friends Historical Library, Swarthmore, Pa.

18. Minutes, April 7, 1959, Swarthmore College Corporation, Friends Historical Library, Swarthmore, Pa.; CCS, remarks to Alumni, "Homecoming November 3, 1962" folder, box B, CCS personal papers. Even with substantial increases in salaries, Swarthmore did not have salaries comparable to those of many large private universities and could not always compete with commercial bids for bright young scholars. Wesleyan University salary survey for 1957–58, "Salaries 1954–58" folder, box 66, CCS presidential papers.

Courtney kept evidence of those who declined a Swarthmore position in favor of a more lucrative one: for example, see Scott E. Pardee to Clair Wilcox, February 6, 1962, "Economics Dept. 1954–1969" folder, box 34, CCS presidential papers.

19. "[29] Institutions Participating in the 1964–65 Faculty Salary Study," "Salaries 1962–65" folder, box 66, CCS presidential papers; "Further Progress: The Economic Status of the Profession," *Bulletin, American Association of University Professors,* summer 1967, pp. 136–142.

20. CCS's files in his presidential and personal papers are full of his annotations on publications that referred to trends in higher education. On the matter of faculty salaries in this era, see also Nathan M. Pusey, *American Higher Education, 1945–1970* (Cambridge: Harvard University Press, 1978), pp. 94–99.

21. CCS, remarks to North New Jersey Alumni Club and Washington Alumni Club, November 13, 1953, and December 16, 1953, "North New Jersey Alumni Club" folder, box A, CCS personal papers.

22. Roland Pennock interview, February 21, 1992, and David Smith interview, April 7, 1991, both in authors' files. Pennock and Smith were in the political science department during Courtney Smith's presidency.

23. Richard Pfaff to Thomas E. Hill, February 2, 1962, "Emeriti Information" folder, box 35, CCS presidential papers.

24. CCS remarks, "Regional Orientation Program for New Faculty," Harrisburg, PA, 30 September 1960" folder, box B, CCS personal papers.

25. CCS remarks at a discussion of the "Religious Basis of Academic Freedom," February 25, 1954, "Panel Discussion, Friends Committee" folder, box A, CCS personal papers; CCS interview notes for Modern Language candidates, February 19, 1955, June 15, 1955, [January] 1956, "Modern Language Department 1954–60" folder, box 52, CCS presidential papers; also see discussion of faculty candidates, "Chemistry Department 1960–69" folder, box 24, CCS presidential papers; CCS, remarks to Men's Sunday Breakfast Club, Trinity Church, Moorestown, N.J., May 22, 1955, "Men's Sunday Breakfast Club—May 22, 1955" folder, box A, CCS personal papers.

26. CCS interview notes, February 1, 1962, "History Department 1961–62" folder, box 43, CCS presidential papers.

27. CCS to Edith Philips and Harold March, December 22, 1959, "Modern Language Department 1954–60," folder, box 52, CCS presidential papers.

28. Joseph V. Ricapito to Elizabeth P. Smith, January 22, 1969, folder R, box G, CCS personal papers.

29. John and Margaret Moore interview, November 16, 1991, in authors' files; Irving E. Dayton to authors, June 10, 1992, in authors' files. John Moore was registrar of the college during Smith's presidency; Dayton was a professor of physics at Swarthmore, 1957–61.

30. Clair Wilcox, quoted in "A Party for Clair Wilcox," *Swarthmore College Bulletin,* 45 (May 1968): 7.

31. CCS notes on candidates, March 27–28, 1957, "Political Science Department 1957–62" folder, box 63, CCS presidential papers; Roland Pennock to CCS, October 4, 1967, "Political Science Department 1966–68," folder, box 63, CCS presidential papers.

32. Teaching Load Committee to Faculty of Swarthmore College, April 2, 1956, CCS to McGeorge Bundy, February 11, 1957, John M. Moore to CCS, March 30, 1957, "Faculty Teaching Loads—1955–62" folder, box 38, CCS presidential papers.

33. CCS to J. Douglas Brown, February 9, 1957, "Faculty Teaching Loads—1955–62" folder, box 38, CCS presidential papers.

34. CCS memorandum of conversation with Robert Enders, May 17, 1960, "Biology Department 1960–63" folder, box 10, CCS presidential papers.

35. "Report on Teaching Load," November 4, 1957, "Faculty Teaching Loads—1955–62" folder, box 38, CCS presidential papers; "Report of the President for the Year 1956–57," *Swarthmore College Bulletin* 35 (April 1958): 23–25.

36. CCS, remarks to faculty and students, "First Collection—2 October 1961" folder, box B, CCS personal papers; Maralyn Orbison to CCS, February 17, 1959, "Asian Studies Program 1959–60" folder, box 7, CCS presidential papers.

37. "Evaluation Report for the Middle States Association of Colleges and Secondary Schools Commission, Institutions of Higher Education, February 16–19, 1958," "Middle States Association—Evaluation 1958" folder, box 51, CCS presidential papers.

CHAPTER 11. "THERE IS STRENGTH . . ."

The phrase is taken from CCS to Mrs. Jack B. Thompson, March 26, 1962, "Ta-Tiz 1955–62" folder, box 76, CCS presidential papers.

1. John Nason interview, February 20, 1992, in the authors' files.

2. Abraham Flexner, *I Remember: The Autobiography of Abraham Flexner* (New York: Simon and Schuster, 1940), pp. 322–23.

3. "Docket Excerpt," section I, reel 0969, grant PA61–354, Ford Foundation Archives, New York.

4. CCS Commencement Address, "Commencement—7 June 1954" folder, box A, CCS personal papers. See also *We're out Ahead but . . .* (Swarthmore, Pa.: Swarthmore College, 1954), copy in "Centennial Fund—pamphlets—n.d. to January 1962" folder, box 23, CCS presidential papers.

5. CCS "Report of the President for the Year 1954–1955," *Swarthmore College Bulletin* 53 (January 1956): 18.

6. CCS, draft "Report of the President for the Year 1962–1963," Annual Report December 3, 1963" folder, box B, CCS personal papers.

7. CCS, draft "Report of the President for the Year 1966–1967," "Commencement Review of the Year—June 12, 1967" folder, box C, CCS personal papers.

8. CCS, draft "Report of the President for the Year 1967–1968," "Commencement Review of the Year—June 10, 1968" folder, box C, CCS personal papers.

9. Kai Bird, *The Color of Truth: McGeorge Bundy and William Bundy, Brothers in Arms* (New York: Simon and Schuster, 1998), p. 137.

10. Clark Kerr, *The Uses of the University* (Cambridge: Harvard University Press, 1964), pp. 6–9; Sheldon Rothblatt, "Clark Kerr and the Pursuit of Excellence in the Modern University," *Minerva* 33 (autumn 1995): 271.

11. Dodds is quoted in Amy Sue Bix, "'Backing into Sponsored Research': Physics and Engineering at Princeton University, 1945–1970," *History of Higher Education Annual* 13 (1993): 12–13.

12. Bix, "'Backing into Sponsored Research'" pp. 13–33. See also Robert Kargon and Stuart Leslie, "Imagined Geographies: Princeton, Stanford and the Boundaries of Useful Knowledge in Postwar America," *Minerva* 32 (summer 1994): 121–43.

13. CCS to members of the faculty, November 24, 1958, "Faculty Meetings—1956–67" folder, box 37, CCS presidential papers.

14. Minutes, Swarthmore College Corporation, December 2, 1958, Friends Historical Library, Swarthmore, Pa.; Claude C. Smith to CCS, November 28, 1958, and CCS notes, December 1–2, 1958, in "NDEA Principles 1958" folder, box 56, CCS presidential papers.

15. CCS notes on telephone conversation with Senator Joseph Clark, [December 1958–January 1959], "NDEA Senate Hearings—1959—January–April" folder, box 56, CCS presidential papers. See Philadelphia Yearly Meeting of the Religious Society of Friends, *Faith and Practice* (Philadelphia: Philadelphia Yearly Meeting, original edition 1955, revised 1972), p. 20.

16. CCS notes of telephone conversation with Pat Malin, December 17, 1958, "NDEA Senate Hearings 1959—January–April" folder, box 56, CCS presidential papers.

17. CCS notes of telephone conversations with Pat Malin, December 17 and 22, 1958; Theodore A. Distler to Dear Colleague, January 14, 1959 (mimeographed), "NDEA Senate Hearings—1959—January–April" folder, box 56, CCS presidential papers; Howard R. Bowen to CCS, February 17, 1959, "NDEA Correspondence—1959, February 10–28" folder, box 55, CCS presidential papers.

18. American Civil Liberties Union, "The National Defense Education Act of 1958 and Civil Liberties in Education," March 9, 1959, attached to Alice Bergwerk to CCS, March 11, 1959, "NDEA Principles 1959–1961" folder, box 56, CCS presidential papers.

19. Excerpt from the *Congressional Record—Senate,* January 29, 1959, "NDEA Senate Hearings—1959—January–April" folder, box 56, CCS presidential papers.

20. CCS to John F. Kennedy, April 23 and 28, 1959, "Education-Loyalty Oath, 2/5/59—5/29/59" folder, box 715, Senate files, pre-presidential series, John F. Kennedy papers, JFK Presidential Library, Boston; CCS notes on telephone conversation with Joseph Clark, April 23, 1959 and, John F. Kennedy to CCS, April 29, 1959, "NDEA Senate Hearings—1959—January–April" folder, box 56, CCS presidential papers.

21. United States Senate, Eighty-sixth Congress, First Session, *Hearings before the Subcommitee on Education of the Committee on Labor and Public Welfare on S. 819, Amending Loyalty Provision of National Defense Education Act of 1958, April 29 and May 5, 1959* (Washington, D.C.: U.S. Government Printing Office, 1959), pp. 77–78; May 4–5, 1959, CCS appointment diary for 1959, box H, CCS personal papers.

22. John Brademas to CCS, February 10, 1959; James Roosevelt to CCS, February 12, 1959, "NDEA Congress and Repeal" folder, box 55, CCS presidential papers; *Biographical Directory of the United States Congress, 1774–1989,* bicentennnial ed. (Washington, D.C.: Government Printing Office, 1989), p. 656; Public Law 87–835, Eighty-seventh Congress, H.R. 8556, October 16, 1962, "NDEA—*National Defense Education Act* 1962 (January–October)" folder, box 54, CCS presidential papers. Senate majority leader Lyndon B. Johnson reportedly blamed the failure of the Kennedy-Clark bill "on the fact that Kennedy and the [Americans for Democratic Action] wanted to eliminate the [loyalty] oath as well

as the disclaimer." Stanley Marcus to Nathan Pusey, December 3, 1959, "NDEA Senate Hearings, May 1959–60" folder, box 56, CCS presidential papers.

23. "V. Civil Liberties and 'McCarthyism'," "Loyalty Oath Bill (S. 2929)" folder, box 769, Senate Series, pre-presidential papers, John F. Kennedy papers, JFK Presidential Library, Boston; CCS to members of the faculty, January 28, 1963, "Faculty—Memoranda to—1953–68" folder, box 37, CCS presidential papers. See also the account of the disclaimer affidavit controversy by Nathan Pusey, then-president of Harvard University, in *American Higher Education, 1945–1970* (Cambridge: Harvard University Press, 1978), pp. 134–37.

24. CCS remarks, "Foxhowe—18 July 1954" folder, box A, CCS personal papers; CCS remarks to Board of Managers, n.d., "NDEA Principles, 1959–1961" folder, box 56, CCS presidential papers. Smith's concerns about federal funding were shared by other educators: see Pusey, *American Higher Education,* pp. 154–57.

25. CCS to Jed Rakoff, October 10, 1962, "Ra misc. 1959–1968" folder, box 65, CCS presidential papers; George Avery interview, August 6, 1991, in authors' files.

26. CCS remarks, "Association of Independent Schools of Greater Washington, 16 October 1956" folder, box A, CCS personal papers; CCS, *The Liberal Arts College,* The Voice of America Forum Lectures, Education Series, no. 5. (Washington, D.C.: Voice of America, 1960), p. 7. It is worth noting that by some measures small liberal arts colleges are very effective training grounds for science: see Thomas R. Cech, "Science at Liberal Arts Colleges: A Better Education?" *Daedalus* 128 (winter 1999): 195–216.

27. Conducting cutting-edge scientific research at the college level remains an issue three decades after the Smith era: Robert Finn, "Scientists at Four-Year Colleges Strive for Research Quality," *The Scientist,* October 27, 1997, pp. 13–14.

28. Edward K. Cratsley to Olaf E. Stamberg, July 12, 1961, "Animal Laboratory" folder, box 6, CCS presidential papers; CCS, announcement regarding computer committee, April 27, 1964, "Computer, 1964–68" folder, box 29, CCS presidential papers; Edward K. Cratsley to C. G. Manly, December 29, 1959, "Physics dept. 1958–1961" folder, box 62, CCS presidential papers; Edward K. Cratsley to R. S. Poor, January 3, 1967, "Physics dept. 1962–1968" folder, box 62, CCS presidential papers; Edward K. Cratsley to A. T. Waterman, February 17, 1954, "Astronomy" folder, box 9, CCS presidential papers; "Progress Report on Astronomic Work Done at the Sproul Observatory with Support from NSF Grants," February 15, 1960, "Astronomy" folder, box 9, CCS presidential papers.

29. See correspondence in "Amos Peaslee, 1954–1962" and "Amos Peaslee, 1963–1970" folders, box 58, CCS presidential papers.

30. *Come to Where the Knowledge Is* (Philadelphia: University City Science Center, [1965]); minutes of the Executive Committee, University Science Center, April 18, 1967, and CCS to Paul J. Cupp [draft], June 26, 1967, "University City Science Center—1967" folder, box 78, CCS presidential papers.

31. Smith's presidential papers are full of newspaper and magazine clippings, particularly from the *New York Times.*

32. One source states that philanthropic giving to higher education grew tenfold from 1940 to 1970, when it constituted 10 percent of American higher education's annual income: Pusey, *American Higher Education,* p. 119.

33. CCS, "Report of the President for the Year 1956–1957," *Swarthmore College Bulletin* 55 (April 1958): 28–29.

34. Richard B. Willis, "Report of the Treasurer," *Swarthmore College Bulletin* 63 (January 1966): 24; Richard B. Willis, "Report of the Treasurer," *Swarthmore College Bulletin* 64 (December 1967): 22.

35. Roger L. Geiger, "What Happened after *Sputnik?* Shaping University Research in the United States," *Minerva* 35 (1997): 349–67.

36. CCS memorandum of discussion with Lalor Burdick, July 11, 1957, Joseph B. Shane to CCS, September 6, 1957, and CCS to Walter O. Simon, December 6, 1957, all in "Pierre S., du Pont—science building, 1954–January 1958" folder, box 33, CCS presidential papers; Crawford H. Greenewalt to CCS, October 18, 1956, and August 8, 1957, "Greenewalt Committee" folder, box 41, CCS presidential papers; CCS, "Report of the President for the Year 1964–65," *Swarthmore College Bulletin* 63 (January 1966): 19; CCS to Walter O. Simon, May 18, 1963, "Walter O. Simon" folder, box 70, CCS presidential papers; "William H. Ward of DuPont, Dead," *New York Times,* March 2, 1961, p. 27.

37. CCS to the Board of Managers, December 18, 1957, "Board of Managers—1954–1965" folder, box 20, CCS presidential papers.

38. CCS, "Report of the President for the Year 1957–1958," *Swarthmore College Bulletin* 56 (January 1959): 21–24; Irving E. Dayton, "The Pierre S. du Pont Science Building, Swarthmore College," *American Journal of Physics* 29 (November 1961): 753–63; CCS appointment diary for 1960, April 23, 1960, box H, CCS personal papers.

39. CCS, "Memorandum of conversation with Tom McCabe (along with Ed Cratsley)," May 22, [1959], "McCabe, Thomas B. 1954–59" folder, box 51, CCS presidential papers; Minutes, June 5, 1959, Swarthmore College Corporation, Friends Historical Library.

40. CCS remarks, October 21, 1961, "Homecoming Day—21 October 1961" folder, box B, CCS personal papers; CCS, *Swarthmore's Centennial Objectives: A Preliminary Statement to the College's Alumni and Friends* (Swarthmore, Pa.: Swarthmore College, 1962).

41. CCS, "Report of the President for the Year 1961–62," *Swarthmore College Bulletin* 60 (May 1963): 19.

42. "Voices from Swarthmore: New Recording Tells Campaign Story," *The Swarthmore Centennial Fund Signal* 1 (May 1963): 5.

43. Wolcott D. Street, November 1, 1963, "Centennial Fund—1963 (9–12)" folder, and "Major Gift Prosects for President Courtney Smith," [January 1964], "Centennial Fund—1964 (1–2)" folder, box 23; minutes of the Centennial Fund Council, February 17, 1963, "Centennial Fund—1963 (1–2)" folder, box 22, CCS presidential papers.

44. CCS draft, "Report of the President for the Year 1962–1963," "Annual Report—3 December 1963" folder, box B, CCS personal papers; "Cash Standing of the Swarthmore Centennial Campaign to Date," November 30, 1963, "Centennial Fund 1963 (9–12)" folder, box 23, CCS presidential papers.

45. CCS remarks, "commencement June 8, 1964" folder, box B, CCS personal papers.

46. CCS, "Report of the President for the Year 1964–1965," *Swarthmore College Bulletin* 63 (January 1966): 14; CCS, "Report of the President for the Year 1965–66," *Swarthmore College Bulletin* 64 (January 1967): 14–15.

47. CCS, draft "Report of the President for the Year 1966–1967," commencement review of the year—June 12, 1967, box C, CCS personal papers; CCS to science departments, February 10, 1967, "Sloan Proposal 1967" folder, box 70, CCS presidential papers.

48. Rebecca S. Lowen, *Creating the Cold War University: The Transformation of Stanford* (Berkeley and Los Angeles: University of California Press, 1997); Richard Norton Smith, *The Harvard Century: The Making of a University to a Nation* (Cambridge: Harvard University Press, 1986), pp. 218–21; Bix, "'Backing into Sponsored Research,'" pp. 13–33; Bird, *The Color of Truth,* p. 137. A highly critical view of the changes in higher education during the cold war may be found in R. C. Lewontin, "The Cold War and the Transformation of the Academy," in *The Cold War and the University,* ed. André Schiffrin, (New York: The New Press, 1997), pp. 1–34.

CHAPTER 12. NETWORKS OF SUPPORT AND SERVICE

1. CCS to the Committee on the Selection of the Rhodes Scholars for the State of Iowa, [November 1937], "Rhodes Scholarship" folder, box I, CCS personal papers; Hyder E. Rollins to CCS, April 18, 1953, "Personal—1953 (4/8—5/23)" folder, box 71, CCS presidential papers; James B. Munn to CCS and EPS, April 19, 1953, "Personal—1953 (5/25—5/28)" folder, box 71, CCS presidential papers.

2. CCS to Murray and Helen Smith, [May 1938], C album, box H, CCS personal papers.

3. H. Wendell Endicott to Sidney J. Weinberg, April 21, 1942, "Navy Veterans Administration" folder, box I, CCS personal papers.

4. H. Wendell Endicott to Sidney J. Weinberg, April 21, 1942, H. Wendell Endicott to Director of Naval Officer Procurement, October 16, 1943, "Navy Veterans Administration" folder, box I, CCS personal papers.

5. Whitney J. Oates to CCS, April 17, 1953, "Woodrow Wilson Fellowship" folder, box H, CCS personal papers; Alexander Leitch, *A Princeton Companion* (Princeton N.J.: Princeton University Press, 1978), pp. 20–21, 167–68, 333, 343.

6. CCS to Richard H. Sullivan, January 2, 1953, "The Markle Foundation, 1953—68" folder, box F, CCS personal papers; CCS appointment diary for 1953, January 26–29, 1953, box H, CCS personal papers. The most recent history of the Markle Foundation briefly reviews the era in which Courtney Smith was active: Lee D. Mitgang, *Big Bird and Beyond: The New Media and the Markle Foundation* (New York: Fordham University Press, 2000).

7. Minutes of the Board of Directors, October 29, 1953, folder 9, box 2, series 1.1, RG 2, Markle Foundation Archives (hereafter Markle minutes), Rockefeller Archive Center (hereafter RAC), Sleepy Hollow, N.Y.

8. Frederick Osborn to Harold Helm, December 19, 1955, folder 587, box 82, Educational Interests Series, RG 2, Rockefeller Family Archives, RAC.

9. Markle Minutes, November 19, 1959; CCS notes on conference with John Russell and Jim Creese, February 15, 1960, "Markle Foundation, 1953–68" folder, box F, CCS personal papers.

10. CCS to Stuart W. Cragin, Jarvis Cromwell, Walter H. Page, and William M. Rees, March 27, 1967, unmarked folder, box F, CCS personal papers.

11. CCS to Stuart W. Cragin, *et al.,* 27 March 1967, Minutes of the Committee on Future Plans, 31 March 1967, and CCS, "Report from Committee on Future Plans," 21 June 1968, "Committee on Future Plans" folder, RG 2.6, John and Mary R. Markle Foundation Archives, RAC; draft Minutes of the Committee on Future Plans, 29 June 1967 and William M. Rees to CCS, 12 June 1968, unmarked folder, box F, CCS personal papers.

12. "Eisenhower Exchange Fellowships" pamphlet, October 14, 1953, "Eisenhower Exchange Fellowships—1953" folder, box 33, CCS presidential papers.

13. Ward Wheelock to CCS, August 27, 1953, and Agenda for Eisenhower Fellowship Committee Meeting, September 24, 1953, "Eisenhower Exchange Fellowships—1953" folder, box 33, CCS presidential papers; CCS appointment diary for 1953, September 16 and 24, 1953, box H, CCS personal papers; John Bird, "They're Learning about America," *Saturday Evening Post,* December 1955.

14. John B. Fox to CCS, July 16, 1954, "Eisenhower Exchange Fellowships—1954–55" folder, box 33; CCS to J. Hampton Barnes, October 11, 1956, and J. Hampton Barnes to CCS, October 15, 1956, "Eisenhower Exchange Fellowships—1956" folder, box 34, CCS presidential papers; CCS to J. Hampton Barnes, August 1, 1966, "Eisenhower Exchange Fellowships" folder, box F, CCS personal papers; Gilmore Stott to J. Roland

Pennock, Robert Keohane, and John Patrick, February 2, 1968, "Eisenhower Exchange Fellowships," box F, CCS personal papers.

15. Minutes of the Quaker College Presidents, January 11, 1954, January 10, 1955, January 8, 1957, January 7, 1957, "Quaker Colleges—1954–57" folder, box 64, CCS presidential papers; Prosser Gifford to CCS, c. 1960, "Quaker Colleges 1958–67" folder, box 64, CCS presidential papers; CCS to Archibald MacIntosh, December 14, 1956, "Quaker Colleges—1954–57" folder, box 64, CCS presidential papers.

16. Claude C. Smith to Joseph B. Shane, March 1, 1954, Howard R. Reidenbaugh to CCS, November 4, 1954, "PACU 1953–54" folder, box 58, CCS presidential papers.

17. Howard R. Reidenbaugh to CCS, November 4, 1954, "PACU 1953–54" folder, box 58, Edward C. Cratsley to CCS, July 28, 1955, "PACU 1955" folder, box 58, Clarence D. Bell to CCS, June 7, 1963, CCS to Edward B. Mifflin, June 8, 1963, "PACU 1963" folder, box 59, CCS presidential papers; "State Council of Higher Education—Senate Bill 569 as amended," PACU *Newsletter* (May 29, 1957) with attached memorandum of Joseph B. Shane to CCS, "PACU 1956–57" folder, box 58, CCS presidential papers.

18. CCS notes on telephone conversations with Harry M. Pluebell, April 26–27, 1957, Harry M. Pluebell to Member President, May 9, 1957, "PACU 1956–57" folder, box 58, CCS presidential papers; CCS appointment diary for 1957, May 14, 1957, box H, CCS personal papers.

19. Frederick W. Ness to CCS, October 4, 1960, "PACU 1958–60" folder, Howard R. Reidenbaugh to CCS, May 17, 1961, "PACU 1961" folder, box 59, CCS presidential papers.

20. CCS appointment diary for 1956, January 11, 1956, box H, CCS personal papers; "Alumni Funds and Annual Giving," n.d., "Association of American Colleges—1953–55" folder, box 7, CCS presidential papers; Guy E. Snavely to CCS, January 20, 1954, "Association of American Colleges—1953–55" folder, box 7, CCS presidential papers.

21. Theodore Distler to CCS, January 16, 1957, CCS to Arthur G. Coons, November 4, 1957, "American Association of Colleges—1957" folder, "Relations with CASC," March 14–15, 1961, CCS to James A. Perkins, January 19, 1961, "American Association of Colleges—1960–61" folder, box 8, CCS presidential papers.

22. CCS appointment diaries for 1956 and 1958, July 6–13, 1956 and January 4–6, 1958, box H, CCS personal papers. The Pugwash Conferences on Science and World Affairs, named for the Nova Scotian village where the first meeting was held, were founded by Albert Einstein and Bertrand Russell and focused on nuclear weapons control and disarmament.

23. American Council on Education, *A Brief Statement of the History and Activities of the American Council on Education* (Washington, D.C.: American Council on Education, 1957).

24. William K. Selden report on Section 4, October 11, 1957, Arthur S. Adams to CCS, October 15, 1957, "A.C.E. Co-op 1957" folder, box 5, CCS presidential papers; "Cooperation in the Colleges," *Newsletter of the Council for the Advancement of Small Colleges, Inc.* 2 (October 1957): 2 (copy in "A.C.E. Co-op 1957" folder, box 5, CCS presidential papers).

25. Minutes of the Commission on International Education, March 16, 1965, "ACE minutes—Commission on International Education—1962–65" folder, box 5, CCS presidential papers; CCS appointment diary for 1965, March 16, 1965, box H, CCS personal papers.

26. John E. Toulmin to CCS, November 23, 1954, CCS to Peter E. Pratt, December 23, 1954, with enclosure of CCS curriculum vitae, "Alumni Name Thirty-five for Harvard

Jobs," *New York Times,* January 15, 1955, "Harvard Board of Overseers, 1954–58" folder, box C, CCS personal papers. Senator Kennedy did not win a seat during that election but subsequently ran and was elected to the overseers.

27. David Rockefeller interview, December 4, 1992, transcript in the authors' files.

28. Benjamin Fine, "Harvard Seeking Seventy-five to One Hundred Million," *New York Times,* November 1, 1956, p. 41; "The University," *Harvard Alumni Bulletin,* June 6, 1953, pp. 699–701.

29. *Board of Overseers at Harvard College: Functions of the Harvard Visiting Committee, 1958* (Cambridge: Harvard University, 1958); "A Guide to Visiting Committee Procedure," n.d., "Harvard Board of Overseers, 1954–58" folder, box C, CCS personal papers.

30. CCS interview of Morton White, November 23, 1955, "Philosophy—Written Report for '58" folder, box C, CCS personal papers.

31. Morton White, "Harvard's Philosophical Heritage: The Evolution of the Discipline of James, Royce & Santayana," *Harvard Alumni Bulletin* (November 9, 1957): 161–64, 172.

32. CCS, "Report of the Committee to Visit the Department of Philosophy," June 11, 1959, copy in "Overseers—Philosophy—1957–59" folder, box C, CCS personal papers.

33. McGeorge Bundy to CCS, September 28, 1959, "Visiting Committee Philosophy—1960" folder, box C, CCS personal papers.

34. CCS and Committee, "Report of the Committee to Visit the Department of Philosophy," [1962], "Overseers—Philosophy—1957–59," box C, CCS personal papers.

35. CCS appointment diary for 1956, October 8 and November 26, 1956, box H, CCS personal papers; Harvard University press release, December 27, 1955, folder 498, box 68, Educational Interests Series, RG 2, Rockefeller Family Archives, RAC.

36. Elliot Dunlap Smith to Douglas Horton, May 1, 1957, "Overseers—Divinity—1956–57" folder, box C, CCS personal papers. James Conant, Pusey's predecessor, was a skeptic who seemed to care little about religious questions: Richard Norton Smith, *The Harvard Century: The Making of a University to a Nation* (New York: Simon and Schuster, 1986), pp. 109–10.

37. CCS notes on Visiting Committee meeting, January 13, 1958, "Overseers—Divinity—1957–61" folder, box C, CCS personal papers.

38. CCS notes on interview with Douglas Horton, November 25, 1957, CCS notes on interview with Elliot Dunlap Smith (former chair of the Visiting Committee), November 25, 1957, "Overseers—Divinity—1957–61" folder, "Report of the Committee to Visit the Harvard Divinity School," February 1962, "Visiting Committee—Divinity" folder, box C, CCS personal papers. In 1958 the Divinity School "set up a Center for World Religions to foster study of . . . the diverse religious communities of mankind": Nathan Pusey, *American Higher Education, 1945–1970: A Personal Report* (Cambridge: Harvard University Press, 1978), p. 37.

39. CCS notes on conversations with John Moore and Robert Cross, on Douglas Horton to Nathan M. Pusey, March 26, 1958, CCS to James R. Reynolds, January 29, 1959, George William Webber to CCS, March 30, 1959, "Overseers—Divinity—1957–61," box C, CCS personal papers.

40. Betty D. Mayo, "Harvard Divinity Dean Scans Post," *Christian Science Monitor,* August 17, 1959; *A Special Opportunity: New Patterns in Theological Education,* (Cambridge: Harvard University, 1962). *A Special Opportunity* was "made up of excerpts from the Report submitted to the Board of Overseers of Harvard College by the Committee Appointed to Visit the Divinity School, under the chairmanship of Courtney Craig Smith and dated March 12, 1962."

41. Elliot Dunlap Smith to CCS, March 18, 1960, "Visiting Committee—Divinity," box C, CCS personal papers. See also a brief history of the Divinity School in this era that dates the school's reconstruction as a scholarly institution to the late 1950s: William A. Coolidge, "Harvard Divinity School, 1954–1972," December 1972, folder 998, box 88, John H. Knowles papers, RAC.

42. CCS to Charles F. Adams, April 14, 1961, Gerard Piel to CCS, July 19, 1967, "Overseers—English Committee" folder, box C, CCS personal papers; CCS appointment diaries for 1963–64 and 1966–67, March 11, 1963, November 24, 1964, April 21, 1966, and April 17, 1967, box H, CCS personal papers.

43. CCS to Catharine Evans, May 17, 1957, "American Friends Service Committee, 1957–1959" folder, box 6, CCS presidential papers.

44. A. Burns Chalmers to CCS, June 28, 1955, "AFSC—1954–56" folder, box 6, CCS presidential papers; "American Friends Service Committee, Inc.—Educational Advisory Committee," October 17, 1957, CCS to George Mohlenhoff, March 16, 1958, "AFSC—Educational Advisory Committee—1957–59" folder, box 6, CCS presidential papers.

45. Philip D. Reed to CCS, February 1, 1955 [correspondence folder], box D, CCS personal papers; Manning M. Pattillo to CCS, February 27, 1957, "Lilly Endowment Committee, 1956–1958" folder, box 48, CCS presidential papers; Curtis G. Benjamin to CCS, January 14, 1960, "Florence Agreement Legislation" folder, box 38, CCS presidential papers; CCS appointment diaries for 1962, January 11, 1962, box H, CCS personal papers.

46. Alfred H. Williams to CCS, February 15, 1957, "Penjerdel—1957–60" folder, box F, CCS personal papers.

47. Press releases, October 3, 1957, and *Introduction to Penjerdel* (Philadelphia: Penjerdel, 1958), "Penjerdel—1957–1960" folder, box F, CCS personal papers. Swarthmore professor Charles E. Gilbert directed one of the studies, which was summarized in his book *Governing the Suburbs* (Bloomington, Ind.: Indiana University Press, 1967).

48. *A Region Takes Shape* (Philadelphia: Perjerdel Inc., 1969).

49. Nathaniel Burt, *The Perennial Philadelphians: The Anatomy of an American Aristocracy* (Boston: Little, Brown, 1963), pp. 167–68.

50. CCS to Benjamin F. Price, July 16, 1957, R. Stewart Rauch Jr. to PSFS Board of Managers, October 7, 1957, Robert B. Whitelaw to CCS, May 13, 1963, Robert B. Whitelaw to CCS, January 13, 1964, "Philadelphia Savings Fund Society—1957–65" folder, Donaldson Cresswell to CCS, December 1, 1964, "PSFS Committees" folder, "Second Interim Report of the Ad Hoc Committee to the PSFS Board" [1967], "Philadelphia Savings Fund Society—1966–68" folder, box F, CCS personal papers; CCS appointment diaries, 1957–1967, box H, CCS personal papers.

51. Minutes of Board of Managers, April 14, 1967, Philadelphia Savings Fund Society, RG 1.2.b, Philadelphia Savings Fund Society Archives, Hagley Museum and Library, Wilmington, Del. Bryn Mawr College President Katharine McBride was the woman and Judge A. Leon Higginbotham Jr. was the African American elected to the board: J. Stewart Rauch oral history, p. 59, RG 12, Philadelphia Savings Fund Society Archives, Hagley Museum and Library, Wilmington, Del.; William Glaberson, "A. Leon Higginbotham Jr., Federal Judge, Is Dead at Seventy," *New York Times,* December 15, 1998, p. b-14.

52. R. Stewart Rauch Jr. to Elizabeth P. Smith, January 24, 1969, folder R, box G, CCS personal papers.

53. CCS notes on offer of PSFS presidency, September 12–23, 1968, "Honors" folder, box D, CCS personal papers.

54. CCS memorandum on conference with Ford Foundation officers, May 11, 1955, "Asian Studies Program—1955–57" folder, box 7, CCS presidential papers.

55. Hugh Borton to John S. Everton, December 15, 1958, with Ford Foundation application, "Asian Studies Program—1958" folder, box 7, CCS presidential papers; Hugh Borton, "Asian Studies and the American Colleges," *Journal of Asian Studies* 18 (November 1958), pp. 59–65; CCS to John S. Everton, December 18, 1958, grant number 58–127, Ford Foundation Archives, New York.

56. Maralyn Orbison to CCS, February 17, 1959 with press release, "Asian Studies Program—1959–60" folder, box 7, CCS presidential papers.

57. CCS to J. Roland Pennock [September 1955], "Three Colleges—1955–59" folder, box 76, CCS presidential papers; CCS to Robert Walker, December 19, 1958, "Art Department—1954–58" folder, box 6, CCS presidential papers.

58. Milton Eisenhower to CCS, August 7, 1956, "Ea-Em 1953–1964" folder, box 33, CCS presidential papers.

59. "Memorandum of Record of the Meeting of the Visiting Committee for the Humanities, the Johns Hopkins University," April 14, 1964, "Johns Hopkins Visiting Committee," box F, CCS personal papers; CCS appointment diary for 1966, May 24, 1966, box H, CCS personal papers; CCS address, February 22, 1968, "Johns Hopkins Inauguration—22 February 1968" folder, box C, CCS personal papers.

60. CCS appointment diaries, 1961–67, November 16, 1961, November 15, 1962, June 27, 1963, November 21, 1963, November 17, 1964, June 15, 1965, November 16, 1966, June 29, 1967, September 28, 1967, November 16, 1967, box H, CCS personal papers.

61. Nathaniel Burt, *The Perennial Philadelphians: The Anatomy of an American Aristocracy* (Boston: Little, Brown, 1963), pp. 143–47.

62. Geoffrey S. Smith to Elizabeth P. Smith, March 5, 1969, "S" folder, box G, CCS personal papers; Glynn Mapes, "Two Ancient Insurers In Philadelphia Flourish Despite Relaxed Ways," *Wall Street Journal,* December 22, 1967; H. Gates Lloyd to CCS, November 20, 1967, "Philadelphia Contributorship" folder, box F, CCS personal papers.

63. *Annual Report, 1968, The Philadelphia Contributorship* (Philadelphia: The Philadelphia Contributorship, 1969).

64. *Greater Philadelphia Movement, Twentieth Annual Dinner, October 24, 1968* (Philadelphia: Greater Philadelphia Movement, 1968).

65. Gustave G. Amsterdam to CCS, October 25, 1968, "Greater Philadelphia Movement" folder, box F, CCS personal papers.

66. Gustave G. Amsterdam to CCS, October 25, 1968, with enclosure from Frederick B. Glaser, assistant professor of psychiatry, Temple University Health Science Center, "Greater Philadelphia Movement" folder, box F, CCS personal papers; Claude Lewis, "Racial Bias Film Moves Audiences Here," *The Philadelphia Bulletin,* November 3, 1968.

67. CCS to L. B. Larabee, January 15, 1968, "A-Am 1964–69" folder, box 1, CCS presidential papers.

68. CCS to Frederick Goldman, May 26, 1964, "La-Liz 1963–68" folder, box 76, CCS presidential papers.

69. See his entry in *Who's Who in America (1966–67)* 34 (Chicago: Marquis, 1966), p. 1976.

70. Ozone Club membership invitation, December 13, 1954, and "Ozone Annual Meeting 1968," [December 1968], "Ozone Etc." folder, box F, CCS personal papers; CCS appointment diaries, 1954–1967, box H, CCS personal papers; untitled Ozone Club History, 1901–55, folder 1, box 1, Ozone Golf Club records, Friends Historical Library,

Swarthmore, Pa.; Ozone Club Minute Book, minutes for December 13, 1940 and attached copy of the July 11, 1948 *Buck Hill Breeze,* box 2, Ozone Golf Club records.

71. CCS to Thomas B. McCabe, July 2, 1954, "McCabe, Thomas B., 1954–59" folder, box 51, CCS presidential papers; CCS appointment diaries, 1954–67, box H, CCS personal papers; documentation in "Sunday Breakfast Club" folder, box F, CCS personal papers.

72. CCS to Eugene Ormandy, December 8, 1960, "Pe-Pl misc. 1956–61" folder, box 58, CCS presidential papers; CCS to W. Atlee Burpee, February 12, 1962, "Pe-Pl misc. 1962–65" folder, box 58, CCS presidential papers.

73. Documents in "Harvard Club of Philadelphia and Harvard Alumni Association" folder, box F, CCS personal papers.

74. *Biographical Directory of the United States Congress, 1774–1989* (Washington, D.C.: U.S. Government Printing Office, 1989), p. 1443.

75. *Current Biography Yearbook 1963,* s.v. "Gordon, Kermit," (New York, NY: H. W. Wilson Company, 1963), pp. 153–55.

CHAPTER 13. "NATURE SHAPED TO ADVANTAGE"

Phrase from CCS, remarks, [c. May 1954], "Scott Fndn—25 anniv." folder, box A, CCS personal papers. CCS cited Alexander Pope as the source of this phrase: it appears to be not a direct quotation but a variation on one in "An Essay in Criticism," which reads, "True Wit is Nature to Advantage dressed": Herbert Davis, ed., *Pope: Poetical Works* (London: Oxford, 1966), p. 74, verse 297.

1. CCS, remarks, [ca. May 1954], "Scott Fndn—25 anniv." folder, box A, CCS personal papers.

2. The Blue Route was a segment of an "outer belt" expressway intended to encircle Philadelphia, similar to other outer belts or beltways that were planned for other major American cities in the mid-century: most large cities had plans for two rings, or belts, of highways, one circling the central business district, and one at the beginning edge of dense urban growth.

3. The interstate highway act did not become law until 1956, but momentum had been building since February 1955 when President Eisenhower submitted a special message to Congress proposing a new national highway system: Richard O. Davies, *The Age of Asphalt: The Automobile, the Freeway, and the Condition of Metropolitan America* (Philadelphia: J. B. Lippincott, 1975), p. 22, 51–55.

4. CCS to John C. Wister, March 15, 1954, "Scott Foundation 1954–1963" folder, box 67, CCS presidential papers; Arnold Nicholson, "People's Garden: The Story of the Arthur Hoyt Scott Foundation, Swarthmore College," *Saturday Evening Post,* April 14, 1945; "Arthur Hoyt Scott Horticultural Foundation: Swarthmore Centennial," September 18, [1963], "Scott Foundation 1954–1963" folder, box 67, CCS presidential papers.

5. Richard J. Walton, *Swarthmore College: An Informal History* (Swarthmore, Pa.: Swarthmore College, 1986), pp. 45–46, 117; Elizabeth Weber and Margaret Helfand, "The Campus That Never Was," *Swarthmore College Bulletin* 96 (September 1998): 8.

6. Cliff Ellis, "Professional Conflict over Urban Form: The Case of Urban Freeways, 1930 to 1970," in *Planning the Twentieth-Century American City,* ed. Mary Corbin Sies and Christopher Silver (Baltimore: Johns Hopkins University Press, 1996), p. 271.

7. Clarence G. Myers to Joseph Shane, August 3, 1955, and Joseph Shane to CCS, August 4, 1955, "Mi misc. 1955–69" folder, box 51, CCS presidential papers.

8. CCS to Board of Managers, January 28, 1957, "Board of Managers, 1954–65" folder, box 20, CCS to Swarthmore Alumni, February 19, 1957, "By-pass (Blue Route) alumni correspondence, 1957 February" folder, box 11, CCS presidential papers; February 4 and 19, March 6, 12, and 29, CCS appointment diary 1957, box H, CCS personal papers.

9. CCS notes, February 4, 1957, "Borough meeting on roads" folder, box A, CCS personal papers.

10. Minutes, Swarthmore College Corporation, October 1, 1957, Friends Historical Library, Swarthmore, Pa.

11. Ellis, "Professional Conflict over Urban Form," *Planning the Twentieth-Century American City*, pp. 272–73; Jon C. Teaford, *The Twentieth-Century American City: Problem, Promise, and Reality* (Baltimore: Johns Hopkins University Press, 1986), pp. 99–100.

12. Minutes, Swarthmore College Corporation, July 10, 1960, Friends Historical Library, Swarthmore, Pa.

13. W. C. H. Prentice to Kermit Gordon, August 17, 1961, "Swarthmore College" folder, box 69, Kermit Gordon papers, John F. Kennedy Presidential Library, Boston.

14. Ibid.; May 29 and September 29, CCS appointment diary 1961, box H, CCS personal papers.

15. Theodore Distler to CCS, March 1, 1961, "Association of American Colleges, 1960–61" folder, box 8, CCS presidential papers; CCS to David Bailey, December 11, 1961, "Harvard Board of Overseers, 1958–65" folder, box C, CCS presidential papers.

16. "A College and a Highway," *Philadelphia Bulletin,* December 6, 1961, p. B-17.

17. "A College and a Highway," p. B-17.

18. CCS, remarks at Swarthmore commencement, "Commencement Review of the Year—11 June 1962" folder, box B, CCS personal papers.

19. CCS to David W. Bailey, August 1, 1962, "Overseers—Philosophy 1959–62" folder, box C, CCS personal papers.

20. CCS, "Report of the President for the Year 1961–62," *Swarthmore College Bulletin* 60 (May 1963): 18; CCS appointment diary for 1962, December, 27, box H, CCS personal papers.

21. CCS to Clarence D. Martin Jr., December 31, 1963, "Blue Route Correspondence, General, 1964–66" folder, box 14, CCS presidential papers; CCS appointment diary for 1963, November, 4, box H, CCS personal papers.

22. Joseph S. Clark to CCS, March 20, 1964, "Blue Route Correspondence, General, 1964–66" folder, box 14, CCS presidential papers; CCS remarks, "Commencement 8 June 1964" folder, box B, CCS personal papers.

23. David Smith interview, August 7, 1991, in authors' files.

24. CCS, "A Summary of Swarthmore College's Position on the Mid-County Expressway (Interstate Route 480)," May 27, 1965, "Blue Route—Official Statements 1961–65" folder, box 20, CCS presidential papers.

25. Ellis, "Professional Conflict over Urban Form," *Planning the Twentieth-Century American City*, pp. 274–75.

26. CCS appointment diary for 1965, April 5 and May 27, box H, CCS personal papers; CCS, "A Summary of Swarthmore College's Position on the Mid-County Expressway (Interstate 480)," May 27, 1965, and press release, "The Mid-county Expressway in the Crum Creek Valley," June 1965, in "Blue Route—Official Statements 1961–65" folder, box 20, CCS presidential papers; "Blue Route Battle: After Ten Years Nether Providence Bows to Crum," *Phoenix,* September 17, 1965, pp. 1, 4.

27. CCS to Elvis J. Stahr, December 31, 1968, "Sm-Sz Misc. 1965–68" folder, box 70, CCS presidential papers; Davies, *The Age of Asphalt,* p. 34.

Blue Route construction began in 1985 and was completed by the early 1990s. Interstate 480 (still popularly known as the "Blue Route") is a reality and the campus has been affected, but it was the time, energy and persistence of Smith's ten-year battle over ideologies of development and prioritization of public resources that resulted in so little being sliced from the campus.

28. John M. and Margaret Moore interview, November 16, 1991, and Eleanor S. Clarke interview, May 10, 1991, in authors' files.

29. CCS, notes, "Commencement—7 June 1954" folder, box A, CCS personal papers; "Twenty-five year plans of development for Swarthmore College," June 1945, attachment to James A. Perkins to CCS, [April 1963], "Perkins, James A., 1954–67" folder, box 60, CCS presidential papers; CCS, "Report of the President for the Year 1955–56," *Swarthmore College Bulletin* 54 (January 1957): p. 20.

30. CCS to Edward K. Cratsley, February 18, 1955, "Six Point Program—Somerville, Athletics, etc." folder, box 70, CCS presidential papers.

31. Irving E. Dayton, "The Pierre S. du Pont Science Building, Swarthmore College," *American Journal of Physics* 29 (November 1961): 761–62.

32. Ibid., pp. 754, 761.

33. See "Animal Lab" folder, box 6, CCS presidential papers.

34. CCS remarks, "1st Collection 27 September 1962" folder, box B, CCS personal papers.

35. "The Fine Art of Eating at Swarthmore," *American School and University* 39 (April 1967): 50.

36. CCS remarks, "Michigan Alumni 22 Jan 64" folder, box B, CCS personal papers. It is not clear what architectural prize Smith was referring to at this time: in 1968 Vincent Kling received the Samuel F. B. Morse medal for architecture for his design of the Sharples Dining Hall.

37. CCS, remarks, [ca. May 1954], "Scott Fndn—25 anniv." folder, box A, CCS personal papers.

38. Thomas A. Gaines, *The Campus as a Work of Art* (New York: Praeger, 1991), p. 87.

## Chapter 14. Student Activism

1. Courtney C. Smith, "The Academic Community and Social Concerns," *Swarthmore College Bulletin* 63 (December 1965): 2–8. All quotations in the following discussion are from this essay unless otherwise noted. Page locations of cited passages are in parentheses.

2. Richard J. Walton, *Swarthmore College: An Informal History* (Swarthmore, Pa.: Swarthmore College, 1986), p. 84.

3. CCS to Richard O. Niehoff, February 4, 1958, "Fraternities 1958–1966" folder, box 39, CCS presidential papers.

4. CCS remarks, "Annual Report, 3 December 1963" folder, box B, CCS personal papers.

5. *The Inauguration of Courtney Craig Smith as Ninth President of Swarthmore College* (Swarthmore, Pa.: Swarthmore College, 1953); untitled news clipping, December 1, 1953, album C, box H, CCS personal papers.

6. Minutes, Swarthmore College Corporation, December 2, 1957, June 5, 1959, Friends Historical Library, Swarthmore, Pa. See chapter 11 for further discussion of the NDEA disclaimer affidavit.

7. Benjamin Fine, "Educator Descries College Snobbery," *New York Times*, February 10, 1955, p. 33.

8. *Swarthmore Today and Tomorrow* (Swarthmore, Pa.: Swarthmore College, 1963), p. 24.

9. CCS remarks, "Commencement—7 June 1954" folder, box A, CCS personal papers.

10. CCS remarks, "Manners and Morals II" folder, c. 1956, box A, CCS personal papers.

11. "Swarthmore College: Tailored to the Individual," *Business Week*, June 8, 1957, p. 140.

When growing beards began to be a visible expression of student identity in the early 1960s, Smith was much more tolerant than many of his generation, telling alumni that "Americans often grow beards when number give safety" and that "most men would like to grow a beard": CCS remarks, "Swarthmore Club of Philadelphia Dinner, 2/8/64" folder, box B, CCS personal papers.

12. CCS, remarks, "1st Collection, 27 September 1962" folder, box B, CCS personal papers.

13. "Twenty-three Test Public Accomodations on Maryland's Eastern Shore," *Phoenix*, February 9, 1962; Peter B. Levy, "Civil War on Race Street: The Black Freedom Struggle and White Resistance in Cambridge, Maryland, 1960–1964," *Maryland Historical Magazine* 89 (fall 1994): 296–300; Wesley Hogan, "How Democracy Travels: SNCC, Swarthmore Students, and the Growth of the Student Movement in the North, 1961–1964," *Pennsylvania Magazine of History and Biography* 126 (2002):43–51.

14. Fred Powledge, *Free at Last: The Civil Rights Movement and the People Who Made It* (Boston: Little, Brown, 1991), pp. 524–25; Clayborne Carson, *In Struggle: SNCC and the Black Awakening of the 1960s* (Cambridge: Harvard University Press, 1981), pp. 72–73, 89–95, 252–58.

15. CCS remarks, "Commencement review of the year 6/10/63" folder, box B, CCS personal papers.

16. "SPAC Plans Stand-In," *Phoenix*, November 12, 1963; statement, Susan Cobbs, Robert Barr, and Barbara Lange, November 19, 1963, "Chester Movement, 1963–64" folder, box 24, CCS presidential papers.

17. Raphael L. Polosky to Susan Cobbs, November 25, 1963, "Chester Movement, 1963–64" folder, box 24, CCS presidential papers; minutes, December 9, 1963, "Faculty Mtgs., 1956–57" folder, box 37, CCS presidential papers.

18. CCS remarks, "1st Collection, 24 Sept 1964" folder, box B, CCS personal papers.

19. Lee Smith Ingram interview, April 2, 1995, in authors' files.

20. "SPAC Initiates Protest; Requests College End Support of Chase Bank," *Phoenix*, March 2, 1965; "Students, President Smith Discuss Chase Open Letter," *Phoenix*, March 9, 1965; Gilmore Stott to CCS, March 21, 1965, "Chase Manhattan Bank Issue" folder, box 24, CCS presidential papers.

21. CCS, notes on conversation with David Rockefeller, March 30, 1965, "Chase Manhattan Bank Issue" folder, box 24, CCS presidential papers.

22. "Board to Keep Chase Stock; Terms Student Plea Unjust," *Phoenix*, April 16, 1965; minutes, Swarthmore College Corporation, April 13, 1965, Friends Historical Library, Swarthmore, Pa.

23. Andy Lyon to CCS, April 21, 1965, "Chase Manhattan Bank Issue" folder, box 24, CCS presidential papers.

24. The Sullivan Principles primarily called for desegregation of workplaces, equal pay for equal work, enhanced job training, a commitment to increasing the number of nonwhite managers, and improving housing and schooling for nonwhites.

25. CCS remarks, "1st Collection, 27 September 1962" folder, box B, CCS personal papers; *Phoenix,* September 28, 1962.

26. CCS remarks, "Alumni Day, 10 June 1967" folder, box C, CCS personal papers.

27. Peter H. Binzen, "Don't Be an Automatic Liberal, Smith Tells Swarthmore Students," *Philadelphia Bulletin,* May 26, 1963.

28. CCS to Joseph S. Clark, draft, n.d., "Draft 1966" folder, box 32, CCS presidential papers.

29. "Report of the Ad Hoc Committee on the Draft, May 1967," "Board of Managers, 1966–69" folder, box 20, CCS presidential papers.

30. CCS to Edith Green, February 28, 1968, "Draft 1968" folder, box 32, CCS presidential papers.

31. CCS remarks, "Rhodes Scholars Sailing Dinner 3 October 1968" folder, box C, CCS personal papers. Smith's remarks provide a particular historical perspective on William J. Clinton's state of mind when the future president sought a deferment in November 1968. While some have described Clinton's action as self-concerned or even devious, this context suggests that it may be equally valid to consider that his action was taken with the explicit knowledge that he could not depend on the experienced Rhodes administrators to negotiate the Selective Service System effectively, and that being able to serve out his Rhodes term depended on his own maneuvering within the system.

32. Clayton D. Ford to CCS, December 2, 1968, "Pl misc. 1962–68" folder, box 63, CCS presidential papers.

## Chapter 15. Two Decades of Student Life

1. CCS notes, "1st Collection, 2 October 1958" folder, box A, CCS personal papers. Smith, in his 1968 address to freshmen, also made similar remarks about the positive qualities that incoming students were bringing to the campus: CCS notes, "Welcome Freshmen, 18 September 1968" folder, box C, CCS personal papers.

2. Peter H. Binzen, " Don't Be an Automatic Liberal, Smith Tells Swarthmore Students," *Philadelphia Bulletin,* May 26, 1963.

3. CCS, "Smith Calls Swarthmore Attitude College's Most Important Asset," *The Phoenix,* January 17, 1965.

4. CCS notes, "Men's Sunday Breakfast Club, 22 May 1955" folder, box A, CCS personal papers.

5. Barbara Keay to CCS, April 14, 1953, "Personal—1953 (4/8–5/23)" folder, box 71, CCS presidential papers.

6. Ralph Lee Smith, "If I Had a Song . . . ," *Swarthmore College Bulletin* 94 (March 1997): 17–18; David King Dunaway, *How Can I Keep from Singing: Pete Seeger* (New York: McGraw-Hill, 1981), pp. 158–59.

7. Smith, "If I Had a Song . . . ," 19.

8. Willis J. Stetson to CCS, May 26, 1954, "Use of College Facilities" folder, box 78; Virginia Rath and Irene Moll to CCS, January 25, 1956 and CCS to Rath and Moll, January 30, 1956, "F-misc., 1957–62," box 37; Ginnie Beth Beam to Irene Moll, [fall 1958], "Phoenix—1955–61" folder, box 61; "Swarthmore Student Folk Festival—1962," "F-misc. 1957–62" folder, box 37, CCS presidential papers; "Pete Seeger, Gary Davis, Ellen Stekert to Perform Today," *Phoenix,* April 13, 1962, p. 1; Pete Seeger to authors, April 14, 1995, in authors' files; Smith, "If I Had a Song . . . ," *Swarthmore College Bulletin* 94 (March 1997): 20.

See also a summary of the Folk Festival's early years in Everett Lee Hunt, *The Revolt of the College Intellectual* (Chicago: Aldine, 1963), pp. 73–75; and Smith, "If I Had a Song . . . ," 16–21, 62.

9. CCS notes, "Forum on Rules, etc.—9 April 1962" folder, box B, CCS personal papers; Richard Barrett, "Smith Speaks on Rules; Stresses Responsibility," *Phoenix,* April 13, 1962.

10. Lawrence Lafore, "Today's College Student," *Philadelphia Bulletin Magazine,* November 18, 1962, p. 4.

11. Hunt, *The Revolt of the College Intellectual* p. 98.

12. CCS notes, circa March 1957, "Open House, 1955–58" folder, box 57, CCS presidential papers.

13. See "Open Houses 1955–68" folder, box 57, CCS presidential papers. According to Burton R. Clark, *The Distinctive College: Antioch, Reed and Swarthmore* (Chicago: Aldine, 1970), p. 224, regarding regulations, "students [at Swarthmore] were not as free as their counterparts at Antioch and Reed."

14. Jeremy J. Stone to CCS, February 19, 1957; CCS notes, circa March 1957; Student Activities Committee Minutes, March 12, 1957, February 12, 1960; "Excerpt from President Courtney Smith's Collection Speech on 24 September 1964"; and Student Affairs Committee, memorandum to CCS, May 1966, all in "Open House, 1955–68" folder, box 57, CCS presidential papers.

15. Jed Rakoff (1963) interview, March 12, 1993, authors' files.

16. "Swarthmore College Student Activities, Parents Day, May 2, 1959," attached to CCS notes, "Parents Day, 2 May 1959" folder, box A, CCS personal papers.

17. CCS to Mrs. J. Donald Patton, November 19, 1959, "P-misc.,1956–66" folder, box 57, CCS presidential papers.

18. CCS notes, "1st Collection, 27 September 1962" folder, box B, CCS personal papers; Carl Wittman, "Pres. Smith Asks for More 'Dialogue' in College Community," *Phoenix,* September 28, 1962, p. 1; Carl Wittman, *Phoenix* editor-in-chief in the fall 1962, has been as identified as a campus leader and later organizer of Students for a Democratic Society, in Doug Rossinow, "The Ideal of Community in the New Left: Swarthmore College in the 1960," 1995, copy in the authors' files.

19. *The Roundup* [Roosevelt High School Yearbook] (Des Moines, Iowa, 1934), p. 52; CCS to the Committee on the Selection of the Rhodes Scholars for the State of Iowa, [November 1937], "Rhodes Scholarship" folder, box I, CCS personal papers; CCS to all of you, October 20, 1938, album C, box H, CCS personal papers; CCS to Murray and Helen Smith, [May 1938], Album C, box H, CCS personal papers.

20. William Murphy interview, October 22, 1994, in authors' files; CCS notes, "Maxwell Club Luncheon, 13 November 1961" folder, box B, CCS personal papers; CCS notes, "Oxford-Cambridge Boatrace Dinner, 1 April 1960" folder, box B, CCS personal papers.

21. CCS notes, "Maxwell Club Luncheon, 13 November 1961" folder, box B, CCS personal papers.

22. John C. Hoy interview, February 11, 1999, in authors' files.

23. In December 2000 Swarthmore College terminated its football program: Jere Longman, "No More Football, Lots of Questions," *New York Times,* December 5, 2000, pp. D1, D4; Welch Suggs, "Swarthmore Kicks Football out of College," *The Chronicle of Higher Education,* December 15, 2000, pp. A55–A56.

24. David Smith interview, August 7, 1991, in authors' files.

25. CCS, memorandum to all Swarthmore students, October 19, 1966, "Office Hours, 1966–68" folder, box 57, CCS presidential papers.

26. See, especially, Open Office Hour on April 20, 1967, "Office Hours, 1966–68" folder, box 57, CCS presidential papers.

27. Rakoff interview; Michael Dukakis (1954) interview, October 9, 1994; and, Paul Peele (1969) interview, October 10, 1994, in authors' files.

28. Frank A. Sieverts, "Courtney Smith at Swarthmore," *The American Oxonian* 56 (April 1969): 68–69.

29. Rakoff interview.

30. Leo M. Leva to CCS, May 10, 1967, "Campus Roads" folder, box 21, CCS presidential papers.

31. Paul Leavin, "LBJ, Smith and McCabe Are ALL Paper Tigers," *Phoenix,* October 6, 1967, p. 2.

32. Hamburg Show script, [1967], "H-misc. 1953–58" folder, box 41, CCS presidential papers.

33. Terry H. Anderson, *The Sixties* (New York: Longman, 1999), pp. 132–35.

34. Robert D. Cross to Helen F. Post, August 3, 1969, "Post, Helen F." folder, box 63, CCS presidential papers.

## CHAPTER 16. "PERSONAL THINGS"

The epigraph is from: CCS to Edward Weismiller, July 6, 1960, W folder, box D, CCS personal papers.

1. Elizabeth Smith Ingram interview, April 2, 1995, authors' files.

2. CCS appointment diaries, April 2–3, 1958, March 6, 1959, April 5, 1959, November 22, 1959, November 19, 1961, November 3, 1963, April 17, 1964, May 12–14, 1967, box H, CCS personal papers.

3. CCS draft address to alumni dinner, fall 1953, alumni dinner folder, box A, CCS personal papers. These lines were scratched out and presumably not delivered.

4. Ingram interview.

5. Ibid.; Samuel Hynes interview, May 7, 1994, authors' files.

6. CCS to Robert Lyle, June 3, 1954, "Invitations Accepted for Future," box D, CCS personal papers; CCS appointment diary, June 28, 1966, box H, CCS personal papers.

7. Joseph H. Willits to Elizabeth P. Smith, June 7, 1964, in "Smith, Courtney" folder, box D, CCS personal papers.

8. George Becker to Elizabeth P. Smith, n.d. [July 1968], "Smith Resignation" folder, box D, CCS personal papers; Charles Gilbert, interview, February 10, 1996, in authors' files; Edward Weismiller interview, November 11, 1994, authors' files; Mr. and Mrs. Robert Cross interview, November 12, 1994, in authors' files.

9. CCS appointment diaries from 1954–67, box H, CCS personal papers; CCS to Edward Weismiller, July 6, 1960, W folder, box D, CCS personal papers; CCS to Oreon Keeslar, June 27, 1967, and CCS to Mrs. A. W. Ehrhorn, June 27, 1967, box I, CCS personal papers; CCS to Murray and Elizabeth Smith, January 22, 1968, CCS album, box H, CCS personal papers.

10. See the discussion of CCS's appreciation of Ortega y Gasset in chapter 9.

11. Elizabeth Smith Ingram interview, April 2, 1995, in authors' files.

12. CCS appointment diaries, March 24, 1954, November 25, 1957, November 25, 1958, box H, CCS personal papers; CCS to Murray D. Smith, April 27, 1957, *Chicago Tribune* folder, box 25, CCS presidential papers.

13. S. Oliver Goodman, "C. D. Smith Named to High RCA Post," *Washington Post,*

June 4, 1960, p. C9; CCS appointment diaries, March 17, 1959, May 5, 1959, June 11–12, 1960, December 12, 1960, May 4, 1961, July 13, 1962, February 27, 1963, May 13, 1963, March 15, 1965, June 30, 1965, April 8, 1967, box H, CCS personal papers.

14. Ingram interview; "Van Syoc, Wayland Bryce," *Directory of American Scholars,* 6th ed. (New York and London: R. R. Bowker, 1974), 3:480; CCS appointment diaries, 1958–67, box H, CCS personal papers.

15. "Golden Pond Is Now Open to the Public," *New York Times,* September 8, 1999, p. A-18. Squam Lake was the setting for the 1980 feature film "On Golden Pond."

16. CCS appointment diaries, June 13–26, 1950, June 13–July 1, 1951, August 3, 1954, August 1–2, 1955, August 1–September 4, 1956, September 6, 1957, August 1–September 6, 1958, August 1–September 8, 1959, August 1–September 7, 1960, August 2–September 4, 1962, August 1–September 4, 1963, August 7–September 8, 1964, August 3–September 6, 1966, July 1, 1967.

17. C. Craig Smith interview, February 12, 1993, in authors' files; Ingram interview.

18. Ibid.; CCS appointment diary for 1953, April 24–August 3, 1953, box H, CCS personal papers.

19. Ingram interview; CCS appointment diary for 1961, June 28–September 5, 1961, box H, CCS personal papers.

20. CCS to J. Russell Smith, September 11, 1961, "Sm-Sz misc." folder, box 70, CCS presidential papers.

21. E. P. Smith to Murray and Elizabeth Smith, n.d. [January 1966], first tan album, box H, CCS personal papers; CCS to Mr. and Mrs. Willie Lasser, n.d. [August 1966], box D, CCS personal papers; CCS appointment diaries, October 3–December 17, 1965 and February 17–25, 1966, box H, CCS personal papers; Ingram interview; Smith interview.

22. CCS appointment diaries, January 10–14, 1959, January 26–February 3, 1963, February 10–17, 1964, February 21–March 2, 1965, March 2–9, 1967, box H, CCS personal papers; Ingram interview.

23. William H. Whyte Jr., *The Organization Man* (Garden City, N.Y.: Doubleday, 1956), pp. 162–65, quote on p. 162.

## Chapter 17. Administration of a College

1. *Philadelphia Bulletin,* April 7, 1953, clipping in "Smith, Courtney" folder, box D, CCS personal papers.

2. Frances Blanshard, *Frank Aydelotte of Swarthmore* (Middletown, Conn.: Wesleyan University Press, 1970), p. 259; Richard J. Walton, *Swarthmore College: An Informal History;* (Swarthmore, Pa.: Swarthmore College, 1986), p. 92; John Moore letter, November 28, 1984, in authors' files; John Moore, interview, November 16, 1991, authors' files.

3. John Nason to Joseph B. Shane, April 15, 1950, "Shane, Joseph B. 1948–54" folder, box 69, CCS presidential papers.

4. Everett Lee Hunt, *The Revolt of the College Intellectual* (Chicago: Aldine, 1963).

5. Joseph Shane to CCS, April 6, 1956, "Dean" folder, box 31, CCS presidential papers.

6. Robert Barr interview, May 7, 1993, in authors' files.

7. Blanshard, *Frank Aydelotte of Swarthmore,* p. 172; Prosser Gifford, interview, November 11, 1994, in authors' files.

8. CCS to Prosser Gifford, May 17, 1956, "Gifford, P." folder, box 41, CCS presidential papers; Gifford interview.

9. CCS, "Report of the President for the Year 1957–58," *Swarthmore College Bulletin* 56 (January 1959): 30.

10. CCS to Richard Pfaff, July 16, 1966, "Pfaff, Richard W." folder, box 60, CCS presidential papers.

11. CCS, memorandum to Faculty, Staff and Student Body, May 26, 1962, "Faculty, Memoranda to" folder, 1953–68, box 37, CCS presidential papers; CCS, "Report of the President for the Year 1961–1962", *Swarthmore College Bulletin* 60 (May 1963): 19–20; resumé of Barbara Pearson Lange, January 1964, "Lange, Barbara—Dean" folder, box 47, CCS presidential papers.

12. John C. Hoy interview, February 11, 1999, in authors' files; Rockefeller Foundation Trustees docket item 64198, April 1, 1964, folder 769, box 89, series 200, RG 1.2, Rockefeller Foundation Archives (hereafter RFA), Rockefeller Archive Center, Sleepy Hollow, N.Y.

13. Terri Shane interview, August 6, 1991; Barr interview; Gifford interview; Gilmore Stott interview, February 10, 1996; and John C. Hoy interview, February 11, 1999, all in the authors' files.

14. Shane interview.

15. Shane notes, "Invitations Accepted for Future" folder, box D, CCS personal papers; CCS to Joseph B. Shane, February 18, 1955, "Shane, Joseph 1955–62" folder, box 69, CCS presidential papers.

16. CCS appointment diaries, 1954–55, 1963–67, box H, CCS personal papers.

17. Stott interview.

18. Samuel Hynes interview, May 7, 1994, in authors' files.

19. Robert D. Cross interview, November 12, 1994, authors' files.

20. Kenneth W. Thompson diary entry, November 12, 1964, folder 200–1964, box GC 484, RG 2, RFA.

21. James Field interview, April 30, 1993, in authors' files.

22. Comments on Annual Report for 1957–58 and Annual Report for 1958–59, box A, CCS personal papers.

23. Cross interview; John and Margaret Moore interview, November 16, 1991, in authors' files.

24. CCS appointment diary for 1959, July 8–10, 1959, CCS appointment diary for 1966, June 26–29, 1966, box H, CCS personal papers; Gilmore Stott to CCS, July 3, 1959, "Rehoboth Meeting—Planning Committee, 1959" folder, box 65, CCS presidential papers; Gilmore Stott to CCS et al., June 23, 1966, "Rehoboth Conference, 1966" folder, box 65, CCS presidential papers. There was an earlier administrative retreat held at Rehoboth Beach in the summer of 1959.

25. CCS to Members of the Administrative Staff, June 24, 1966, "Rehoboth Conference 1966" folder, box 65, CCS presidential papers.

26. Monroe Beardsley et al. to CCS, May 2, 1966, "Commission on Educational Policy, 1966 (1–9)" folder, box 28, CCS presidential papers.

27. CCS notes on Beardsley et al. to CCS, May 2, 1966, "Commission on Educational Policy 1966 (1–9)" folder, box 28, CCS presidential papers; Hynes interview; Charles Gilbert interview, February 10, 1996, in authors' files.

28. Gilbert interview.

29. CCS, "Report of the President for the Year 1965–66," *Swarthmore College Bulletin* 64 (January 1967): 7, 12. The title "Commission on Educational Policy" was not determined until July 1966, when Courtney wrote to Chuck Gilbert saying it was "an excellent name"; apparently he made the editorial addition for the published version of his June

speech. CCS to Charles E. Gilbert, July 11, 1966, "Commission on Educational Policy 1966 (1–9)" folder, box 28, CCS presidential papers.

30. CCS to Charles E. Gilbert, July 11, 1966, "Commission on Educational Policy 1966 (1–9)" folder, box 28, CCS presidential papers.

31. Gilmore Stott to Members of the Administrative Staff, October 24, 1966, "Rehoboth Conference 1966" folder, box 65, CCS presidential papers.

32. CCS notes, August 1966, "Commission on Educational Policy 1966 (1–9)" folder, box 28, CCS presidential papers.

33. CCS memorandum, September 19, 1966, and Commission of Educational Policy to Members of the Faculty and Administration, September 30, 1966, both in "Commission on Educational Policy 1966 (1–9)" folder, box 28, CCS presidential papers.

34. News release, October 25, 1966, "Commission on Educational Policy 1966 (1–9)" folder, box 28, CCS presidential papers.

35. CCS appointment diary for 1966, November 25–27, 1966, box H, CCS personal papers.

36. David Smith to CCS, January 25, 1967, "co-education 1966–67" folder, box 25, and CCS to George E. McCully, November 4, 1966, "Committee on the Library 1966–68" folder, box 29, CCS presidential papers; Charles E. Gilbert to CCS, May 3, 1967, "Vassar May 5–6" folder, box C, and CCS appointment diary for 1967, February 19, 1967, April 23, 1967, August 26, 1967, August 31, 1967, September 1, 1967, and September 23, 1967, box H, CCS personal papers.

37. Bob Goodman, "Pres. Smith Opens 'Year of Decision' in Collection," *Phoenix,* September 29, 1967, p. 1.

38. CCS, "President Courtney Smith's Talk at the Alumni Dinner on June 8, 1968," "Alumni Day speeches" folder, box 2, CCS presidential papers.

39. Comission on Educational Policy, *Critique of a College* (Swarthmore, Pa.: Swarthmore College, 1967), pp. 291, 293.

40. Ibid., pp. 296–97.

41. Ibid., p. 297.

42. Clark Kerr, who served on the college's Board of Managers immediately after the Smith presidency, believed that Smith was the last of "three strong presidents" at Swarthmore, and that subsequently power devolved substantially to the new provost and the board of managers: Clark Kerr interview, August 28, 1995, in authors' files.

43. Joseph H. Willits to CCS, February 1, 1968, "Commission on Educational Policy 1968 (1–3)" folder, box 28, CCS presidential papers; Harris Wofford, "In Search of Liberal Education," *Saturday Review,* July 20, 1968, pp. 50–51, 61; George Von der Muhll to Roland Pennock, January 17, 1969, "V" folder, box G, CCS personal papers; Barr interview; Hynes interview; Harrison Wright interview, May 8, 1994, in authors' files; Gilbert interview.


CHAPTER 18. THE FINAL YEAR


1. Commission on Educational Policy, *Critique of a College* (Swarthmore, Pa.: Swarthmore College, 1967).

2. Ibid., p. 293.

3. Ibid., e.g., p. 291.

4. The Yankelovich report of 1972, based on surveys conducted since the mid-1960s, provides a useful view of the rapid changes in the attitudes of American students, changes

that to some degree were reflections of changes in behavior: Daniel Yankelovich, *The Changing Values on Campus: Political and Personal Attitudes of Today's College Students* (New York: Washington Square Press, 1972).

5. *Critique of a College,* pp. 401–26.

6. CCS, "Report of the President for the Year 1967–68," June 10, 1968, in "Commencement Review of the Year, 10 June 1968" folder, box C, CCS personal papers.

7. "Revision of SCOLP Recommendations," January 12, 1968, "Committee on the Library, 1966–68" folder, box 29, CCS presidential papers.

8. Three issues of *The Egg* are preserved in "Phoenix 1962–68" folder, box 61, CCS presidential papers.

9. See CCS's edited copies of the faculty meeting agendas in "Faculty Meetings 1968, Feb.–Apr." folder, and "Faculty Meetings 1968, May–Dec., [and Jan.] 1969" folder, box 37, CCS presidential papers.

10. CCS, "President Courtney Smith's Talk at the Alumni Dinner on June 8, 1968," "Alumni Day Speeches" folder, box 2, CCS presidential papers.

11. CCS remarks, "Report of the President for the Year 1967–68," "Commencement Review of the Year, 10 June 1968" folder, box C, CCS personal papers.

12. Ibid.

13. Ibid.

14. Ibid.

15. Minutes of the Committee on Future Plans, June 20, 1968, RG 2.6, Markle Foundation Archives, Rockefeller Archive Center, Sleepy Hollow, N.Y.

16. Tamara G. Strickland and Stephen P. Strickland, *The Markle Scholars: A Brief History* (New York: John and Mary R. Markle Foundation, 1976), pp. 11, 66–67.

17. CCS to Faculty and Staff, July 16, 1968, folder "Smith, Courtney—resignation," box D, CCS personal papers; this folder also contains several hundred letters regarding the Swarthmore resignation and Markle appointment.

18. "President of Swarthmore Heads Markle Fund Here," *New York Times,* July 17, 1968, p. 22.

19. Edward Joseph Shoben Jr. to CCS, July 27, 1968, folder "American Council on Education, 1967–69," box 2, CCS presidential papers; "Oral History of the Samuel Craig Smith/Myrtle Dabney Smith Family," typescript dated October 6, 1990, supplied to the authors by Elizabeth Smith Ingram.

20. CCS remarks, June 12, 1968, "Welcome Civic Conference 12 June 68" folder, box C, CCS personal papers.

21. CCS to Bill H. Wilcox, July 22, 1968, "Greater Philadelphia Movement" folder, box F, CCS personal papers.

22. CCS notes on offer of PSFS presidency, September 12–23, 1968, "Honors" folder, box D, CCS personal papers; Board of Managers minutes, October 14, 1960—January 10, 1969, Philadelphia Savings Fund Society records, Hagley Library and Museum, Wilmington, Del.

23. CCS remarks, "Welcome Freshmen 18 Sept 1968" folder, box C, CCS personal papers; CCS remarks, "1st Collection, 26 Sept 1968" folder, box C, CCS personal papers. Courtney recently had clipped *New York Times* articles about student demands for change at universities; see "9 Oct 68—Wilmington College Convocation" folder, box C, CCS personal papers.

24. Frederick A. Hargadon to Leland DeVinney, October 5, 1968, and Leland DeVinney to Frederick A. Hargadon, November 21, 1968, folder 769, box 89, series 200, RG 1.2, Rockefeller Foundation Archives (hereafter RFA), Rockefeller Archive Center, Sleepy

Hollow, N.Y.; "The Admission Policy Committee's Study of Negro Student Recruitment and Enrollment: A Chronology," "Admissions Policy Committee, 1968" folder, box 2, CCS presidential papers; minutes, Swarthmore College Corporation, January 25, 1969, Friends' Historical Library, Swarthmore, Pa.

25. "The Admission Policy Committee's Study of Negro Student Recruitment and Enrollment: A Chronology," "Admissions Policy Committee, 1968" folder, box 2, CCS presidential papers.

26. According to the dean of admissions there were "about fifty" black students at Swarthmore at the beginning of the 1968–69 academic year; at the end of the semester Vice President Shane reported that forty-seven were enrolled: Fred[erick] Hargadon to Frank C. Pierson, August 14, 1968, "Admissions 1968–69" folder, box 2, CCS presidential papers; Joseph B. Shane, memorandum, January 9, 1969, "Black Crisis Sept 68–Jan 69" folder, box 10, CCS presidential papers.

27. Fred[erick] Hargadon, "Admissions Report No. 1," September 1968, "Admissions 1968–69" folder, box 2, CCS presidential papers.

28. "The Admissions Policy Committee's Study of Negro Student Recruitment and Enrollment: A Chronology," "Admissions Policy Committee 1968" folder, box 2, CCS presidential papers (this document appears to have been prepared by Frederick Hargadon, dean of admissions); Patrick Henry, "An Open Letter to the Swarthmore Community," October 16, 1968, "Admissions 1968–69" folder, box 2, CCS presidential papers; authors' notes on an alumni panel discussion, "1969–1989: The Sit-in Twenty Years after," June 10, 1989, in authors' files.

29. "As preconditions for SASS cooperation" ca. October 18, 1968, "SASS 1968–Jan 69" folder, box 67, CCS presidential papers.

30. CCS, "The Future of Swarthmore," *Swarthmore College Bulletin* 65 (October 1968): 1–9.

31. June Jackson Christmas, "A Historical Overview: the Black Experience at Vassar," *Vassar Quarterly* 84 (spring 1988): 3–15; David R. Goddard and Linda C. Koons, "A Profile of the University of Pennsylvania," in *Seventeen Institutions under Pressure,* ed. David Riesman and Verne L. Stadtman, (New York: McGraw-Hill, 1973), pp. 227, 232, 244; Paul Sigmund, "Princeton in Crisis and Change," in *Seventeen Institutions under Pressure,* pp. 254–60; W. J. Rorabaugh, *Berkeley at War: The 1960s* (New York: Oxford University Press, 1989), p. 85.

32. Report of interview with CCS, April 17, 1965, folder 769, box 89, series 200, RG 1.2, RFA.

33. Brent Staples, *Parallel Time: Growing Up in Black and White* (New York: Pantheon Books, 1994), pp. 147–48.

34. "The Admissions Policy Committee's Study." The CEP earlier referred to "middle levels of administration," including the committees intended to coordinate different elements of the college's operations, as the primary source of problems in "the effective performance" of the college: *Critique of a College,* pp. 292–94.

35. Fred[erick] A. Hargadon to students, faculty, administration, and board of managers of Swarthmore College, December 30, 1968, "Admissions Policy Committee 1968" folder, box 2, CCS presidential papers.

36. Adoption of a black studies program was not substantially at issue in the last months of the Smith administration, and one was created in the next year. For a review of thirty years of black studies, see Nell Irvin Painter, "Black Studies, Black Professors, and the Struggles of Perception," *The Chronicle of Higher Education,* December 15, 2000, pp. B7 ff.

37. Fred[erick] A. Hargadon to students, faculty, administration, and board of managers of Swarthmore College, December 30, 1968, "Admissions Policy Committee 1968" folder, box 2, CCS presidential papers.

38. "The Admissions Policy Committee's Study."

39. Clinton A. Etheridge Jr. to CCS, December 23, 1968, in "SASS 1968–January 1969" folder, box 63, CCS presidential papers.

40. Verne A. Stadtman, "Constellations in a Nebulous Galaxy," in *Seventeen Institutions Under Pressure,* 9; Rorabaugh, *Berkeley at War,* p. 84; Todd Gitlin, *The Sixties: Years of Hope, Days of Rage,* rev. ed. (New York: Bantam Books, 1993), p. 340.

41. CCS to members of the faculty, December 31, 1968, in "SASS 1968–January 1969" folder, box 63, CCS presidential papers. Two days later Smith sent a private letter to Dean Hargadon expressing his "dismay at the inappropriateness and lack of justification in SASS's remarks that concerned you and your work in admissions, including Negro admissions": CCS to Frederick A. Hargadon, January 2, 1969, in "SASS 1968–January 1969" folder, box 63, CCS presidential papers.

42. Gilmore Stott, memorandum of meeting, January 6, 1969, in "SASS 1968–January 1969" folder, box 63, CCS presidential papers.

43. Minutes of the Council on Educational Policy, January 6, 1969, in "Commission on Educational Policy 1968–69" folder, box 28, CCS presidential papers.

44. David Cowden to faculty, staff, and students, January 8, 1969, in "SASS 1968–January 1969" folder, box 63, CCS presidential papers.

45. Student Council to college community, January 8, 1969, in "SASS 1968–January 1969" folder, box 63, CCS presidential papers.

46. E.g., Rorabaugh, *Berkeley at War,* pp. 84–85.

47. CCS included a copy of this document in an informational packet he sent to the board of managers on January 9. S. Brown, "Why We Can't Wait," n.d., in CCS to board of managers, January 9, 1969, in "Board of Managers, 1966–69" folder, box 20, CCS presidential papers.

48. Minutes, Swarthmore College Corporation, January 25, 1969.

49. Swarthmore Afro-American Students' Society to the administration and faculty at Swarthmore College, January 9, 1969, "SASS 1968–January 1969" folder, box 63, CCS presidential papers.

50. "SASS Members Occupy Admissions Office," "Press Conference Convenes in Commons," "Meeting Shifts to Clothier," "Moderates Gather Forces before Mass Meeting," "Student-wide Session Held in Clothier," *Phoenix,* supplement, January 10, 1969, pp. 1–3.

51. Tom Fox, "Twenty Seize Office at Swarthmore," *Philadelphia Daily News,* January 10, 1969 (quote); Frances X. Geary, "Swarthmore Sit-in Halts Classes, Registration," *Philadelphia Bulletin,* January 10, 1969; "Negro Insurgents at Swarthmore Study Proposals," *Philadelphia Bulletin,* January 12, 1969; Harry G. Toland, "Quaker Way vs. Confrontation," *Philadelphia Bulletin,* January 13, 1969; Drew Pearson and Jack Anderson, "Blacks Harass Schools Which Sought Reform," ca. January 12, 1969, clipping in "SASS 1968–January 1969" folder, box 63, CCS presidential papers.

52. Harvey T. Satterthwaite to Joseph B. Shane, January 10, 1969, "Black Crisis Sept 68–Jan 69" folder, box 10, CCS presidential papers.

53. Thomas O. Taylor to CCS, January 13, 1969, "Black Crisis Jan 69 (13–19)" folder, box 10, CCS presidential papers.

54. E.g., Dori Goggin to CCS, January 12, 1969, "SASS 1968–January 1969" folder, box 63, CCS presidential papers.

55. "Initial Report Re: Student Protest at Swarthmore College," [January 3, 1969], *WIN: Peace and Freedom through Non-violent Action* (March 1972): 71–72. Copy in Peace Collection, Friends Historical Library, Swarthmore, Pa.

56. CCS remarks, "President Courtney Smith's Statement to the Faculty and Students of Swarthmore College presented at 1:45 P.M. on 13 January 1969 in Clothier Memorial Hall," January 13, 1969, "Black Crisis Jan 69 (13–19)" folder, box 10, CCS presidential papers.

57. Janet Mather to Elizabeth P. Smith, January 16, 1969, "Condolence letters—Alumni" folder, box G, CCS personal papers.

58. "SASS Statement," *Phoenix,* supplement, January 14, 1969, pp. 6–10.

59. CCS to members of the faculty, January 14, 1969, "SASS 1968–January 1969" folder, box 63, CCS presidential papers.

60. "SASS–Faculty Meeting Reported to Plenary Session," and "SASS, Faculty Representatives Meet," *Phoenix,* supplement, January 15, 1969, pp. 4–6; "Faculty Communications Committee–SASS Clarification," *Phoenix,* supplement, January 16, 1969, pp. 1–4.

61. Dorothy Rowden to Elizabeth P. Smith, January 17, 1969, folder "R," box G, CCS personal papers; CCS to Gilmore Stott, January 14, 1969, "Wheaton College Board 1968–69" folder, box F, CCS personal papers.

62. Paul Good, "Requiem for Courtney Smith," *Life* 66 (May 9, 1969): 89.

63. John M. Moore to Aimee Gurbarg, Ellen Brady, and Todd LaPorte, November 27, 1976, in author's files. We thank John C. Moore, registrar of the college during the Smith administration, for providing this document to us.

64. Morris A. Bowie to Edward Cratsley, Joseph Shane, Susan Cobbs, and Gilmore Stott, January 16, 1969, and Morris A. Bowie to Vincent dePillis, January 20, 1969, "CCS Death, 1/16/69" folder, box 70, CCS presidential papers. The condition of Smith's health immediately prior to his death cannot be fully ascertained. Smith had seen doctors regularly for several years, and it was reported that his most recent electrocardiograms "were perfectly normal." He exercised regularly at home. But recent weeks had taken a toll: he had experienced a severe illness late in November 1968, which he described as "a full-blown case of the flu, with temperature and all the trimmings," and for about three weeks before his death he had been working exceptionally long, tension-filled hours. Incidentally, Smith had heard in December of a college official who had suffered a heart attack during student disturbances at Fordham University. Vincent M. Barnett Jr. to CCS, December 20, 1968, "Middle States Association Evaluation 1967–1968" folder, box 52, CCS presidential papers.

65. Russ Benghiat, Doug Blair, Bob Goodman, "Crisis '69: Semester of Misunderstandings and Frustrations," *Phoenix,* January 29, 1969, p. 6, quoting the *Philadelphia Bulletin.* This issue of *Phoenix* is the single best summary of the events of the crisis.

66. Ibid., pp. 6, 8.

67. Lewis Pyenson to Darwin H. Stapleton, November 17, 1991, in author's files. Van de Kamp told Betty Smith that "I had planned to talk to the SASS people, but a remark of your son made me change my mind. I have to live with my anger." Olga and Peter van de Kamp to Elizabeth Smith, January 16, 1969, "V," folder box G, CCS personal papers.

68. Peter van de Kamp, "1969 January—based on what I said at the Chaplin seminar February 1," "Black Crisis Feb 1969" folder, box 11, CCS presidential papers.

69. "Subversion of Reason," *New York Times,* ca. January 20, 1969, p. 30.

70. Claudio Spies to Elizabeth Smith, January 20, 1969, folder "S," box G, CCS personal papers.

71. Corrine Foster to Elizabeth Smith, January 16, 1969, folder "B," box G, CCS personal papers; Agnes B. Doty to Joseph B. Shane, January 18, 1969, "Black Crisis January 1969 (20–26)" folder, box 11, CCS presidential papers.

72. Quoted in "Swarthmore Sit-in Ended after Death of Dr. Smith," *Delaware County Times,* January 17, 1969, p. 1, and Frank Heick and Al Haas, "Swarthmore Students End Eight–Day Sit-in after President Dies," *Philadelphia Inquirer,* January 17, 1969.

73. "Speakers at Memorial Service for President Courtney Smith," January 20, 1969, "CCS Death 1/16/69" folder, box 70, CCS presidential papers.

74. Quotes from "Two Thousand Attend Rites for Swarthmore President," *Philadelphia Bulletin,* January 20, 1969, p. 6.

75. "Burial Rites Here for Courtney Smith," undated newspaper clipping, "Articles c. death" folder, box G, CCS personal papers.

76. Edward K. Cratsley to the Swarthmore college community, ca. January 28, 1969, "Black Crisis Sept 68–Jan 69" folder, box 10, CCS presidential papers.

77. *Wall Street Journal,* March 24, 1969.

78. Robert Cross, "President's Report, 1970–71," *Swarthmore College Bulletin* 68 (1971): 6 (quote); Richard J. Walton, *Swarthmore College: An Informal History* (Swarthmore, Pa.: Swarthmore College, 1986), pp. 90–92.


## CONCLUSION

1. David Halberstam, *The Best and the Brightest* (Greenwich, Conn.: Fawcett, 1973). See also a later work that considers government service by two members of Smith's college cohort during the cold war: Kai Bird, *The Color of Truth: McGeorge Bundy and William Bundy, Brothers in Arms* (New York: Simon and Schuster, 1998).

2. Graduating from Swarthmore in 1934, Perkins received his Ph.D. in political science from Princeton in 1937. After a brief stint at teaching, he held a variety of administrative posts at Princeton, in wartime Washington, in Swarthmore (vice president under Nason, 1945–1950), and at the Carnegie Corporation of New York, culminating with the presidency of Cornell University, 1963–69.

3. Quoted in Arthur M. Schlesinger Jr., *A Thousand Days: John F. Kennedy in the White House* (Boston: Houghton Mifflin, 1965), p. 127.

4. The term "multiversity" was coined by Clark Kerr, a Swarthmore graduate who became chancellor of the University of California system, in his book *The Uses of the University,* 4th ed. (Cambridge: Harvard University Press, 1995).

5. Eugene Lang, one-time chairman of the Board of Managers of Swarthmore College, has gone so far as to argue that "the philosophy of liberal arts is the philosophy of a democratic society in which citizenship, social responsibility, and community are inseparable": Eugene M. Lang, "Distinctively American: The Liberal Arts College," *Daedalus* 128 (winter 1999): 140.

6. As a recent historian of the rise of modern Western politics has pointed out, "ordinary people" became part of the government process in the 16th and 17th centuries by engaging in "the choosing, the learning, the inventing" that came about by dialogue, albeit dialogue that sometimes was interrupted by violent social action: Wayne te Brake, *Shaping History: Ordinary People in European Politics, 1500–1700* (Berkeley and Los Angeles: University of California Press, 1998), p. 11.

7. Robert Putnam, *Bowling Alone: The Collapse and Revival of American Community*

(New York: Simon and Schuster, 2000). Putnam, a Swarthmore graduate, argues that "the performance of our democratic institutions depends on measurable ways upon social capital," i.e., citizens' interconnectivity beyond familial relationships (pp. 19, 349).

8. Martin Trow, "From Mass Higher Education to Universal Access: The American Advantage," *Minerva* 37 (1999): 313.

9. Scholars generally acknowledge that academic leadership is only one piece of the puzzle, but also that it is one of the easier factors to assess. See, for example, David Riesman and Verne L. Stadtman, eds., *Seventeen Institutions under Pressure* (New York: McGraw-Hill, 1973); W. J. Rorabaugh, *Berkeley at War: The 1960s* (New York: Oxford University Press, 1989); and Donald A. Downs, *Cornell '69: Liberalism and the Crisis of the American University* (Ithaca, N.Y.: Cornell University Press, 1999). See also Stephen Sivulich, "After Thirty Years, We Can Still Learn from Kent State," *Chronicle of Higher Education,* April 28, 2000, pp. B6–B8.

10. See chapters on Michigan and the San Francisco State College in *Seventeen Institutions under Pressure,* above.

# Bibliography

Aloian, David, ed. *College in a Yard II.* Cambridge: Harvard Alumni Association, 1985.

Anderson, Terry H. *The Sixties.* New York: Longman, 1999.

Baltzell, E. Digby. *An American Business Aristocracy.* New York: Collier Books, 1962.

Barrett, Paul M. *The Good Black: A True Story of Race in America.* New York: Dutton, 1999.

Barzun, Jacques. *The House of Intellect.* New York: Harper and Brothers, 1959.

Bender, Thomas, and Carl E. Schorske, eds. *American Academic Culture in Transformation: Fifty Years, Four Disciplines.* Princeton, N.J.: Princeton University Press, 1997.

Bird, Kai. *The Color of Truth: McGeorge Bundy and William Bundy, Brothers in Arms.* New York: Simon and Schuster, 1998.

Bissell, Richard. *You Can Always Tell a Harvard Man.* New York: McGraw-Hill, 1962.

Blanshard, Frances. *Frank Aydelotte of Swarthmore.* Middletown, Conn.: Wesleyan University Press, 1970.

Bloom, Allan. *The Closing of the American Mind.* New York: Simon and Schuster, 1987.

Blum, John Morton. *Years of Discord: American Politics and Society, 1961–1974.* New York: W. W. Norton, 1991.

Bowen, William G., and Derek Bok. *The Shape of the River: Long-Term Consequences of Considering Race in College and University Admissions.* Princeton, N.J.: Princeton University Press, 1998.

Brokaw, Tom. *The Greatest Generation.* New York: Random Press, 1998.

Carson, Clayborne. *In Struggle: SNCC and the Black Awakening of the 1960s.* Cambridge: Harvard University Press, 1981.

Chalmers, David. *And the Crooked Places Made Straight: The Struggle for Social Change in the 1960s.* Baltimore: Johns Hopkins University Press, 1991.

Chauncey, Henry, ed. *Talks on American Education.* New York: Teachers College, Columbia University Press, 1962.

Chomsky, Noam, et al. *The Cold War and the University: Toward an Intellectual History of the Postwar Era.* New York: The New Press, 1997.

Clark, Burton R. *The Distinctive College: Antioch, Reed and Swarthmore.* Chicago: Aldine Publishing, 1970.

*Critique of a College.* Swarthmore, Pa.: Swarthmore College, 1967.

Crowley, Joseph N. *No Equal in the World: An Interpretation of the Academic Presidency.* Reno: University of Nevada Press, 1994.

*Decennial Report, Harvard College Class of 1938.* Cambridge: Class of 1938, 1948.

239

*Distinctively American: The Residential Liberal Arts Colleges.* Theme issue of *Daedalus* 128 (winter 1999): 1–272.

Downs, Donald A. *Cornell '69: Liberalism and the Crisis of the American University.* Ithaca, N.Y.: Cornell University Press, 1999.

Dzuback, Mary Ann. *Robert M. Hutchins: Portrait of an Educator.* Chicago: University of Chicago Press, 1991.

Federal Writers' Project. *Iowa: A Guide to the Hawkeye State.* New York: Viking Press, 1938.

Flexner, Abraham. *I Remember.* New York: Simon and Schuster, 1940.

Fosdick, Raymond B. *Adventure in Giving: The Story of the General Education Board.* New York: Harper and Row, 1962.

*Free Enterprise in Education: Remarks at the Fifteenth Annual Forum on Education of the Tuition Plan at Hotel Ambassador in New York, February 9, 1955.* New York: The Tuition Plan, 1955.

Gaines, Thomas A. *The Campus as a Work of Art.* New York: Praeger, 1991.

Gannon, Robert I. *The Poor Old Liberal Arts.* New York: Farrar, Straus and Cudahy, 1961.

Gillespie, Maralyn Orbison, ed. *Swarthmore Remembered.* Swarthmore, Pa.: Swarthmore College, 1964.

Gitlin, Todd. *The Sixties: Years of Hope, Days of Rage.* Rev. ed. New York: Bantam Books, 1993.

Goheen, Robert F. *The Human Nature of a University.* Princeton, N.J.: Princeton University Press, 1969.

Gray, Rockwell. *The Imperative of Modernity: An Intellectual Biography of José Ortega y Gasset.* Berkeley and Los Angeles: University of California Press, 1989.

Gunther, John, and Bernard Quint. *Days to Remember: America, 1945–1955.* New York: Harper and Row, 1956.

Halberstam, David. *The Fifties.* New York: Villard Books, 1993.

Harrison, Brian, ed. *The History of the University of Oxford.* Vol. 8. Oxford: Clarendon Press, 1994.

Hesburgh, Theodore M. *Patterns for Educational Growth.* South Bend, Ind.: University of Notre Dame Press, 1958.

Hunt, Everett Lee. *The Revolt of the College Intellectual.* Chicago: Aldine, 1963.

Hutchins, Robert Maynard. *The Higher Learning in America.* New Haven: Yale University Press, 1936.

Hutchinson, Dennis J. *The Man Who Once Was Whizzer White: A Portrait of Justice Byron R. White.* New York: Free Press, 1998.

Kerr, Clark. *The Uses of the University.* New York: Harper and Row, 1963.

Kimball, Bruce A. *Orators and Philosophers: A History of the Idea of Liberal Education.* Expanded ed. New York: College Entrance Examination Board, 1995.

Leitch, Alexander. *A Princeton Companion.* Princeton, N.J.: Princeton University Press, 1978.

Lowen, Rebecca S. *Creating the Cold War University: The Transformation of Stanford.* Berkeley and Los Angeles: University of California Press, 1997.

McClintock, Robert. *Man and His Circumstances: Ortega as Educator.* New York: Teachers College Press, 1971.

Michener, James A. *Kent State: What Happened and Why.* New York: Fawcett Crest, 1971.

Miller, Douglas T., and Marion Nowak. *The Fifties: The Way We Really Were.* Garden City, N.Y.: Doubleday and Company, 1977.

National Committee on the Preparation of a Manual on College and University Business Administration. *College and University Business Administration.* 2 vols. Washington, D.C.: American Council on Education, 1952–55.

Ortega y Gasset, José. *Mission of the University.* New Brunswick, N.J.: Transaction Publishers, 1992.

Pelikan, Jaroslav. *The Idea of the University: A Reexamination.* New Haven: Yale University Press, 1992.

Philadelphia Yearly Meeting, Society of Friends. *Faith and Practice.* Rev. ed. Philadelphia: Philadelphia Yearly Meeting, 1972.

Pilat, Oliver. *Drew Pearson: An Unauthorized Biography.* New York: Harpers Magazine Press, 1973.

Powledge, Fred. *Free at Last: The Civil Rights Movement and the People Who Made It.* Boston: Little, Brown, 1991.

President's Commission on Higher Education. *Higher Education for American Democracy.* 4 vols. Washington, D.C.: U.S. Government Printing Office, 1947.

Pusey, Nathan M. *American Higher Education, 1945–1970: A Personal Report.* Cambridge: Harvard University Press, 1978.

Riesman, David, and Verne L. Stadtman, eds. *Seventeen Institutions under Pressure.* New York: McGraw-Hill, 1973.

Rorabaugh, W. J. *Berkeley at War: The 1960s.* New York: Oxford University Press, 1989.

Rosovsky, Henry. *The University: An Owner's Manual.* New York: W. W. Norton, 1990.

Rudolph, Frederick. *The American College and University: A History.* Athens, Ga.: University of Georgia Press, 1990.

Ruml, Beardsley, and Donald H. Morrison. *Memo to a College Trustee: A Report on Financial and Structural Problems of the Liberal College.* New York: McGraw-Hill, 1959.

Schiffrin, André, ed. *The Cold War and the University: Toward an Intellectual History of the Postwar Years.* New York: The New Press, 1997.

Schlesinger, Arthur M., Jr. *A Thousand Days: John F. Kennedy in the White House.* Boston: Houghton Mifflin, 1965.

Schudson, Michael. *The Good Citizen: A History of American Civic Life.* New York: the Free Press, 1998.

Smith, Courtney C. *The Liberal Arts College.* Voice of America Forum Lectures. Washington, D.C.: Voice of America, 1960.

Smith, G. Kerry, ed. *Current Issues in Higher Education, 1954.* Washington, D.C.: Association for Higher Education, 1954.

Smith, Richard Norton. *The Harvard Century: The Making of a University to a Nation.* Cambridge: Harvard University Press, 1986.

Staples, Brent. *Parallel Time: Growing Up in Black and White.* New York: Pantheon Books, 1994.

Stillwell, Paul, ed. *The Golden Thirteen: Recollections of the First Black Naval Officers.* Annapolis, Md.: Naval Institute Press, 1993.

Strickland, Tamara G., and Stephen P. Strickland. *The Markle Scholars: A Brief History.* New York: John and Mary R. Markle Foundation, 1976.

Synnot, M. G. *The Half-Opened Door: Discrimination and Admissions at Harvard, Yale and Princeton, 1900–1970.* Westport, Conn.: Greenwood, 1979.

Walton, Richard J. *Swarthmore College: An Informal History.* Swarthmore, Pa.: Swarthmore College, 1989.

Whitehead, Alfred North. *The Aims of Education and Other Essays.* New York: The Free Press, 1967.

Whitfield, Stephen J. *The Culture of the Cold War.* 2d ed. Baltimore: Johns Hopkins University Press, 1997.

Whyte, William H., Jr. *The Organization Man.* Garden City, N.Y.: Doubleday, 1956.

Wright, Richard. *Black Boy: A Record of Childhood and Youth.* New York: Harper and Brothers, 1937.

Wriston, Henry M. *Academic Procession: Reflections of a College President.* New York: Columbia University Press, 1959.

Yankelovich, Daniel. *The Changing Values on Campus: Political and Personal Attitudes of Today's College Students.* New York: Washington Square Press, 1972.

# Index

Acheson, Dean, 155

Ad Hoc Black Admissions Committee, 185

Admissions Policy Committee, 177, 178, 180, 181

African-Americans. *See* race and race relations

Albertson, Mary, 90

American Air Cadets, 17

American Alumni Council, 87, 93

American Association of Independent College and University Presidents, 113

American Association of University Women, 39

American Civil Liberties Union, 95

American Council of Learned Societies, 53

American Council on Education, 98, 106, 107; Commission on International Education, 107

American College Public Relations Association, 87

American Friends Service Committee, 110; Educational Advisory Committee, 110; American Philosophical Society, 113

Amherst College, 85, 91

Animal Laboratory, 124

Arch Street (Quaker) Meeting, 114

Arden House, 104

Ashmead, John, 21, 24, 32

Association of American Colleges, 80, 86, 95, 98, 106, 107; Commission on Liberal Education, 106, 107; position on express highways, 122

Association of American Universities, 53, 54

Association of Graduate Schools, 53, 54, 56

Association for Higher Education, 86

Atomic Energy Commission, 97

Arthur Hoyt Scott Foundation, 118

Arthur Hoyt Scott Outdoor Auditorium, 119

Aydelotte, Frank, 27, 31, 42, 45, 46, 62, 65, 92, 114, 116; American Secretary of Rhodes Trust, 103, 104, 162; Board of Managers of Swarthmore College, 66; director of Institute for Advanced Study, 42, 61, 104; his education and professorships, 59–60; on liberal arts education, 76–77; president of Swarthmore College, 59–61, 76, 161, 167, 173; recommends Courtney C. Smith, 65–66

Bailey, Stephen, 30, 32

Barnard College, 157

Barnard, Boyd T., 65, 66

Barr, Robert (and spouse), 145, 158, 162, 163, 168, 183, 192

Barzun, Jacques, 82, 84

Beardsley, Monroe, 166, 168

Becker, Dorothy, 158

Becker, George, 65, 66, 158

Bekavac, Nancy, 185

Bell, Aldon Duane, 162

Bell, Clarence, 115

Bentley, Gerald E., 41

Berkeley, University of California at, 179, 181

Bermuda, 26

Biddle, Clement, 95

Bill of Rights, G.I., 38, 41

Black, Hugo, 155
Black Interests Committee, 185
Black Studies (Curriculum) Committee, 180, 182
Blue Route, 115, 118–23, 165, 223, 225
Bogardus, George, 24
Borton, Hugh, 111, 112
Bowdoin College, 85
Bond, Richard C., 65
Bowden family, 158
Bowie, Morris A., 185
Brademas, John, 96, 115
Branscomb, Harvie, 107
Brimmer School, 30
British Columbia (Canada), 26
Bronk, Detlev, 66
Brookings Institution, 168
Brown University, 79
Browning, Robert, 186
Bryn Mawr College, 91, 96, 105, 107, 111, 112
Buckhill Falls, Pa., 85
Buckley, William F., Jr., 129
Bundy, McGeorge, 108

Cambridge, Md., 129, 130
campus disturbances and radicalism, 174–76, 189
Carleton College, 20, 62, 116
Carnegie Corporation of New York, 18, 53, 54, 56, 98, 106, 116
Carnegie Hall, 186
Carnegie philanthropies, 188
Cedar Falls (Ia.) state normal school, 15
Century Club, 114
Chambers, E. K., 29
Chase Manhattan Bank, 131
Chester (Pa.), schools, 130
Chronicle of Higher Education, 9
Civil Rights movement, 129, 130, 153, 179
Clark, Joseph S., 95, 96, 116, 122, 132
Clarke, Eleanor S., 65
Clinton, William J., 174, 227
Cleveland, J. Harlan, 30
Clinton, William J., 132
Cobbs, Susan, 70, 145, 158, 161, 163–65, 168, 187
Colby College, 116

cold war, 188, 217, 237
colleges and universities. See under names of institutions
Commission on Educational Policy, 115, 167–74
Commission on Liberal Education, 106, 107
Committee on Education Beyond the High School, 86, 99
Compton, Mr. and Mrs. Randolph, 53
Conant, James, 220
Cooper, W. S., 18
Commonwealth Edison (Chicago), 20
Cornell College, 28
Cornell University, 168
Council for the Advancement of Small Colleges, 106
Cox, Edward H., 90
Cratsley, Edward, 70, 90, 98, 114, 161, 163, 165, 168, 187
Critique of a College ("red book"), 171, 174, 178
Cross, Robert, 153, 187
Cummins, Albert, 20

Damon, Al, 24, 32
Dana Dormitory, 101, 124, 125
Dana Foundation, 100, 101
Danforth Foundation, 100, 101, 116, 168
Dartmouth College, 20
Decrouez, Mr. and Mrs. Pierre, 158
Dedham (Mass.) Polo and Country Club, 26
Delaware County (Pa.), 119–21
Delaware County (Pa.) Commissioners, 119
Delaware County (Pa.) Planning Board, 119
Denworth, Hilda Lang, 65
Des Moines, Ia., 15, 16, 18
Dexter Academy, 15
Dodds, Harold Willis, 41, 57, 94
Dollard, Charles, 56
Donner Foundation, 100
Douglas, Paul H., 155
Downes, Captain Edwin H., 34, 35
Drake University, 16, 20
draft, military, 132, 174, 227
Du Bois, W. E. B., 78

du Pont, Pierre S., 99
du Pont Science Building, 98, 99, 123, 124
DuPont Company, 86, 98, 99
Duane, Morris, 113
Duff, James A., 128

Earlham College, 116
Earth Day, 9
East Harlem (N.Y.) Protestant Parish, 109
Eisenhower, Dwight D., 86, 96, 105, 223; on industrial-military complex, 188
Eisenhower, Milton, 112
Eisenhower, Ruth, 112, 113
Eisenhower Exchange Fellowships, 98, 105, 162
Elliot, T. S., 71
Ellis, Walter, 32
Elton, Lord and Lady, 155
Elverson, Lew, 151
Embree, Edwin, 63
Endicott, Bradford, 26
Endicott, H. Wendell, 26, 27, 71, 77, 103
Endicott Johnson Shoe Co., 26
Endicott, Priscilla Maxwell, 26
environmental issues, 9, 121, 175
Etheridge, Clinton, 180, 181

Federal Reserve Bank of Philadelphia, 110
Feldman, Jerry, 122
Fenton Junction, Ia., 15
Field, James, 168
First Presbyterian Church (Princeton, N.J.), 42
First Presbyterian Church (Winterset, Ia.), 16
Flexner, Abraham, 60, 61
Folk festival, 145, 146, 192
Ford Foundation, 86, 87, 100, 101, 110–12, 116
Foreign Policy Association, 64, 71
foundations, 18, 53–57, 59, 61, 63, 86, 87, 92, 93, 97–101, 106, 108, 110–12, 116, 118, 123, 216. See also name of foundation
Fox, George, 59
freeway revolts, 122
Friends. See Quakers

Friends General Conference, 116
Friends Historical Library, 100, 105
Fulbright, J. William, 69
Fund for the Advancement of Education, 86
Furniss, Edgar Stephenson, Jr., 78

Gaines, Thomas A., 125
General Education Board, 53, 54, 55, 56, 57, 98; grants to Swarthmore College, 61, 92; ranks Swarthmore College, 59; Southern fellowship program, 56–57
General Electric Educational Foundation, 110
George School, 156, 161
Gifford, Prosser (and spouse), 162, 163
Gilbert, Charles (Chuck), 166–68, 221, 231
Gilpatric, Chadbourne, 30, 108, 116
Girl Scouts, 155
Goheen, Robert, 45, 78
Gold, Bob, 122
Gordon, Kermit, 30, 115, 116, 120, 155, 168
Gordon, Lincoln, 113
Greater Philadelphia Movement, 113, 176
Green, Edith, 132
Greenewalt, Crawford, 86, 99, 113
Greenwich, Conn., 193
Grow, Captain H. B., 35, 37
Guilford College, 116
Gulf Health and Welfare Council, 39
Gwynn, Fred, 32

Hall, Gus, 129
Hallowell Dormitory, 101, 124, 125
Hallowell, Thomas, 101
Hargadon, Frederick A., 163, 168, 177, 180, 235
Hargadon report, 177, 179, 180
Harral, Henry D., 122
Harris, Seymour, 155
Harvard Club of Philadelphia, 114, 115
Harvard University, 9, 20, 21, 26, 31, 32, 38, 44, 62, 88, 91, 93, 101, 102, 104, 119, 191; alumni, 115, 116; African-Americans, 22; Board of Overseers, 95, 98, 107–10, 115, 116, 132, 154, 162, 166; Divinity School, 107, 109–10,

Harvard University (*continued*)
220; English Dept., 110; faculty, 73,
77; Faculty of Arts and Sciences, 108;
Freshman Union library, 21; Harvard
Alumni Association, 107; Harvard Col-
lege, 107; Harvard Union, 21; Jewish
quota, 22; Leverett House, 21, 22, 23,
24; Lowell House, 22; Philosophy
Department, 107–9; presidents, 79, 107,
109; Thayer dormitory, 21; visiting
committees, 107–10; Widner Library,
21, 23
Haverford College, 62, 85, 91, 96, 105,
111, 112
Hazen Foundation, 116
Heald, Henry, 86
Heald, Mark, 168
Health and Welfare Council, Inc.:
Delaware County, Pa., 121; Gulf, Fla.,
39
Heider, Dave, 122
Hesburgh, Theodore, 79
Hester, James, 45, 66
Higginbotham, A. Leon, Jr., 221
higher education, problems of, 175
highways, 119–23
Hiss, Alger, 129
Hi-Y, 20
Horton, Douglas, 109
Hoy, John C., 163
Humphrey, Hubert, 155
Hunt, Everett, 70, 145, 161, 166
Hutchins, Robert, 76
Hynes, Samuel, 166, 168

Independence Foundation, 100
Ingram, Greg, 156
Institute for Advanced Study, 41, 42, 104
interstate highway act, 223
Iowa, 15
Iowa Methodist Hospital (Des Moines,
Ia.), 17
Iowa State Teachers College, 20
Insull, Samuel, 20

J. P. Morgan Trust, 104
James Foundation, 101
Javits, Jacob, 95
Jefferson, Thomas, 15

Jenkins, Elsa, 162
Jenkins, Howard M., 65, 90
Johns Hopkins University, 112, 113, 116
Johnson, Lyndon B., 108, 115, 122, 215
Jones, Ernest, 26
Jones, Fenwick, 30
Julius Rosenwald Foundation, 63

Katharine Gibbs School, 25
Kemp, Isabella, 53
Kennedy, John F., 95, 96, 107, 108, 115,
116, 121, 153, 188, 220
Kerr, Clark, 93, 232, 237
Kimball, L. F., 57
King, Martin Luther, 174
Kling, Vincent G., 99, 124, 225
Kresge Foundation, 100, 101

Lafore, Lawrence, 148
Lake Forest College, 163
Lang, Eugene, 237
Lange, Barbara P., 145, 163, 168
Lawrence, David, 120
Leader, George, 106, 119
Lee, William F., 65, 114
Lewis, C. S., 29
liberal arts education, 84, 90, 94, 102,
103, 106, 110, 167, 188, 189, 193;
Smith's remarks on, 79–82, 101, 116;
financing, 86, 87; traditions, 76, 77;
Lilly Endowment, 100, 108
Lincoln University, 113
Longwood Foundation, 98, 99, 123
Los Angeles Town Hall, 80
loyalty oaths, 63, 215
Luttrell, John, 30

MacVeagh, F. W., 23, 77
McBride, Katherine, 107, 111, 112, 221
McCabe, Thomas, 65, 66, 99, 100, 105,
114, 119
McCabe Library, 100, 124, 125
McCarthy, Joseph, 128
McCarthyism, 73, 84, 128, 146, 189, 210
Madison County (Ia.), 15, 16, 198
Malin, Patrick M., 95
Marblehead Neck (Mass.), 30, 158
Markle, John F., 104
Markle, John F. and Mary: Foundation,

98, 104, 105, 112, 154, 157, 162, 185;
Committee on Future Plans, 105, 175,
176; CCS appointed president, 175,
176; history, 218
Markle Medical Scholars Program, 104,
105
Martin, Clarence D. Jr., 120, 122
Martin, Edward, 128
Masonic order, 16
Matthiessen, F. O., 27, 103
*Mauretania,* 69, 158
Mayne, Wiley, 24, 115
Mellon, Andrew W.: Foundation, 100
Middle States Association, 91
Mifflin, Edward B., 115
military-industrial complex, 9, 188
Miller, Samuel H., 109
Milner, Florence, 21
minorities. *See* race and race relations
Moe, Henry A., 45, 66
Mohlenhoff, George, 110
Moore, John M., 70, 90, 161, 166, 168
multiversity, 188
Munn, James B., 23, 31, 39, 77, 103,
202
Murphy, William (Bill), 21, 22, 23, 24,
32, 150, 200
Murray, Admiral George D., 38
Murray, James E., 95
Muskie, Edmund S., 111
Myrdal, Gunnar, 155

Nason, John W., 45, 61–65, 68, 70, 71,
92, 108, 114, 116, 148, 161–63
National Committee for the Florence
Agreement, 110
National Defense Education Act, 94–97,
116, 128, 165, 215, 216
National Institutes of Health, 93, 97
National Science Foundation, 93, 97
Navy, United States, 32–40, 77, 193;
African-Americans (Negroes), 33–
38, 62, 63, 190; Camp Robert Smalls,
34; liaison officers' school, Hampton
Institute, 33–35; Naval Reserve, 32,
33, 40; unit at Swarthmore College,
62
NBC radio network, 20
Nelson, James, 30, 32

New Brunswick (Canada), 26
*New York Times,* 9, 71, 86, 98, 129, 176,
216; CCS obituary, 186
New York University, 86
*Newark* (N.J.) *Sunday News,* 69
Nixon, Richard M., 96
North, Helen, 166

Oates, Whitney J., 46, 53, 54, 55, 57, 103
Old Cambridge (Mass.) Baptist Church,
109
Old Dominion Foundation, 101
Oppenheimer, Robert, 108
*Organization Man, The,* 160
Ortega y Gasset, José, 82–84, 157
Ossorio, Alfonso, 24
Outward Bound, 130
Oxford University, 27, 28, 60, 62, 71, 88,
113, 156; Smith's studies at, 25, 27, 30,
31, 44, 77, 102, 104, 119, 162; Merton
College, 29, 30
Ozone Club, 114, 157

Panofsky, Erwin, 155
Peabody, Dean, 166
Pearson, Drew, 184
Peaslee, Amos, 97
Pendle Hill, 110
Penjerdel, Inc., 111, 176
Pennock, Roland, 186
Pennsylvania Association of Colleges and
Universities, 80, 98, 105, 106, 122
Pennsylvania, Commonwealth of: Assem-
bly (legislature), 115, 121; Department
of Highways, 122; governors, 119–22;
police, 184
*Pensacola* (Fla.) *Journal,* 38
Pensacola Naval Air Station, Fla., 33, 35–
40; racial discrimination, 35–38
*Pensacola* (Fla.) *News,* 38
Perkins, James A., 116, 188, 237
Pettingell, Win, 21, 24
Pfaff, Richard W., 162, 163
Phi Beta Kappa, 23, 25, 77
Philadelphia, Pa., 98
Philadelphia Contributorship, 113
*Philadelphia Evening Bulletin,* 68, 120
*Philadelphia Inquirer,* 120
Philadelphia Flower Show, 115

Philadelphia Orchestra Association, 115
Philadelphia Savings Fund Society
 (PSFS), 111, 112, 176
Philips, Edith, 90
*Phoenix, The,* 100, 131, 132
Pierce, Winnifred Poland, 168
Ponte Vedra Beach, Fla., 114, 159
Pope, Alexander, 223
Prentice, William H.C. (and spouse), 114,
 120, 145, 158, 162, 163
Presbyterian Church, 16, 42, 77
Presser Foundation, 100
Princeton, N.J., 41, 42, 69
Princeton University, 32, 41, 42, 43, 44,
 53, 66, 77, 78, 88, 91, 94, 101, 104,
 119; African-American students, 179;
 alumni, 115; American Civilization
 Program, 43, 44, 103; Bicentennial Pre-
 ceptorships, 44, 78–79; English Depart-
 ment, 41, 42, 103; Forrestal Center, 94;
 Woodrow Wilson Fellowship Program,
 53, 103
Proctor, Elizabeth (Betty) Bowden. *See*
 Smith, Elizabeth P.
Proctor, Emma Bartoll Bowden, 30
Proctor, George Newton, 30, 158
Proctor, Rose Stearns, 30, 158
Pugwash conferences, 107, 219
Pusey, Nathan, 79, 107, 109

Quakers (Religious Society of Friends),
 41, 62, 65, 92, 133, 184; addressed by
 CCS, 85; American Friends Service
 Committee, 110; Arch Street Meeting,
 114; beliefs, faith, traditions and values,
 59, 72–74, 95, 168, 172, 175, 176,
 184, 189; colleges, 105, 107; found
 and influence Swarthmore College, 59,
 94, 154, 168, 172, 175; Friends General Conference, 116; in Philadelphia,
 164; on Board of Managers of
 Swarthmore College, 65; Ozone Club,
 114, 157; schools, 116, 156, 161;
 students at Swarthmore College, 61,
 92
Quaker College Presidents, 98, 105
Queen Elizabeth II, 159
*Queen Elizabeth,* 69, 159

race relations and racism, 22, 33–39, 43,
 113, 128, 129, 163, 174, 175, 177–87,
 189, 190, 193
Radcliffe College, 77
Rakoff, Jed, 152
Rauch, R. Stewart, Jr., 111–13
Religious Society of Friends. *See* Quakers
*Revolt of the College Intellectual, The,*
 161
Rhodes, Cecil, 27
Rhodes Scholar Program and Rhodes
 Trust, 27, 28, 42, 45, 46, 60, 69, 76, 88,
 96, 99, 102, 104, 115, 155, 191; assis-
 tants to American Secretary, 45, 66, 98,
 162, 163; fiftieth anniversary, 69; of-
 fices at Princeton and Swarthmore, 28,
 42, 66, 162; selection committees, 28,
 45; Smith's leadership, 9, 46, 154, 158
Rhodes Scholars, 27, 30, 32, 42, 60, 61,
 69, 77, 96, 102, 108, 113, 132, 162,
 163, 168, 174
Rhys, Hedley, 166
Riesman, Robert, 32
Robeson, Paul, 129
Rockefeller, David, 107, 131
Rockefeller Foundation, 53, 108, 116,
 163, 165, 177, 179
Rollins, Hyder E., 31, 32, 41, 103, 202
Roosevelt High School (Des Moines, Ia.),
 18, 19
Ruml, Beardsley, 86
Rusk, Dean, 57
Russell, John, 104, 176

San Francisco State College, 181, 191
Schall, Ellen, 186
Schlesinger, Arthur M. Jr., 116, 200
Scott, Hugh, 95
Scott Paper Co., 100
Scranton, William, 122
"Seafarer, The," 185
Seeger, Pete, 146
Selective Service System, 132. *See also*
 draft, military
Shane, Joseph, 70, 98, 105, 114, 118, 119,
 161, 163–66, 192
Shanley, J. L., 54
Sharples Dining Hall, 100, 124, 125

Sharples, Philip, 100, 105
Sherrerd, William D., Jr., 53
Sidwell Friends School, 156
Sikes, Robert, 38
Simon, Walter O., 98
Simpson College, 20
Sloan, Alfred: Foundation, 100, 101
Slocum, Richard W., 65, 68
Smedley Park, 121
Smith, Carleton, 16, 18, 68, 157, 158
Smith, Carol Dabney, 46, 69, 156, 157, 159
Smith, Claude C., 65, 71, 95, 106, 113
Smith, Courtney Craig, 9; administrative skill and style, 43, 44, 46, 163, 164, 166, 189–93; African-American interests and views, 43, 179, 180; American Friends Service Committee, 110; Association of American Colleges director, 106, 107; Brooks Brothers, 129; Cambridge, Mass., residences, 31, 32; childhood, 16, 17, 68, 77; children, 68: Courtney Craig Smith, Jr., 32, Carol Dabney Smith, 46, Elizabeth (Lee) Bowden Smith, 39; clubs, 114, 115, 157; college scholarships offered, 20; Commission on International Education, 107; Commission on Liberal Education, 106, 107; critiques of, 90, 152, 153, 189, 191; death, 185, 185, 188, 236; Des Moines, move to, 18; dialogue and discourse, 10, 24, 81, 82, 132, 174, 189, 192; dignity (decorum), 23, 24, 151, 189, 190; Eisenhower Exchange Fellowships, 105, 162; elitist views, 190, 193; engagement and wedding, 25, 26, 30, 31; ethics, 24, 151; European travel, 23, 25, 28–30, 69, 159; family and home life, 154–60; Ford Foundation, committee of grantees, 110; foundation service, 188; General Electric Educational Foundation, 110; golf, 26, 114, 150, 157; Greater Philadelphia Movement, 113, 176; Gulf Health and Welfare Council, 39; Harvard University: Board of Overseers, 98, 107–110, 115, 154, 162, 167, Class of 1938 Alumni Committee, 107, doctorate, 32,

188, 189, employment at, 21, 23, 68, English literature major, 22, 23, 27, 77, graduate studies, 31, 191, graduation, 23, 188, sports, 22, 23, 150, teaching fellow, 32, tutor, 31, 77, undergraduate years, 21, 22, 23, 24, 26, 78, 102, 103, 129, 191, visiting committees, 107–10; high school, 19, 20, 150, 191; humor and wit, 71, 74, 75, 157; instructor at Harvard and Radcliffe, 32; interviews of potential faculty, 88–90; Johns Hopkins University, visiting committee, 112, 113; leadership, 58, 109, 189–93; liaison officer for Negro personnel, 35–39; liberal arts, 90, 189: advocate, 76–84, 102, 103, 123, speeches regarding, 79–80, 116; Lilly Endowment, 110; lobbying, 106; Markle Foundation trustee, 104, 105, 154, 157, 162, 218: presidency, 112, 175, 176, Committee on Future Plans, 105, 175, 176; memorial service and interment, 187; mentored and mentoring, 102, 103; National Committee for the Florence Agreement, 110; National Defense Education Act, 94–97, 116, 128; Navy, service in, 32–40, 71, 77, 78, 188, 189, 192: commission and training, 33–35, honorable discharge, 40, Naval Air Station, Quonset Point, R.I., 33, Naval Air Station, Pensacola, Fla., 33, 35–40, 190, Naval Training School, Hampton, Va., 33–35, release, 41; networks of colleagues and friends, 88, 102–17, 157, 191; Oxford (England) residences, 28–29, 69; Oxford University, represents, 113; Oppenheimer, Robert, 108; Ozone Club, 114, 157; parents, 15; Penjerdel, Inc., 111, 176; Pennsylvania Association of Colleges and Universities, 106; Pensacola, Fla., life at, 39; personality and style, 23, 24, 88, 103, 186, 187; Phi Beta Kappa, 23, 25, 188; Philadelphia businessmen, 175; Philadelphia Contributorship, 113; Philadelphia Savings Fund Society, 111, 112, 176; Ponte Vedra Beach, Fla., 114, 159; Princeton, N.J., residences, 41, 158; Princeton

Smith, Courtney Craig (*continued*)
University: American Civilization Program, 43, 78, 79, Acting Chairman, 43, courses taught, 43, 78; Princeton University, English Department: advisor to English Club, 42, appointment, 41, 45, 103, Bicentennial Preceptor, 44, 46, 78, courses taught, 43, 44, promotions, 42, 45, salary, 44, 45, teaching ability, 44, 45; Protestant ethics, 17, 20; publications and writings, 42, 43, 79, 178, 179; Pugwash conferences attended, 106; Quaker belief and values, 72–74, 147, 176, 184, 189; Quaker College Presidents, 98, 105; Radcliffe College, teaching at, 77; Rhodes scholarship, 23, 26, 27, 28, 174, study at Oxford University, 28, 29, 30, 77, 102, 188, 191; Rhodes Scholar Program and Rhodes Trust: American Secretary, 46, 68, 154, 174, 191, Assistant to American Secretary, 45, 104, attends 50th anniversary reunion, 69, New Jersey Committee of Selection, chairman, 45, 55, 132, Princeton office, 42, 103, 104, speaks to departing classes, 116, 132, rowing (crew), 29, 150; sabbatical, 159, 160, 165; science, views on, 84, 97; siblings, 16; social justice, 127–28; speaking and speeches, 17, 19, 20, 38, 39, 68, 71–75, 79–82, 85, 87, 96, 100, 106, 116, 128, 129, 151, 164, 173, 174, 176, 178, 184, 185, 190, 227; sports, 150; Squam Lake, N.H., 46, 114, 156, 158, 160, 162, 168; squash, 23, 68, 150; Sunday Breakfast Club, 114, 115; Swarthmore College: administrative staff, 149, 158, 161–66, 176, 179, 192, administrative style, 163, 164, 166, 192, 193, admissions, 133, 151, 177–85, 192, alumni, 154, 186, 191, Alumni Day, speaks at, 178, architecture, praise of, 126, appointed president of, 67–68, 104, benefits through networks, 115, 116, building needs, 123, Blue Route opposition, 115, 118–123, campus road opposition, 152, Centennial Campaign and Fund, 99, 100, 110, 115, Collections, speaks at, 71, 176, commencement, speaks at, 122, 173, 174, Commission on Educational Policy, 115, 167–71, "Courtly Courtney," 151, dialogue and discourse at, 82, "dirty-desk Courtney," 166, draft, military, 132, 174, 227, faculty, 85–91, 132, 166–70, 190, 192, first day as president, 69, 70, Folk festival, 145, 146, 192, freedom of speech at, 128, 129, funding for, 91–101, 115, 116, 154, 164, groundbreakings for buildings, 123, 124, inauguration, 71–74, introduced to students and faculty, 68, liberalism, concerned by, 132, manners and morals, 129, 146, 147, office hours for students, 151, 152, Parrish Hall, 164, *The Phoenix,* irritated by, 131, 132, 149, 150, presidency, views of, 74, 75, 147, presidential assistants, 162, 163, president's house, 154, 168, racial understanding at, 174, 184, 185, recommended for president of, 66, 67, resignation, 170, 175, 176, salary, 68, selecting faculty, 88–90, Sharples Dining Hall, 125, sports, 116, 151, staff retreat, 156, 166, 167, Student Council, meetings with, 149, 152, student critiques and views of Smith, 152, 153, 210, students, 125, 145–54, 184, 185, 192, 226, student activism, 116, 127–33, 152, Swarthmore Afro-American Students Society (SASS) demands, 180–85, 192, views of, 72–73, 129, 173–75, 184, 189, 190, 192, 193, 227; tennis, 23, 26, 150; Three College Presidents, 112; tutoring: for Bradford Endicott, 26, at Harvard, 31, Vietnam War, 174; Woodrow Wilson Fellowship Program, 45, 46, 132; appointed co-director, 54; appointed national director, 54; creates national program, 55–58, 103; obtains foundation support, 56–58
Smith, Courtney Craig, Jr., 32, 69, 156, 159
Smith, Dabney. *See* Smith, Carol Dabney
Smith, David, 166
Smith, Elizabeth (Betty) Proctor, 25, 30, 46, 67, 68, 69, 70, 105, 114, 151, 155, 159, 162; faculty assessments of, 156

Smith, Elizabeth (Lee) Bowden, 39, 69, 151, 156, 159
Smith, Elliott Dunlap, 109
Smith, Florence Dabney, 16, 18, 19, 20, 23, 25, 30, 68, 157
Smith, Helen, 18
Smith, Lee. *See* Smith, Elizabeth (Lee) Bowden
Smith, Myrtle Dabney, 15, 16, 17, 18, 19, 20, 157, 158
Smith, Murray, 16, 18, 20, 68, 77, 157
Smith, Nichol, 29
Smith, Peggy Remington, 156
Smith, Samuel Craig, 15, 16, 20, 200; death, 18, 102
Smith College, 25, 30, 68, 155
social justice, 127, 129
Sorlien, Robert Parker, 24
South Africa, Union, 131
Southern Illinois University, 157
Southwell, Tom Anderson, 24
Soviet Union, 98
Special Committee on Library Policy, 167–69, 171, 172, 178
Special Committee on Student Life, 167, 169, 171, 172, 178
Spies, Claudio, 186
Sproull, Robert, 168
Sputnik crisis, 86, 98
Squam Lake (N.H.), 46, 114, 156, 158, 160, 162, 168
Stahr, Elvis, 30
Standard Oil Co. of N.J., 162
Standlake (England), 69, 158, 159
Stanford University, 101, 163
Stott, Gilmore, 30, 42, 45, 145, 163, 166, 168, 181, 192
Strider, Robert E. Lee, 24
Student Nonviolent Coordinating Committee (SNCC), 129
Sullivan, Leon, 131
Sullivan principles, 131, 226
Sunday Breakfast Club, 114, 115
Swain, Joseph, 59
Swarthmore, Pa., 118; government, 118, 119; police, 184
Swarthmore Afro-American Students' Society (SASS), 113, 174, 177–85, 187; demands of, 180–84, 192; alumni views of, 184
Swarthmore College, 9, 10, 20, 24, 27, 28, 58, 104; administration and administrative staff, 119, 132, 133, 145, 147–49, 152, 153, 161–166, 172, 176, 178, 179, 184, 189, 191; admissions, 133, 163, 177–80, 183; Admissions Policy Committee, 177, 178, 180, 181; African-Americans (Blacks) at, 62, 63, 113, 128, 163, 177–87, 193; alumni, 65, 71, 92, 93, 99, 100, 119, 150, 151, 154, 157, 164, 168, 170, 184, 186; Alumni Association, 62, 92; Alumni Council, 85; Alumni Fund, 62, 87, 92; Alumni Gospel Choir, 193; Animal Laboratory, 124; architecture, praise of, 126; Asian Studies, Three College, 112; Black Studies (Curriculum) Committee, 180, 182; Board of Managers, 59, 61, 65, 67, 87, 95, 96, 99, 110, 128, 132, 133, 153, 157, 165, 186: appoints Courtney C. Smith president, 67, appoints Edward Cratsley acting president, 187, considers SASS demands, 181, divestment of stock, 131, 132, Blue Route opposition, 119, 120, Presidential selection committee, 65–69, reviews CEP recommendations, 173, 174, 178, student appearance, 129; building program, 100, 123; Campus Club, 156; campus design and preservation, 118–26, 152; Centennial Campaign and Fund, 99–101, 165; Clothier Hall, 183, 184, 186; Collections, 68, 71, 130, 145, 148, 150; Commission on Educational Policy, 115, 167–70, 173, 178, 231; community, sense of, 191, 192; Council on Educational Policy, 169, 182; "crisis, the," 182–86; Crum Creek and Meadow, 118, 119, 122, 123; Dana Dormitory, 101, 124, 125; dialogue, failure of, 187; du Pont Science Building, 98, 99, 123, 124; education at, 76, 193; *Egg, The,* 173; employees, 183; endowment, 59; faculty, 73, 85–91, 96, 118, 123–125, 128, 130, 133, 147, 148, 156, 165, 166, 168, 172, 174, 176, 178, 187, 189, 191: memorial resolution for CCS, 186, rela-

Swarthmore College (*continued*)
  tions with CCS, 85–91, responds to
  SASS demands, 181–185, salaries, 85–
  88, 213; finances, 85–87, 92–101; folk
  festival, 146, 147; fraternities, 63, 64;
  Friends Historical Library, 100, 124;
  Hallowell Dormitory, 101, 124, 125;
  Hamburg Show, 153; history of to
  1953, 59–64; honors program, 60, 61,
  76, 92, 145; Inter-fraternity Council,
  162; Jews at, 63, 128; library, 100, 124,
  125, 167; library committee, 167–69,
  171–73, 178; McCabe Library, 100,
  124, 125, 172; Navy unit, 62; open
  houses, 152; parents, 150, 154; Parrish
  Hall, 145, 167, 183, 186; *The Phoenix,*
  63, 68, 145, 149, 150, 151, 153; presidency, 189–93, *see also* Aydelotte,
  Frank; Cross, Robert; Nason, John;
  Smith, Courtney C.; Swain, Joseph;
  press coverage, 184; provost, 169, 170;
  Quaker traditions and values, 172, 173,
  175, 176; rank among liberal arts colleges, 193; Rehoboth Conferences, 156,
  166, 168, 231; sciences, 98, 99, 101,
  123, 124; Sharples Dining Hall, 100,
  124, 125, 225; sororities, 61, 92; sports,
  59, 61, 62, 151, 228; Sproul Observatory, 100; Student Affairs Committee,
  147, 148, 173, 178; Student Association
  and Student Council, 63, 149, 162, 179,
  182, 186; student governance, 146–49,
  153, 168; student life committee, 168,
  169, 171, 172, 178; student rules, 148,
  149, 152, 153, 168, 172, 228; students,
  61, 63, 72, 73, 118, 125, 128–130, 132,
  145–153, 165, 172, 174, 178–87, 189,
  191; "Superweek," 169, 173, 178; Tarble Social Center, 124; Teaching Load
  Committee, 90, 91; veterans at, 63;
  vice-president, 188; Wade House summer program, 130; Willits Hall, 123;
  Worth Health Center, 124, 125, 185
Swarthmore College Alumni Gospel
  Choir, 193
*Swarthmore College Bulletin,* 68, 127, 178
Swarthmore Political Action Committee
  (SPAC), 130, 131
Szilard, Leo, 155

Taylor, Hugh S., 56
Theater of the Living Arts, 113
Thorp, Willard, 43, 103
Three College Presidents, 112
*Time,* 69
Tuition Plan Forum, 79

Union League (Philadelphia), 105
United Nations: Economic and Social
  Commission, 72
United States: Atomic Energy Commission, 97; Bureau of Public Roads, 120;
  Commissioner of Education, 86; Con-
  gress, 121, 128, 132; Council of Eco-
  nomic Advisors, 120; Department of
  Commerce, 120, 122; Department of
  Defense, 93; Department of Housing
  and Urban Development, 111; federal
  program growth, 168, 175; funding of
  science, 94, 101, 212; House of Repre-
  sentatives, 38, 96; National Defense
  Education Act, 94–97, 116, 128, 215,
  216; Office of Education, 87; Senate,
  95, 96, 107, 108, 111, 122, 132
University City Science Center, 97
University Club, 114
University of California, 93, 179, 181
University of Chicago, 20
University of Iowa, 15, 20
University of Michigan, 157, 191
University of Missouri, 31
University of Notre Dame, 79
University of Pennsylvania, 97, 179
University of South Dakota, 96
urban problems, 130, 175
Urey, Harold, 155

Valentine, Alan, 45, 66
van de Kamp, Peter, 186, 236
Van Syoc, Bruce, 157
Van Syoc, Florence, 157. *See also* Smith,
  Florence Dabney
Vanderbilt University, 107
Vassar College, 116, 179
Vietnam War, 132, 133, 153, 174
Voice of America, 80

Wade House, 130
War Production Board, 27, 103

Ward, William H., 65, 99
Webber, George William, 109
Weismiller, Edward R., 28, 30, 31, 32
Wellesley College, 72
Wesleyan University, 85, 91
West Virginia University, 116
Wheaton College, 116, 162, 185
Wheelock, Ward, 105
White, Bertha Dean, 62
White, Byron, 29
White, Morton, 108
Whitton, Rex, 120
Whyte, William H., Jr., 160
Wiener, Norbert, 155
Wilcox, Clair, 65, 90
Wilkinson, C. H., 29
Williams, Alfred H., 110, 114
Williams College, 85
Williams, E.T., 155
Willits, Joseph H., 116
Wilmington College, 116
Wilson, Woodrow, 44, 78

Winterset, Ia., 15, 16, 187
Winterset Cemetery, 187, 198
Winterset Savings Bank, 16, 18
Wistar Association, 113
Wittman, Carl, 228
women's rights, 153
Wood, Robert, 111
Woodrow Wilson Fellowship Program, 9,
    45, 46, 54, 88, 98, 99, 103, 104;
    Courtney C. Smith appointed co-
    director, 54; inaugurated, 53; founda-
    tion support, 53–57; histories, 206;
    Worth Health Center, 124, 125
Wriston, Henry, 79
Wyeth, Andrew, 155
Wyeth, Jamie, 155

Yale Divinity School, 62
Ylvisaker, Paul N., 111
Yeats, William Butler, 72
Yankelovich report, 232, 233
Yellow Route, 118, 119